MERCENARIES

Also by Michael Lee Lanning

THE ONLY WAR WE HAD: *A Platoon Leader's Journal of Vietnam*

VIETNAM 1969–1970: *A Company Commander's Journal*

INSIDE THE LRRPS: *Rangers in Vietnam*

INSIDE FORCE RECON: *Recon Marines in Vietnam* (with Ray W. Stubbe)

THE BATTLES OF PEACE

INSIDE THE VC AND NVA (with Dan Cragg)

VIETNAM AT THE MOVIES

SENSELESS SECRETS: *The Failures of U.S. Military Intelligence*

THE MILITARY 100: *A Ranking of the Most Influential Military Leaders*

THE AFRICAN AMERICAN SOLDIER: *From Crispus Attucks to Colin Powell*

INSIDE THE CROSSHAIRS: *Snipers in Vietnam*

DEFENDERS OF LIBERTY: *African Americans in the Revolutionary War*

BLOOD WARRIORS: *American Military Elites*

THE BATTLE 100: *The Stories Behind History's Most Influential Battles*

MERCENARIES

Soldiers of Fortune, from Ancient Greece to Today's Private Military Companies

MICHAEL LEE LANNING

BALLANTINE BOOKS • NEW YORK

A Presidio Press Mass Market Original

Copyright © 2005 by Michael Lee Lanning

Published in the United States by Presidio Press, an imprint of The Random House Publishing Group, a division of Random House, Inc., New York.

PRESIDIO PRESS and colophon are trademarks of Random House, Inc.

ISBN 0-345-46923-2

Cover photographs: © Alamy

Printed in the United States of America

www.presidiopress.com

9 8 7 6 5 4 3 2 1

OPM

To Michael Thomas Neary

ACKNOWLEDGMENTS

The original idea for this book came from Chris Evans. Many people contributed to its completion, including Rick Kiernan, Sara Pearson, Tim Spicer, Tom Hargrove, Dan Cragg, and Linda Moore-Lanning.

Special thanks goes to my research assistant Meridith Moore Lanning. This book would not have been possible without her.

CONTENTS

MERCENARIES

·1·

First Mercenaries

They go by many names—mercenaries, soldiers of fortune, wild geese, hired guns, legionnaires, contract killers, hirelings, condottieri, contractors, and corporate warriors—these men who have fought for money and plunder rather than for cause or patriotism. Soldiers of fortune have always played significant roles in warfare, they are present on the battlefields of today, and they certainly will be a part of whatever combat occurs in the future.

For centuries the marching song and drinking toast of these hired soldiers has been, "Long live war, long live death, long live the cursed mercenary." On land, in the air, and on the sea, these soldiers of fortune have influenced kingdoms, religions, and peoples of all nations since the beginning of time.

Humans have roamed the earth for about a million years, and their presence long predates their ability to create lasting records. Nothing exists to prove exactly when men first adapted stones and clubs as tools for hunting and weapons for fighting their neighbors over choice hunting grounds, caves, water sources, or women. Except for a few cave paintings, there are no archives of man's activities until about five thousand years ago.

Based on these five thousand years or so of recorded history, there is no reason to think that early man was any different from his modern counterpart in the preparation for and execution of war. Whether for territorial expansion, personal gain, or just the pure pleasure of it, war is most certainly as old as mankind itself—and as warfare evolved, so did the profession of soldiering for hire.

Archaeologists can provide insights into the long period of unrecorded history. The occasional fire pit, rock chip, or bone fragment prove man's existence, but little is known about his daily life or his eventual evolution into bands that warred with each other.

A rare look at early man occurred with the discovery in 1991 of a frozen corpse in an Alpine glacier at 10,500 feet on the Italian/Austrian border. Testing showed that what became known as the Iceman died about 5,300 years previously. Scientists initially thought the Iceman, nicknamed Otzi, had likely frozen to death in an early season snowstorm, but they could not explain why he was leaving a lush valley to make a difficult mountain crossing so late in the season. At first it was assumed that Otzi was a hunter armed with a copper-blade ax, a quiver of arrows, and a stone knife. More recent investigations have proven the Iceman to be a warrior who died not as a result of the cold, but at the hands of multiple enemies.

In 2001, Italian researchers discovered an arrowhead embedded in Otzi's shoulder. Further investigation revealed that both of his hands had cuts. Blood tests on the residue from the Iceman's arrows and knife showed that at least three men had fought against the lone warrior on the mountaintop. Just why he was crossing the mountains or why his enemies killed him remains a mystery. Regardless, the world's oldest existing corpse is that of a warrior who died in direct combat.

There is no record of the first mercenary, but the profession was born the first time three required conditions were met: one, a war to fight; two, someone or a group preferring to pay for a substitute; and three, a fighter or a group of them willing to hire out to do the fighting. Wars raged, men died, kingdoms fell, and mercenaries fought long before anyone developed a desire or method to make a permanent record of these events. Even when records began to be kept, mercenaries received little attention in the battle archives. As would be the case throughout the future, the victors recorded the results of warfare, and few leaders have ever desired reports that detract from themselves and their own great accomplishments.

The earliest existing records of organized warfare are in the Standard of Ur, exhibited at the British Museum in London, and in the Stele of Vultures, housed at the Louvre in Paris. Both of these relics originated in the third millennium B.C. in the region of modern Kuwait and southwestern Iraq, known then as Sumeria. The multipaneled Standard of Ur, composed of shell and lapis lazuli inlaid on wood and made about 2650 B.C., depicts men of all walks of life, including charioteers and armed soldiers, leading what appear to be prisoners of war to their king.

Although likely several hundred years older, the Stele of Vultures is not as well preserved. One fragment from the original stone memorial displays soldiers wearing helmets and carrying spears. Another portion, which provides the relic its name, shows vultures carrying off the heads of vanquished enemies.

Although neither of these relics documents the use of mercenaries, the first written fragmented records of actual combat do reflect the use of hired soldiers. In about 3000 B.C. Upper and Lower Egypt united to form the Egyptian Empire. During the next five hundred years the Egyptians began construction of the Great Pyramids and then ruled the entire region with little opposition for the next thousand years.

Around 1479 B.C., the Mitanni and other tribes along the Euphrates River united under the leadership of the King of Kadesh and challenged Egypt's control over the regions of modern Palestine and Syria. Egyptian King Thutmose III responded by marching an army of about twenty-five thousand against the enemy alliance. The two armies met at Megiddo, where the Egyptians proved victorious.

While the Battle of Megiddo ensured Egyptian hegemony over the region for the next several centuries, the lasting significance of the fight is that it is the earliest warfare in which chroniclers accompanied the army and recorded details of the campaign. Unfortunately, from this first record of warfare few details survive. The story of the campaign was recorded on a roll of leather and later stored in the Temple of Amon. Unfortunately, the scroll itself was later either destroyed or lost, but there are sufficient references to it in other documents to verify its existence. None of these references, however, provide details on the actual fight or the presence of mercenaries on either side.

Because of the size of King Thutmose's army and his kingdom, however, it can be assumed that at least some of his warriors served for money rather than for any loyalty to the kingdom. What is known for certain is that over the next two centuries the Egyptians actively recruited mercenaries and began to make them an integral part of their army.

There were two primary reasons for the increase in Egypt's use of hired soldiers. First, as Egypt increased in wealth and power, its citizens preferred to enjoy their riches rather than face the hardships of the battlefield and the possible loss of limbs or life. Second, large numbers of poor and/or displaced tribes were readily available to fight for money. The Nubians of North Africa provided the greatest numbers of "local" talent for the Egyptian ranks, but the largest and most influential groups of mercenaries for the pharaohs' armies came from tribes in the Aegean Islands and along the Anatolian coast.

These tribes, collectively known as "Sea Peoples," apparently fled across the Mediterranean or by eastern land routes because of widespread famine in their homelands.

The exact origins of these refugees are unknown, as is their ultimate fate. None of the tribes maintained their individual histories for a significant period after their arrival in Africa, and they either assimilated or died out over the next few centuries. Even the name Sea Peoples is a modern label and was first used in 1881 by historian Gaston Maspero as a collective name for the wandering tribes.

The Egyptians did not greet the Sea Peoples as future citizens but rather as an immediate source of soldiers. New arrivals from across the Mediterranean joined the army for sustenance as well as payment. The tribe largest in numbers and importance was the Sherdens. Based on what little archaeological evidence is available, the Sherdens called their homeland Shardana in Anatolia, even though they had already migrated to Sardinia and Corsica before journeying to Egypt. The primary skills they brought were those of warriors. Too small in numbers to challenge the Egyptians, they readily became soldiers for hire.

Little is known about the early military activities of Sherden, Nubian, and other tribes in Egypt. While at least some number of mercenaries served in the Battle of Megiddo, there is no proof of the large-scale use of hired soldiers until the Battle of Kadesh in about 1290 B.C. This battle also marks the earliest conflict from which sufficient details survived to allow succeeding generations to know the numbers, formations, and tactics of the participants.

While Egyptians were enjoying their riches and power, a group of people known as Hittites established a kingdom in Asia Minor in what is today Syria. The Hittites took control of various Egyptian territories and advanced into present-day Lebanon and Israel. King Ramses II assembled his army and marched eastward to defend his kingdom. Although Egyptian nobles still occupied most of the leadership positions, the ranks were filled with Nubians, Sherdens, and other soldiers who fought for money rather than for loyalty to Egypt.

Ramses II finally met the Hittites along the Orontes River near the town of Kadesh in present-day Syria. Neither side was able to gain an advantage, and both armies soon retreated from the battlefield. Although Ramses returned home with reports of a great victory, primarily brought about by his claim of personal leadership and bravery, the Battle of Kadesh was indecisive at best. The major influence of the brief fight was to introduce self-promotion and positive public relations to warfare—and to show that mercenaries were to be an important factor in future battles.

Ramses II and the succeeding pharaohs employed mercenaries in all aspects of military operations. Within a century after the Battle of Kadesh, few Egyptians served in the pharaoh's army in any capacity. The comfortable, prosperous Egyptian citizens enjoyed the benefits of their positions with no desire to serve as soldiers to defend their privileges. Egyptian leaders, recognizing the threat of an army composed of outsiders who fought for money rather than loyalty to the pharaoh, offered land grants and other rewards to assimilate the mercenaries into the general population.

Some of the efforts to maintain the loyalty of the mercenaries proved successful, but the general lack of will of native Egyptians to risk their own lives in defense of their kingdom began to erode its power. Egypt's primarily mercenary army had managed to successfully defend the kingdom for more than seven hundred years after the Battle of Kadesh before finally falling to the Persians in 525 B.C. and then to Alexander the Great and the Greeks in 332 B.C. Egypt then remained under the control of a succession of foreign powers until the latter part of the twentieth century A.D.

During the final years of the Egyptian Empire, the pharaohs added Greek mercenaries to their ranks. Unfortunately for the Egyptians, their Persian enemies also employed Greeks in their armies. By the time the two kingdoms met in the Battle of Pelusium in 525 B.C., Greek soldiers of fortune dominated both armies.

In addition to gaining control over Egypt, Persia's victory also showed that mercenaries on occasion changed sides. Shortly before the battle, the Greek Phanes of Halicarnassus became unhappy with his Egyptian employers and defected to Persia, where he revealed the Egyptian battle organization and plans. When the Persian and Egyptian armies met at Pelusium, the pharaoh brought out Phanes's sons, who had remained in Egypt. In full view of Phanes and his now-Persian allies, the Egyptians cut the throats of the traitor's sons. Their blood was caught in large bowls, mixed with water, and passed among the Greek mercenaries loyal to the pharaoh to drink before the battle.

While this particular story was recorded by the classical historian Herodotus, most of the details of mercenaries in Egypt and the armies of its enemies remained unknown. The tomb of Ramses mentions the Sherdens and Nubians but, like subsequent pharaohs, the Egyptian leader made little mention of his mercenaries in his personal history. There are a few unofficial, graffiti-like notations, likely made by soldiers of fortune, that proclaim "I was there."

All in all, there are just enough actual records to show that Egypt and its enemies used mercenaries. Interestingly, one of the most complete records of early military actions and mercenaries comes not from a true official record, but rather from religious documents.

Information about the composition of armies and the use of hired soldiers by the kingdom of Israel are found throughout the books of the Old Testament of the Holy Bible. I Chronicles lists the specific military skills of the Twelve Tribes that established the kingdom of Israel in what was then Canaan. The nomadic, Arabian desert–dwelling Hebrews began slowly settling into the

region about 1800 B.C. It was not until Moses led a group
of Hebrews out of Egyptian slavery in about 1250 B.C.
that all twelve tribes united.

The Hebrews found that their claim to the lands was
challenged by Canaanites who had previously occupied
the territory for about fifteen hundred years and who
stood ready to defend what they thought was their homeland. Philistines, who arrived as a part of the general mi-
gration of Sea Peoples at about the same time as Moses'
tribe, also claimed much of the coastal regions.

Warfare among the three groups was infrequent for several centuries, with the Canaanites and Philistines maintaining an advantage with their larger, better organized
armies. Along with a strong chariot force, these armies
also contained many mercenaries from other Sea Peoples
as well as Bedouin tribesmen.

The Hebrews initially defended their territory with a
conscription army from the Twelve Tribes, but discovered
that making farmers and herders into soldiers drastically
reduced crop and animal production. Israel's leaders, like
those of other ancient kingdoms, quickly determined that
hired soldiers from external sources freed local citizens to
maintain an economic output that supported both the
kingdom and the army. The Bible's Judges 9:4 and 11:3
relate how Hebrew leaders in about 1250 B.C. supple-
mented their armies with "vain" (idle) men hired for
pieces of silver.

Generally, however, the Hebrews limited their use of
mercenaries, or hirelings as they were known, over the
next two centuries until the stronger Philistines began to
threaten their existence. During the latter years of this period, King Saul actively increased his recruitment of mercenaries. According to I Samuel 15:52, "When Saul saw
any strong man, or any valiant man, he took him unto
him."

King Saul increased the security of his kingdom, but it

was not until David replaced him on the throne that Israel enjoyed its first golden age. David, a sheep herder, worked for Saul as a musician until the age of seventeen, when he killed the Philistine giant Goliath with a sling and a few stones. Hebrew prophets anointed David to be the next king, causing Saul to become threatened and jealous of the young warrior.

David's success on the battlefield made him realize that his skills were better used as a warrior rather than as a shepherd or musician. When Saul did not encourage him to remain in his army, David sought employment as a mercenary in the employment of Israel's Philistine enemies. David assembled an army of five hundred fellow mercenaries from his native Judean tribe and defeated various tribes of Sea Peoples and desert nomads that opposed both Israel and Philistia.

Although the Israelis and Philistines continued their war, David did not participate in fights against his fellow Hebrews. Against other opponents he showed no mercy. David's mercenaries not only killed enemy soldiers, they also massacred their opponents' women and children and looted their homes and villages.

When Saul finally fell in battle with the Philistines, David returned home to assume the leadership of his Judah homeland. Not long afterward the other Hebrew tribes accepted him as their king as well. David ruled the kingdom for forty years until his death in about 965 B.C. Both David and his son Solomon, who succeeded him, steadily decreased their reliance on mercenaries as their own population increased and flourished. It is noteworthy, however, that the kingdom of Israel was strongest during the period shortly after David took power. Although the kingdom's decline came more from its number of enemies than anything else, its loss of power closely paralleled its reduction in use of mercenaries.

Israel, however, never completely ceased hiring foreign

soldiers, nor did the armies of its opponents. Members of the Sea Peoples, nomadic tribes, escaped slaves, refugees, and other displaced people continued to seek employment as warriors. Regardless of the ruler, the state of the economy, or the perceived threat, a man could always find a job if he was willing to accept the dangers and hardships of military life. This was true as well in the many islands and city-states of Greece, where young Greeks began to step forward to fill the ranks of armies throughout the Mediterranean region. They quickly became the most influential soldiers for hire who had ever marched upon the battlefield.

· 2 ·

Master Mercenaries: The Greeks

Mercenaries continued to serve throughout the last millennium B.C. wherever armies fought. During this period, the warriors whose nationality would become synonymous with hired soldiers came to the forefront. By 400 B.C. the very names *Greek* and *mercenary* went hand-in-hand.

Various tribes had settled mainland Greece, Crete, and the hundreds of surrounding islands as early as 7000 B.C. Over the next centuries they had fought among each other as well as against outside invasions by Mycenaean and later Dorian armies. Natives, invaders, and immigrants merged over the passage of time until the mixed population blended into a general homogeneous population that practiced the same culture and worshiped similar gods. From 1000 to 600 B.C. the Greeks expanded their territory throughout the Aegean and Ionian Seas.

As the Greek city-states became stronger during this period, their populations increased over the years to the point where they could not support themselves. The amount of fertile farmland was limited. Mountains, ravines, and rocky slopes covered 80 percent of Greek territory, and there simply was insufficient arable land to support the people. During the seventh and sixth centuries B.C., the larger city-states began to absorb by political and military means the smaller territories, but crop and animal production remained insufficient to feed the entire populations. Some of the city-states, particularly Sparta, prac-

ticed infanticide to decrease their numbers. Baby boys
who did not appear strong enough to become warriors and
girls who seemed too weak to be the bearers of future soldiers were thrown off cliffs to their deaths.

Despite the difficulties in feeding their families, the
Greeks prided themselves on their athletic abilities, and
sports contests were common. As early as 776 B.C. representatives of the various city-states met in competition at
Olympia—the origins of the Olympic Games that exist
today. Even more than athletes, the Greeks saw themselves as brave, proficient soldiers. They not only practiced their combat skills, but also readily accepted
military innovations shown by invaders as well as those
they conquered. For example, from the Carians they
learned to put handles on their shields and add crests to
their helmets.

Each of the city-states maintained an army and a navy.
Greek men at age eighteen were expected to serve for two
years and then remain on call to the active forces for
emergencies for the next thirty years. But their military
requirement did not end then. Even men over age fifty
were expected to serve in garrison and support roles when
needed.

In time, food shortages in the Greek city-states increased. Leaders and citizens realized that their greatest
resource for export was qualified, motivated soldiers willing to assume the mercenary life. When these men left
their homes (many never to return), in their own minds
they remained members of the city-state from which they
originated. Many banded together in companies composed of a network of family, friends, and neighbors. Entire units marched out of their city-states seeking
employment from anyone who would feed, support, and
pay them. Some brought their own arms and armor while
others depended on their hosts for these supplies. Wives,
children, and other camp followers joined the mercenary

companies so that they resembled traveling villages that mirrored their native city-state.

As is true of armies today, most recruits came from the lower classes and the disenfranchised. Social status within city-states carried over so that those from the upper classes assumed the leadership positions. Thus, Greek mercenary units maintained their identity regardless of their employer. They allowed no citizens of other countries to join their ranks, as the Greeks maintained a family relationship within their units. Also as is true today, some Greeks joined the mercenaries not for money, but out of a desire for adventure and to wander the world as armed warriors.

By the middle of the sixth century B.C., the Greek city-states were providing mercenaries to kingdoms throughout the Mediterranean as well as to other Greek colonies to fight their battles. By the arrival of the fifth century B.C., more Greeks served as mercenaries outside their country than in standing armies within the city-states.

Also by that time, almost every battle fought anywhere in the region involved Greek mercenaries. Most battles had Greeks fighting on both sides. Often adversaries were from city-states that opposed each other in Greece. Even if they found themselves fighting against units from their own city-state, the Greeks remained loyal to whomever was paying them.

Persia became the largest employer of Greek mercenaries in the latter part of the sixth century B.C., when Cyrus, soon to be known as "the Great," decided to dominate his homeland as well as the surrounding region. Cyrus began his conquest when his father died in 556 B.C. He first united his own country through military might and then steadily conquered his neighbors. Along the way he folded defeated armies into his own and hired thousands of Greek mercenaries. Many of these Greek units acted as personal bodyguards to Persian generals while others formed elite organizations of hoplites (heavily armed foot soldiers) that spearheaded attacks.

By the time of Cyrus's death twenty-five years later, the Persian Empire extended from the eastern Indus River border in India to the Aral, Caspian, Black, and Mediterranean Seas. Included in the empire was the west coast of Asia Minor, known as Ionia, which was inhabited by Greek colonists. In 512 B.C. the Ionian Greeks briefly rebelled against their Persian occupiers, then did it again more substantially in 499 B.C. During this latter rebellion the Ionian Greeks requested help from city-states in Greece itself. Athens and Eritrea responded with about twenty-five warships, but the Persian army, supported by Greek mercenaries from throughout the region, quickly put down the rebellion.

Persia was not accustomed to having its hegemony challenged, and Darius, current emperor, swore vengeance against Greece. In 492 B.C., Darius invaded and conquered the kingdoms of Macedonia and Thrace on the northern Greek border. Two years later, in the late summer, Darius led a 20,000-man army of his fellow Persians, supported by mercenary forces—Ionian Greeks, Indians, Medes, Egyptians, Cypriots, Phoenicians, Bactrians, Ethiopians, and others—onto the plains of Marathon twenty-six miles north of Athens.

Athenian leaders responded with an army of ten thousand supported by another one thousand soldiers from the city of Platae. Although Athens and Sparta were often at war against each other, the Athenian leaders believed that their fellow Greeks would join them in opposing an invasion by barbarians. The Spartans responded that their religious beliefs precluded their participation until after the next full moon.

For several days in mid-September the armies of Athens and Persia faced each other across the Marathon plain while both sides awaited reinforcements. Early one morning the Persian cavalry rode away, perhaps on reconnaissance or to gather supplies. Whatever the reason, the Athenian commander Miltiades took advantage of their absence by ordering an attack. Armed with swords, spears, and shields, the Athenian infantry attacked the Persian flanks, which were defended by Ionian Greek mercenaries. They pushed back their fellow Greeks and then enveloped the Persian center.

At the end of the day more than six thousand Persians, along with Ionian Greek and other mercenaries, lay dead on the battlefield. Athenian casualties totaled only 192 men. The Spartans arrived shortly after the battle ended and could only admire the success of their fellow Greeks and former enemies.

The overall celebration, however, was short lived. Those Persians who escaped the battlefield boarded their ships off the coast and sailed for what they thought would be an undefended Athens. Miltiades dispatched a runner to Athens to inform the city of his victory and to warn it of a possible attack. He then forced-marched his army southward and arrived at the city-state before the Persian army and navy. The Persians, wanting nothing more to do with the army that defeated them at Marathon, sailed for home.

Marathon, through the writings of Greek historian Herodotus and others, quickly became celebrated as history's first great decisive battle between the West and the East. They touted the run of Miltiades' messenger over the more than twenty-six-mile route to Athens, which established the basis for the future Olympic event known as the marathon. Historians mostly ignored the fact that much of the battle had been between native Greek and Greek mercenaries.

During the decade following the Battle of Marathon, the Greek city-states drifted back to internal fighting. Not until an even larger Persian army and navy threatened them did the city-states once again unite against the common enemy. In 480 B.C. an allied navy of the Greek city-states finally defeated the Persian naval forces and ended their threat against Greece's homeland.

Once again, however, victory over the Persians did not lead to peace. In 458 B.C., Athens and Sparta began the First Peloponnesian War to determine Greek rule. After a yearlong, indecisive war, the two city-states agreed to a truce that lasted fifteen years before they renewed their hostilities in the Great Peloponnesian War, which lasted more than twenty-five years. Throughout the war both Athens and Sparta relied on mercenary troops from other city-states as well as regional tribesmen. Although the war accomplished little beyond creating massive bloodshed and continuing the employment of mercenary troops, Sparta did emerge as a stronger city-state, which opened the way for an eventual unification of the Greeks under the command of Philip of Macedonia.

Despite their defeat by the Greeks, the Persians maintained the largest empire of the age, but not everyone in Persia was happy. In 404 B.C. the king of Persia, Darius II, died, leaving his throne to his son Artaxerxes II. Cyrus, the new king's younger brother, believed that the crown should belong to him and assembled an army to take by force what had not been granted him by inheritance. Details about the civil war that followed are the result of the writings of Xenophon, an Athenian-born writer, student of Socrates, and mercenary soldier.

Xenophon understood Persia's dependence on its Greek soldiers of fortune. According to Xenophon, "Since the Persians themselves recognize the parlous state of their own forces, they give up, and no one makes war without Greeks anymore, either when they fight each other or when Greeks make war upon them. They have decided to use Greeks even in order to fight Greeks."

Cyrus also understood the importance of Greek mercenaries to the success of his rebellion against his brother. Although the Greek city-states had been warring among each other as usual, Cyrus convinced more than thirteen thousand Greeks to join his force. He also convinced the Spartan Clearchus to command the hired army.

Many of the Greeks in Clearchus's ranks came from opposing city-states that had stood in battle against each other over past decades. Old differences were put aside, however, as the hired army swore allegiance to Clearchus and to Cyrus. Xenophon, who joined the mercenary force as a minor leader, later wrote a book entitled *Anabasis* (Greek for "expedition") that described the army and its activities.

About the Greeks' motives, Xenophon wrote what is undoubtedly the best source on mercenaries of the period. "Most of the soldiers have not sailed out to take this paid service because they had no livelihood, but because they heard of the nobility of Cyrus. Some actually brought servants along, others had even spent money beforehand. Some of these had run away from their parents, others had even left children in the hope they would come back with money for them, having heard that the other mercenaries with Cyrus were active and prosperous."

Cyrus combined the Greek mercenaries with Persians loyal to him to field about fifty thousand men. From Sardis in Asia Minor he marched his army toward Babylonia. As they neared the Euphrates River, the mercenaries—despite their loyalty to their employer and their professionalism as soldiers—demanded a pay raise before they would continue. Because this was not an unusual mercenary tactic, Cyrus agreed to a 50 percent increase in their gold payment. The mercenaries pocketed their pay raise and continued the march.

In mid-September 401 B.C. near the town of Cunaxa, Cyrus and the rebel army met the legions loyal to Artaxerxes. Some historians claim that Cyrus's army numbered as many as a million soldiers, but a total of about one hundred thousand is more reasonable, and most agree that Artaxerxes' army outnumbered his brother's by at least two-to-one. The Greek mercenaries moved to the right wing of Cyrus's force and quickly pushed back the left flank of Artaxerxes' front line. They then pivoted to the center, and victory was almost in hand when Cyrus left his secure position in the rear and joined the attack. Within moments Cyrus fell to an enemy spear—wielded by a Carian mercenary in service as a bodyguard to Artaxerxes, according to most accounts.

Cyrus's death immediately changed the course of the battle. Although the Greek mercenaries and their Persian allies had been on the verge of winning, the loss of Cyrus left the rebellion without a leader. His Persian followers knew there would be no mercy from a victorious Artaxerxes and quickly deserted their units, fled the battlefield, and returned to their homes.

The Greek mercenaries were now not only leaderless, but more important, they were jobless. Clearchus and his ranking generals met with Artaxerxes' subordinates to discuss surrender terms. The Persians were not hospitable. They killed Clearchus on the spot and hauled his principal subordinates to Babylon, where they were placed on public display and then beheaded. Artaxerxes sent word to the Greeks that their choice was simple—slavery or death.

Despite the loss of their senior leaders, the Greek legions remained disciplined under the command of their junior officers. Death was not an option, and the proud Greeks had no desire to become Persian slaves. Pragmatically, they looked to the future not as Spartans or Athenians, but as Greeks. The thirteen thousand mercenaries decided they would fight their way out of Persia back to their home city-states and do so with leaders they elected from their own ranks.

The histories of the period vary on just who the Greeks selected to lead them. At least five names appear in one document or another, but the generally accepted commander of what would become known as the Ten Thousand is the Spartan soldier-writer Xenophon. As many authors would discover and rediscover over the succeeding centuries, history is not necessarily what happens, but what gets written. Xenophon's epic *Anabasis* is the most detailed and lasting of the written histories of the time, and this Greek leader did not hesitate to promote himself. Xenophon notes only a few of the senior officers' names as well as some of the braver hoplites. He includes his own name more than two hundred times in the book as well as in twenty speeches he made to "his troops" during their long trek.

As Artaxerxes watched the Greek army begin its withdrawal from the battlefield, he followed but did not immediately attack. Doubtlessly he remembered how near he had come to death and defeat when the Greeks turned on his flank in the battle. But he had no plans to let them escape; he called for reinforcements. The Greeks would be punished with death like their leaders or be forced to submit to slavery.

Realizing that a direct march westward would take them through the heart of Persian power, the Greeks instead headed north into the mountains of present-day Iraq, where they were able to slow the pursuing Persians in the narrow passes. The Ten Thousand next crossed the Syrian desert and then marched through what is now Albania to the Greek colonies on the Black Sea. Along the way they fought several major battles and many skirmishes as they lived off the land. Enemy engagements, disease, and starvation reduced the Greek army to about six thousand over their six-month journey.

According to Xenophon, the exhausted mercenaries joyously cried, *"Thalasa! Thalasa!"* [The sea! The sea!], when they finally reached their objective. From boats borrowed from the Greek colonies and additional vessels captured from other communities on the Black Sea, the survivors of the Ten Thousand made their way back home.

Xenophon settled on an estate near the Spartan frontier. Despite his Athenian roots, he remained in the service of Sparta for the rest of his life. He spent little time, however, as a soldier. Instead, he began his career as an author, writing history as he saw it, or wished it to be seen. By the time of his death in about 354 B.C., he had earned the reputation as the true chronicler of the Ten Thousand and one of the foremost historians of his age.

Upon reaching Greece, the Ten Thousand did not rest long. In their absence Sparta had attacked a weakened Athens that had shifted its emphasis and spending from the military to arts and education. In the war that Sparta eventually won in 404 B.C., the survivors of the Ten Thousand were in the middle of the conflict—frequently fighting on both sides.

In 395 B.C. the city-states again resumed their wars, and the veterans of the Ten Thousand often found themselves in mortal combat with each other once more. During this period the combatants also hired soldiers from other city-states as well as from the various Mediterranean tribes.

Along with the continued use of mercenaries, the city-states experimented with military innovations. Their soldiers used various spear lengths and positioned themselves in different sizes of formations, known as phalanxes. The city-state of Thebes even went so far as to organize an elite unit of three hundred homosexual warriors known as the Sacred Band. This unit guarded the Theban leader and acted as a "strike force" to influence specific points on a battlefield.

For a quarter century the Greek city-states warred among each other until Thebes gained the upper hand by defeating the Spartans at the Battle of Leuctra in 371 B.C. While the victory gained a brief peace for Greece, the long civil war had depleted the resources and manpower of the city-states, leaving them vulnerable to outside enemies.

In the far northern area of the Greek peninsula lay a tribal region known as Macedon. Like the Greeks, the Macedonians had little unity and fought against each other as well as neighbors who raided their villages and stole their property. After an invasion and defeat by the Illyrians in 359 B.C., Philip II, although only twenty-three years of age, took charge of his tribe and began to unite the diverse Macedonian groups. As a boy Philip had been held hostage in Thebes, where he learned to appreciate their culture and military system. He adopted the Greek phalanx for his army as their primary formation and modified it to make it even better by increasing the length of the soldiers' spears and adding additional ranks.

One by one, Philip united the Macedonian tribes by first defeating them with his phalanxes, then incorporating the vanquished armies into his own. To ensure the loyalty of his former enemies, he had his own officers intermarry with the women of the defeated tribes. Philip also indulged in this practice and married Olympia of the house of Molossia in 357 B.C. A year later Olympia gave birth to a son they named Alexander. Philip arranged for the very best classical and military education for his son, including private tutoring from the Greek philosopher Aristotle. Alexander also acquired a copy of Xenophon's *Anabasis,* and the classic tale of the Ten Thousand was never far from his reach.

Unlike Xenophon and his fellow Greeks, Philip believed that an army that fought for their king and their kingdom rather than for money and plunder were the key to victory. He knew that the Greek city-states had accomplished much with hired soldiers, but he also realized that they had become too dependent on foreign mercenaries. As a result, he assembled a professional, full-time army of citizen soldiers paid for by the lucrative gold and silver mines in Macedonian territory.

Philip, however, did not completely eliminate mercenary support. On occasion he hired specialists such as archers and cavalry, but generally the Macedonian ruler used hired soldiers in noncombat roles, including manning occupation garrisons in recently captured territory and instructing new recruits in the art of warfare. Actual combat remained the responsibility of his professional Macedonian army.

Over the next two decades Philip and his countrymen defeated his neighbors and moved south against the Greek city-states. At his side was Alexander, who at sixteen years of age commanded a large portion of his father's army. Philip and Alexander's victory at the Battle of Chaeronea in 338 B.C. gave control of all of Greece to Macedonia.

Upon Philip's death two years later, Alexander took full command of the Macedonian army. Although he mostly placed his fellow Macedonian officers in charge of the subordinate armies, he welcomed the defeated Greeks into his ranks. He paid his soldiers as citizens of the empire rather than as mercenaries. Alexander also installed Greek language, culture, and politics as an integral part of his expanding kingdom.

Alexander turned from Greece toward Persia. In a series of battles, Alexander defeated the Persians and finally put an end to the Persian Empire with his victory at Arbela-Gaugamela in 331 B.C. Along the way Alexander used the wealth of captured territories to pay his army. He also continued his father's policy of mercy and allowed defeated armies to join his own. On several occasions Alexander found his most proficient enemies to be Greek mercenaries in Persian employment. Nevertheless, he welcomed the survivors into his ranks after defeating them in battle. Alexander also copied Philip's policy of having his officers intermarry with women of defeated tribes. More than ten thousand of his officers married Persian women, effectively joining East and West.

After defeating the Persians, Alexander and his army continued east toward India. Alexander never knew defeat, but his own officers finally convinced the young general that they had been away from home too long and that it was time for a rest. Legend has it that Alexander wept because there were no more territories to capture, but in fact if he cried at all it was likely because he knew that even more riches in India and beyond would now not be his.

Alexander died at age thirty-three, likely of malaria, on his way home. His empire did not survive long after his death. Family members and subordinates began a struggle that fragmented Alexander's kingdom within a year. Awaiting nearby were other leaders anxious to assume power over the region—and mercenaries would play an important role in their rise and fall as well.

· 3 ·

Carthage and Rome

During the century following Alexander's death, the city-states and former kingdoms that made up his empire resumed fighting among themselves. Greeks continued to serve as mercenaries to neighboring city-states and to other emerging powers around the Mediterranean. Celtic bands from Gaul (areas of modern France) began raiding the northern Greek territory in the fourth century B.C. When the Celts were unable to defeat the Greeks, they too stayed on as mercenaries in the continuing civil wars.

Meanwhile, Carthage in North Africa began its campaign to control the entire Mediterranean. Phoenician settlers from the eastern Mediterranean had established colonies throughout North Africa as early as 800 B.C. The colony at Carthage soon gained control of the shipping lanes at the narrow point between North Africa and Sicily. Profits from shipping and other commerce paid to build a navy and man an army composed almost entirely of native Libyan and Nubian mercenaries. As Carthage gained power over the succeeding centuries, it hired soldiers from Spain, Gaul, Italy, and any other area where men were willing to fight for money.

By 500 B.C., Carthage had become a kingdom unique in history in that its armies were almost exclusively made up of mercenaries. Fabulously wealthy, Carthage had one huge weakness in that its population was small. Fortunately for these few people, they did produce extremely proficient military leaders to organize and lead their soldiers of fortune.

About a century after the first Phoenicians landed in North Africa, clusters of villages in central Italy united to form the city and future empire of Rome. Unlike Carthage, Rome had sufficient manpower to fill its army with citizen soldiers who willingly fought for the glory of Rome rather than for gold coins.

Over the next five hundred years, Rome added most of the rest of the Italian peninsula to its empire by force and diplomacy. Rome was sacked by the Gauls in 390 B.C., but this defeat only delayed the city's advance in power. During this period the Romans introduced the military innovation of giving state-provided equipment to its soldiers, and standardized arms, armor, and uniforms.

A third power vied with early Carthage and Rome for control of the Mediterranean. Greek colonists settled the city-state of Syracuse on the island of Sicily shortly after the Phoenicians landed in Carthage. Although their origins were Grecian, the citizens of Syracuse considered themselves independent and soon joined the wars among the Greek city-states. Syracusans were enthusiastic supporters of military actions, but not keen on risking their own lives in combat. While the citizens of Syracuse commanded their army and navy, they, like the Carthaginians, depended on mercenaries to be their sailors and soldiers.

Syracuse attained a degree of power on par with other Greek city-states as well as with that of Rome and Carthage. The mercenaries of Syracuse defeated an invasion by Athens in 413 B.C. and by Carthage in 387 B.C. and its power did not diminish until Rome defeated the city-state in 212 B.C., giving the Romans control of all of Sicily.

By the time Rome defeated Syracuse, it had already fought the First Punic War with Carthage over other parts of Sicily. At the beginning of the First Punic War, the Romans had an advantage in land forces while the

Carthaginians had the better navy. Rome improved its naval force by hiring Greek mercenary captains and other officers. Rome also had the advantage of being able to draw sailors and soldiers from the Italian peninsula's large population of 6 million.

Rome ultimately defeated Carthage in a war that lasted from 264 to 241 B.C. The long conflict exhausted both sides, and although Rome was the victor, it did not occupy the Carthage homeland itself. As a result, Rome agreed to fairly lenient terms for the defeated Carthaginians. The most stringent military stipulations of the victory called for Carthage to give up its claims to islands in the vicinity of Sicily and Italy, to return all prisoners, and to agree to no longer recruit mercenaries in areas controlled by Rome.

However, the most damaging part of the truce for Carthage was Rome's demand of an annual indemnity of silver. Precious metals gained from commerce and warfare had been the key to the small number of Carthaginians being able to hire a large number of mercenaries to fight their battles. With their silver going to Rome in retribution for the war, the Carthaginians had little left to pay their soldiers of fortune. Mercenaries returning to Carthage from the First Punic War expected to be paid, and when they were not, they rebelled against their employers. Other mercenaries stationed in Carthaginian colonies also rose in rebellion.

Hamilcar Barca took charge of the small army composed of Carthaginian citizens, formed an elephant corps, and moved against the rebellious mercenaries. Barca ruthlessly fought the rebels. He crucified opposing officers and had his elephants trample other prisoners. By 237 B.C., Barca had ended the uprising and returned the surviving mercenaries to his army's control. Shipping and commerce had by then resumed, and Carthage began to make enough money to pay both Rome and their own hired warriors.

Barca then moved his now loyal army into Spain to gain new territory for Carthage. When Rome complained about these renewed Carthaginian military operations, Barca explained that his purpose was to gain resources from the rich Spanish silver mines so Carthage could continue to pay its restitution for the First Punic War.

When Barca died in 229 B.C., his son-in-law Hasdrubal replaced him. Hasdrubal continued what he called peaceful expansion rather than conquest as he extended Carthaginian territory in Spain. In 221 B.C. a Spaniard murdered Hasdrubal, and Barca's oldest son assumed command of the Carthaginian army. Hannibal was only in his mid-twenties, but he was a battlefield veteran, for as a boy of only about nine he had accompanied his father on campaigns during the First Punic War. Near the end of that unsuccessful war, Hannibal had sworn to his father an eternal hatred of Rome and promised to dedicate his life to fighting the empire.

Shortly after assuming command, Hannibal moved his army farther into Spain. Rome demanded that the Carthaginians return to their original territory and turn Hannibal over for trial as a war criminal. The Roman ambassador explained the empire's demands: "Here I give you peace or war; choose which you will." When Hannibal's representatives responded that they would not comply, the Roman ambassador declared, "Then I give you war."

Hannibal had no trouble accepting that declaration. War with Rome was exactly what he wanted, and he was determined to take it to the heartland of the empire rather than continue to fight in Spain. In September 218 B.C., Hannibal set out from Spain with an army of fifty thousand, mostly mercenaries from North Africa, Spain, and other regions bordering the Mediterranean. About forty war elephants and their hired handlers accompanied the force.

Over the next fifteen years Hannibal added his name to

those of Xenophon and Alexander as the greatest leaders
of mercenaries in the history of the world. Hannibal began with an epic crossing of the Alps to reach northern
Italy from Spain. Along the way he faced rugged terrain,
harsh weather, and hostile tribesmen. Despite the hardships, he arrived in Italy even stronger than when he had
begun his trek. Along the way he recruited defeated
tribesmen, including many Gauls, into his ranks as mercenaries. In addition to the opportunity to fight their traditional Roman enemies, Hannibal promised his soldiers
from Gaul regular payment and the right to loot the Italian
countryside.

During 217 B.C., Hannibal and his army defeated the
Romans at Lake Trasimeno and then ravaged the fertile
Campania region. The Romans began a series of delay-
ing actions as they withdrew southward, but Hannibal
surrounded them at Cannae in 216 B.C. and killed more
than fifty thousand Romans at the cost of only seven
thousand of his own soldiers.

Hannibal then continued his march against Rome but
soon faced the difficulties of being far from home. Although he could loot the countryside for supplies for his
army, he could not so easily replace lost soldiers. Hannibal
hoped to turn Italian cities against Rome and add their men
to his army. However, Rome let it be known that any city or
town that turned traitor to the empire would be dealt with
harshly. Death, enslavement, and total destruction of
homes and businesses were among the consequences.

In addition to the lack of replacements, Hannibal faced
the problem of not having siege equipment with which to
attack walled Italian cities. In 207 B.C., Hannibal sent
word to his brother Hasdrubal in Spain to come to his assistance in Italy. Hasdrubal crossed the Alps along the
same track that his brother had used a decade earlier. With
Hasdrubal marching south, Hannibal turned his army
back northward to destroy the Roman forces caught in

between and to unite the two armies for an attack against Rome.

Hannibal's and his brother's mercenaries did not fail them, but the Carthaginians encountered something that they had not previously confronted—a better general. Gaius Claudius Nero, in command of a Roman citizen army, outflanked Hasdrubal along the Metaurus River and destroyed his mercenary army. Hannibal's first news of his brother's defeat was when Hasdrubal's head was tossed across the lines into his camp.

With Hasdrubal's army absent from Spain, the Romans there quickly occupied all of the Iberian Peninsula. On the Italian peninsula, Hannibal now was forced to retreat rather than attack. Over the next four years he kept the Roman army busy so they could not invade Carthage itself, but Hannibal did not gain another victory.

Roman general Scipio, who had defeated the remaining Carthaginians in Spain, knew that occupation and defeat of Carthage itself was the only way to win what had become known as the Second Punic War. In 202 B.C. he landed his army in North Africa. Upon hearing of the invasion of Carthage, Hannibal rushed his army home to defend the city.

In October the two armies met at Zama, about five miles southwest of Carthage. Once again Hannibal found himself being outgeneraled. Scipio used Roman cavalry along with North African forces who opposed Carthage to envelop Hannibal's attacking army. By the end of the day, one-half of Hannibal's fellow Carthaginian and mercenary soldiers lay dead on the battlefield. Most of the rest were taken prisoner.

Scipio likely could have moved on to Carthage itself and destroyed the city, but once again Rome was lenient with its vanquished enemy. The Romans offered a generous peace accord that spared Carthage and even allowed Hannibal to maintain his position of leadership. Regardless of the past, most Romans admired Hannibal and recognized his abilities in molding a large number of divergent peoples and tribes into history's greatest mercenary army. Roman chroniclers recognized Hannibal's leadership by writing that "he never required others to do what he could not and would not do himself."

Despite Rome's generosity, Hannibal continued to plot against the empire and was eventually exiled to Syria. There, he again tried to organize an army against Rome but was unsuccessful. In 183 B.C. he chose suicide rather than be captured by the Romans.

For a half century after the Battle of Zama, the Carthaginians and Romans remained at peace. However, despite the passage of years, many Roman leaders believed that Carthage had not been sufficiently punished for its invasion of the Italian peninsula. Roman leader Marcus Cato began each of his speeches with the declaration, "Carthage must be destroyed."

Cato did not find much support until Carthage's rejuvenated commerce began to take revenue from the Roman Empire. In 150 B.C., Rome dispatched an army to North Africa on the pretext of supporting its Nubian allies from neighboring Carthage. Over the passage of years since Zama, the citizens of Carthage had enjoyed the wealth gained from trade but, unlike earlier times, had spent little to nothing on employing mercenaries to defend their territory.

Aware of its military weaknesses, Carthage proposed to surrender its arms, pay additional monetary reparations, and even offered three hundred children of its leading families as hostages in order to avoid conflict. Rome refused the offers and informed the Carthaginians that they had to abandon their city and move into the African interior. The people of Carthage refused, closed the city's gates, and prepared to fight to the death. The siege took three years before the Roman army finally breached the city's walls.

Romans were not so generous in victory this time. They leveled the city, poisoned the wells, and salted the fields so nothing would again grow there. Adult males were put to the sword, the females ravished, and children enslaved. Without its mercenaries to defend them, what had once been the most powerful empire on the Mediterranean ceased to exist.

The fall of Carthage eliminated Rome's major competition for control of the Mediterranean. Over the next three centuries Rome expanded its empire to become the largest of its age, stretching from Britain eastward to Babylonia and from the North Sea to Egypt's Nile River. During this period the Romans faced formidable foes from both external and internal sources. Caesar defeated the primary external enemy to Rome's expansion in 52 B.C. when he destroyed the Gaul army at Alesia. Caesar rewarded his army by giving each soldier a prisoner as a slave. The victorious army brought the captured Celtic leader Vercingetorix back to Rome, where he was paraded through the streets, imprisoned for many years, and then publicly executed.

During the early part of this expansion, Rome relied on citizen soldiers just as it had in the wars against Carthage. Many of these soldiers came from agricultural regions and successfully combined the careers of part-time soldiering with farming and herding.

By the end of the Second Punic War, however, much of the countryside of the Italian peninsula lay in waste from the campaigns of Hannibal. Small farmers could no longer make a living, and most sold their holdings to wealthy neighbors. Many migrated to the cities, where they found menial jobs that barely supported their families. This movement from small farms to large estates created a twofold problem in manning the Roman armies. Poor citizens no longer felt they were a part of the empire and were reluctant to risk their lives in the military. Large landowners also lost interest in military service, as they preferred to stay put and enjoy their wealth and status.

When Gaius Marius gained the title of consul and supreme commander in 107 B.C. he reorganized the Roman army from one dependent on citizen militiamen to a full-time professional force. Soldiers were now volunteers who served full-time for a fair wage. These soldiers, although they often expressed more loyalty to their commanders and legions than to Rome and its Senate, were professionals rather than mercenaries. They were citizens of Rome serving the military needs of the Roman state.

As the Roman Empire expanded, the army continued to recruit professional soldiers from its captured territories. Although their loyalty was gained by placing them in positions of leadership and through payment, they, like their Roman allies, were more professional than mercenary. Eventually, however, Rome's expansion exceeded its abilities, and in some cases motivation, to man its army with professionals. Territorial gains and manpower limitations finally forced the Romans to hire soldiers of fortune.

The Roman army as well as its senior leadership went through many transitions. Commanders of successful legions became jealous of each other, as did the leaders of the government and Senate in Rome. The massiveness of the empire, along with disagreements over who should be in command and how the people should be governed, led in A.D. 395 to the separation of its territory into the Eastern Empire, headquartered in Constantinople, and the Western Empire centered in Rome.

By early in the fifth century neither the Eastern nor Western Empires could depend entirely on their professional Roman armies. Attempts were made to reinforce their legions with units of soldiers from captured territories, but even these efforts ultimately failed to produce sufficient manpower. Rome was proud that it was the first vast empire to achieve its greatness with limited assistance from hired soldiers, but ultimately need exceeded pride and both the Eastern and Western Empires began to recruit mercenaries.

The increased importance of cavalry encouraged the Romans to seek mounted soldiers of fortune. Light cavalry bowmen from the Asiatic tribes of Huns, Alans, Avars, and Bulgars added the firepower of bows and arrows to the Roman legions. The Romans also recruited heavy cavalry, experienced with the lance and pike, from the Germanic tribes that occupied the vast plains between the Danube and the Black Sea. These included Goths, Lombards, Vandals, Gepidae, and Heruli. The Eastern Empire recruited infantrymen from many of its own occupied provinces, including Anatolia, and added Germans and Slavs to its ranks of foot soldiers. Gaulish infantrymen joined the Western Empire as did Franks and Burgundians from the northern regions. The Romans recognized that these "barbarians" fought better under their own leadership, and so the Romans formed entire units of mercenaries led by mercenaries known as *federati*.

The decline of the Western Roman Empire began about the same time that Rome started employing large numbers of soldiers of fortune. Although many of the mercenaries did turn against their employers, they were not the cause of Rome's decline. The practice of hiring others to fight its battles was only a part of the eventual end of the Western Empire. Internal struggles within the Roman government and an ever-increasing number of enemies eventually brought an end to the Western Empire when it fell to successive waves of barbarians in 476.

During the years before the fall of Rome, the Romans of the East had further distanced themselves from their Western brothers. The two empires, long disagreeing on religious interpretations and practices, went their separate ways. The Eastern Empire thrived while their Western counterparts from Rome and the Italian peninsula perished.

The Eastern Empire had to depend almost entirely on armies formed from captured tribes and on mercenaries. Good leadership, ironhanded discipline, and well-paid soldiers allowed them to rule much of southern and southeastern Europe and western Asia for the next thousand years. Its eventual fall came not from a dependence on mercenaries but rather from the rise of the Muslims, believers in the religion founded by Mohammed in A.D. 610. Over the centuries the Muslims had gained in power until the Ottoman Turks overran most of the empire and finally swept into Constantinople itself in 1453, ending the reign of the Eastern Roman Empire.

Among the final Eastern Empire soldiers standing were the personal bodyguard company of Emperor Constantine XI. When the last of his loyal hired guards fell, Constantine took a sword and charged into the ranks of Muslim invaders, declaring "God forbid that I should live an emperor with no empire!"

The millennium between the fall of the Western Roman Empire and the end of the Eastern Empire mirrored the change in warfare and culture of the period. Before the fall of Rome to barbarian Visigoths in 410, empires rose to honor and enrich kings and emperors. By the time of the fall of Constantinople to the Muslim Turks, men were killing each other in the name of their gods. Christians fought Muslims, Catholics battled Protestants. Meanwhile, "godless" barbarians fought each other and anyone else they encountered. One particular aspect of warfare, however, remained the same from Rome to Constantinople and beyond—all sides continued to rely on soldiers who fought for profit rather than for a cause, a religion, or patriotism.

· 4 ·

Middle Ages

The Middle Ages began with the fall of the Western Roman Empire in the fifth century and ended with the collapse of the Eastern Roman Empire in the fifteenth. These intervening ten centuries saw the spread of religious beliefs, the discovery of new continents, and a continuous environment of warfare with mercenaries playing significant roles. ·

This period was not unlike those before or after in that religious leaders could not spread their messages, explorers could not venture to discover, artists could not create, and educators could not teach unless they resided in a kingdom or country that fielded an adequate army and navy to protect and defend its citizens. Most independent and strong kingdoms of the Middle Ages maintained their armed forces through a feudal system that provided land in exchange for military service. To lead these forces, the kings called upon fellow members of the royalty and other titled citizens. These elites also served their kings as independent warriors known as knights.

The problem with this system was that once a serf owned or at least occupied land, he became reluctant to leave his crops and livestock for any extended period. As a result, feudal armies proficiently defended their home areas, but they were uninterested in offensives that required travel in order to conquer new lands.

Kings continued to require military service from their

serfs during the Middle Ages, but they also looked elsewhere for armies willing to undertake long and often dangerous campaigns. They did not have to look far or long because overpopulated cities and underproducing farms yielded men who were looking for work and willing to become soldiers.

In the eleventh century an army of mercenaries at the Battle of Hastings achieved the most influential victory ever attained to date and established control of the British Isles. Prior to that time the Vikings had ruled Scandinavia, Northern Europe, and much of Britain. The Vikings came from the cold regions of the North, where little could be gained through agriculture. As a result, Vikings took to the sea to raid and plunder, with warfare becoming their principal employment.

While some tribes of Vikings took over the British Isles, other occupied France. Both groups intermarried with the locals but still considered themselves first and foremost Vikings. Common bloodlines ran between both groups, but this did not prevent them from fighting among each other once there were no other readily available territories to raid or capture. Claims of crowns and territory reached a crisis with the death of Edward the Confessor, king of England, in 1066. Three men claimed the throne. Harold Godwin, brother-in-law of Edward; King Harald of Norway, Harold Godwin's brother; and William, duke of Normandy and a distant relative of Edward's.

Both Harald and William assembled armies to sail to Britain to claim the throne they thought rightly theirs. Harald arrived first with a force of about ten thousand, made up almost entirely of Viking warriors. Godwin marched to meet Harald's army and soundly defeated it at Stamford Bridge near York in late September.

Godwin had no time to celebrate his victory, as word reached him that William had landed to the south at Sussex and was marching inland. On October 1, Godwin halted briefly in London to add replacements to his army of about seven thousand. These poorly trained militiamen, known as *fyards,* were basically draftees levied from the employees of landowners. At the heart of Godwin's army were two thousand professional soldiers of Viking heritage known as housecarls.

William's army also totaled about seven thousand (some accounts claim about double that number), several thousand of whom were fellow Normans evolved from intermarriage between Vikings and residents of Normandy. The remainder of William's army were mercenaries from across Southern Europe who joined the Normans for pay and promises of land. These hired soldiers not only were experienced combatants, they also brought with them the skills of cavalrymen and archers. Other mercenaries were armed with crossbows—medieval weapons that would become widely used on the battlefield.

On October 12, 1066, the two armies met about eight miles northwest of Hastings. William attacked, but Godwin's army repelled several assaults. Godwin's housecarls and serfs held until an arrow struck their leader in the eye. They began a retreat with the Normans in full pursuit. On December 25, William entered London and received the crown of England. Some of William's fellow Normans and their hired mercenaries returned home to Normandy, but many remained with their king. There, they intermarried with the Saxons and developed the laws, customs, and traditions that established England as a power for the future.

The 1066 Battle of Hastings not only became a staple of history books and school texts, it also established the lethality of the crossbow as a weapon of war and created a new industry. Regions and cities, with little else to export, began to specialize in training mercenaries to use specific weapons or teaching them other battle skills. The Italian cities of Pisa and Genoa became synonymous with soldiers armed with crossbows available for hire.

Italian crossbowmen joined the ranks of Germanic cavalrymen and Swiss pikemen as mercenaries known for their combat specialties. Southern France and Spain continued to be fertile recruiting ground for infantrymen armed with swords and shields. Individual mounted knights also hired out their services to whomever was willing to pay their wages. Many were the younger sons or illegitimate offspring of titled landowners. Some had titles themselves and sought to fight as "swords for hire" for adventure as well as wealth.

Although they were known to demand additional payment before going into battle, mercenaries knew that their personal reputation and that of the region from which they came depended on their loyalty as well as their abilities on the battlefield. For many of them fighting for pay was their lifelong profession, and they understood that future employment depended upon current performance.

Mercenaries played a role in every conflict on the Continent as well as in the civil wars in the British Isles themselves during the decades following the Battle of Hastings. For more than a century English nobles assembled their serfs and hired mercenaries from the Continent to challenge control of the throne. As with all wars, there was loss of life and destruction of property. All the armies, especially those of mercenaries, were accused, usually correctly, of murder and pillage.

By the early years of the thirteenth century the Norman conquerors and the defeated Saxons still disagreed over who should rule, but the two had united in many ways, developing and advancing culture and government. On June 15, 1215, English barons forced King John to sign a charter that guaranteed certain civil and political liberties to the people of the kingdom. Among the many provisions of the Magna Carta were limitations on the future use of mercenaries within Britain. Article 51 stated, "As soon as peace is restored, we will remove from the kingdom all foreign knights, bowmen, their attendants, and the mercenaries that have come to it."

It took two more years for the internal strife in Britain to end, but peace did in fact bring the expulsion of mercenaries from the Isles. That is not to say, however, that England did not hire mercenaries for its future wars outside their home islands.

The Magna Carta actually had little influence on the future of mercenaries during the remainder of the Middle Ages. Numbers of mercenaries did decrease somewhat in the thirteenth century, but this was more the result of changes in warfare than in any opposition to hiring soldiers. As cities became bigger and wealthier, they added to their physical defenses with higher walls, deeper moats, and other structures. It took months and even years for an enemy to besiege and defeat these fortified cities, greatly increasing the time and costs of hiring mercenary forces. As a result, both attackers and defenders of castles and fortified cities began to rely on full-time professional citizen soldiers rather than hire part-time mercenary help.

This brief lull in the expansion of mercenaries ended when cities and kingdoms reached new levels of wealth through trade and exploration. Not only could they increase their fortifications, but they could also now pay hired armies as well. Even those powers that previously spoke out against mercenaries renewed the practice of hiring soldiers of fortune. Although Catholic leaders condemned the use of hired soldiers in their Third Lateran Conference of 1179, less than fifty years later, papal mercenaries played an important role in the wars over control of the Italian peninsula.

The Norman conquest of England at the Battle of Hastings led to a unification of Britain but not to peace with the remaining regions of France. England and France disagreed over who should occupy the French throne, and in 1337 an English army invaded the mainland of France.

This began what became known as the Hundred Years' War—although it lasted nearly two decades more than a century. Britain won the major battles but ultimately could not maintain an effective army so far from home.

Mercenaries played roles in many of the battles of the Hundred Years' War, but the primary military advancement came from professional British archers. Since expelling its mercenaries in the previous century, the British had developed the longbow—an aptly named weapon that was longer than the ordinary archer's weapon of the period. The longbow required physical strength and extensive training in firing quickly and accurately.

At Crecy in 1346 the British longbowmen numbered seven thousand, and their arrows launched at a range of 250 to 300 yards, which greatly exceeded in distance those of the mercenary Genoese crossbowmen who made up the heart of the French army. French leaders blamed their Genoese crossbowmen for the defeat. When the hired soldiers retreated in panic beneath the shower of arrows of the English longbowmen, the French king ordered his own men to turn against the Genoese, shouting, "Quick now, kill all the rabble. They are only getting in our way!"

Sixty years later the British longbowmen proved their mastery over mounted French knights at the Battle of Agincourt in 1415. British archers killed more than five thousand French, including five hundred noblemen, and lost only about two hundred of their own.

The battles of Crecy, Agincourt, and many others of the long Hundred Years' War led to significant changes in the art of warfare itself. The longbow proved to be superior to the crossbow in range as well as in the number of arrows launched per minute. Mounted soldiers, mostly knights, were no longer the superior force on the battlefield. The many dead nobles on the fields of Agincourt had proven that archers and foot soldiers had renewed their mastery of direct combat.

By the time the Hundred Years' War finally ended in 1453, warfare had become much more sophisticated. Successful commanders developed means of combining their cavalry, archers, and foot soldiers into teams that complemented and supported each other on the battlefield. Maneuver, including flanking movements and envelopments, became even more important in the difference between defeat and victory.

· 5 ·

Italy and the Condottieri

The Hundred Years' War influenced the future of soldiers who fought for pay and booty. Although the war lasted for more than a century, combat was not continuous. Often years passed with neither the British nor the French able to field large armies because of financial difficulties and manpower shortages. The bubonic plague, known as the Black Death, that spread across Europe in the fourteenth century also diverted attention from the hostilities.

In 1360 the French and English agreed to the Peace of Bretigny, which did not actually end the war but did establish a truce that lasted until 1414. The long war and its frequent periods of inactivity had produced large numbers of experienced, unemployed soldiers, and these common soldiers as well as untitled knights found themselves without jobs and unwelcome in the countries for whom they had fought. Several knights, mostly illegitimate sons of nobles as well as legitimate offspring with too many siblings to claim title and territory, took advantage of the peace by organizing free companies. These companies, ranging from hundreds to thousands, contained foot soldiers, archers, cavalrymen, and all the trappings necessary to make the companies small armies within themselves.

Although these free companies that emerged from the Peace of Bretigny introduced a technique of mercenary warfare new to France, the concept was not entirely a novel one. In 1281 soldiers in northeastern Spain had formed an organization called the Catalan Company to fight as mercenaries in the war over Sicily between the Angevin and Aragonese dynasties. Near the end of the twenty-year conflict, Roger di Flor, a German soldier of fortune, assumed command of the company.

Di Flor, formally known as Rutger von Blum before becoming a soldier of fortune, brought wisdom and skills to the company. He had participated in the Crusades as a member of the Knights Templar, where he fought against the Ottoman Turks at the Battle of Acre in 1191, likely assisting in the execution of two thousand seven hundred Muslim captives. His stay with the Templars, however, was brief. Although the order of Christian knights was vicious on the battlefield, they were pious monks when not in combat, and di Flor, who fought well but refused to pray and meditate, was forced to leave. Apparently he stole a Templar galley that he used to shuttle Muslim fugitives from Acre to Cyprus for a high fee. Di Flor briefly also used the galley as a pirate vessel before journeying to Sicily.

By the end of the war in Sicily in 1302, di Flor had risen to command the Catalan Company. Peace ended the company's employment, so di Flor sought others who would pay for a well-organized combat unit. He found a willing employer in the Byzantine Empire, where its leader, Andronicus II, was facing an increasing threat from the Ottoman Turks. When they landed at Constantinople, the Catalans had a formal organization of cavalrymen, crossbowmen, archers, and foot soldiers armed with javelins, spears, and swords. They marched under their own flag and seal.

In service to Byzantium, the Catalan Company won several battles, but di Flor was so ruthless in torturing and killing his enemies and looting the countryside of his allies that the Byzantine emperor arranged for his assassination in 1305. Di Flor's death, however, did not bring an end to the company. Its well-organized chain of command took control and raided and ravished the countryside in revenge for their leader's execution. They then migrated to Greece, where that once powerful empire was again being torn apart by internal strife. There the company, now commanded by Ramón Muntaner, added Greeks and some of their former Turkish enemies to its ranks.

After conducting independent raids for several years and fighting for whomever would pay their bills, the Catalan Company began working for the Duke of Athens in 1310. The company captured more than thirty castles held by the duke's enemies before the Athenian leader decided he no longer needed a company of soldiers of fortune. When he attempted to dismiss the company without paying, the mercenaries rebelled, slaughtered the duke's troops, and assumed control of Athens.

For the next seventy years the Catalan Company ruled Athens, requesting and receiving a series of dukes from their Spanish home provinces to sit on the city's throne to provide credibility to a city actually ruled by soldiers of fortune. The passage of decades, however, weakened the company as it lived off the fruits of its former victories. In 1388 an army from Florence defeated the company and its survivors disbanded.

The Catalan Company earned its place as the first independent, self-sufficient mercenary company in Western Europe. In addition to the wealth and power it enjoyed for nearly a century, it also gained fame for its most important leader. Roger di Flor, although born a German, was adopted as a hero of Spain. Today several major hotels and other landmarks still bear his name on the Spanish mainland.

The free companies that emerged after the Peace of Bretigny raided and looted the French countryside on the pretext of continuing the fight in the name of England. This brief employment ended with an order from King Edward III, which instructed any English companies that were fighting and plundering "as if it were still time of war" to cease operations immediately. Those who failed to do so were to be arrested by knights dispatched to France from London.

Not able, or at least not willing, to fight both France and England, the veterans of the Hundred Years' War looked elsewhere to earn their living with sword and shield. They did not have to venture far. On the Italian peninsula were dozens of cities, principalities, and territories vying with one another for land, power, and influence.

During the nearly one thousand years since the fall of the Western Roman Empire, the Italian peninsula had gone through a series of wars, from dealing with external invaders to internal revolutions. By the fourteenth century the area had settled into three regions of power. The kingdoms of Sicily and Naples ruled the south, the Papal States controlled Rome and the central region, and the cities of Venice, Florence, and Milan vied for hegemony in the north.

The powers within the three regions shared several characteristics. Manufacturing, commerce, and trade had allowed them to amass great riches, but the merchants and craftsmen who built this wealth had no desire to risk their lives to defend it. In addition, the populations of the city-states were too small to effectively man their armies.

These factors led to the active recruitment of mercenaries. However, unlike in previous times, warfare now required not only a large number of soldiers but also military units that offered combined skills, detailed organization, and superior leaders.

The companies that made their way to Italy had gone through several reorganizations and many leaders before signing their contracts as *condottieri,* Italian for "to hire" or "to contract." The Company of St. George, composed of Swiss, Germans, and native Italians, apparently was the first to arrive on the peninsula and fought against Milan in 1349. It then disbanded, only to be reestablished by Alberigo de Barbiano in the 1370s.

During this same period the Great Company, which originated in Hungary with Hungarian and German soldiers, contracted with the city of Florence as its mercenary army. The Great Company, under the command of Werner of Urslingen, grew to a force of ten thousand cavalry and infantry, becoming virtually a city within itself with more than twenty thousand camp followers.

Werner and his Great Company arrived in Italy bearing a letter from the king of his native country. Louis of Hungary wrote the leaders of Florence recommending Werner and his company as condottieri, but also warning, "There is no faith or pity in those who follow battle; and the said duke Werner has been accustomed to doing on other occasions very dangerous things under the protection of his company. So be on your guard."

Werner established the philosophy of his company with his credo worn on his breastplate, "Lord of the company; enemy of God, of pity, and mercy." Though the credo did not mention profit, Werner and his soldiers of fortune certainly succeeded in that arena as well. Through their contracts with various powers, ransoms of captured foes, and general looting, the Great Company prospered. When Werner died of natural causes in 1354, many members of the company, much like their Italian patrons, had reached the point where they were too wealthy to need to continue in this line of work, and most retired. The few who remained in the company would eventually face defeat by another group of condottieri known as the White Company.

The White Company, so named for their warriors' highly polished armor, was formed as a free company of former English soldiers shortly after the Peace of Bretigny. For a while the company prospered by continuing to raid and loot villages in southern France. When King Edward III ordered that English mercenaries cease operations in France in 1361, the White Company crossed into Italy to offer its services to the highest bidders.

Shortly after the White Company reached Italy, an English soldier of fortune named John Hawkwood assumed command of the mercenary band, which now contained Germans and French as well as English soldiers. Hawkwood, born the son of a tanner in Essex in about 1321, had risen in the ranks of the English army despite his common birth. Having fought in the Battle of Crecy in 1346 and earned his knighthood a short time later, Hawkwood understood the merits of combining cavalry, infantry, and archers. He was a strict but fair disciplinarian, and he was an apt negotiator. He could also be ruthless. After the Battle of Faenza he discovered two of his subordinate officers arguing over who would rape a young nun. Hawkwood drew his sword, declared "half each," and cut the woman in two.

Hawkwood and the White Company served as condottieri for the next three decades throughout the Italian peninsula. The mercenaries changed sides several times during their long service, usually because of better offers and occasionally due to disagreements with their employers. The company served in hire of the pope and the Papal States, with the antipapal alliance, and for the city of Florence. In one instance the company found satisfactory employment under the papal banner, but ended its contract when ordered to destroy a city that Hawkwood had promised would be spared.

This English mercenary thoroughly understood his position as a leader of men who fought for profit rather than cause. During one of his campaigns two friars greeted him with the prayer, "God give you peace." Hawkwood, the professional soldier, responded, "God take away your alms. For as you live by charity, so do I by war, and to me it is as genuine a vocation as yours."

It was during their service with the city of Florence that the company and Hawkwood gained the most influence and earned their greatest wealth. Hawkwood married the daughter of a Florentine aristocrat and secured the title of captain—general of all of the city's armies—and spent his final days in luxurious retirement in Florence. The White Company continued under new commanders until the rise of internal Italian armies brought an end to the free mercenary units at the end of the century.

When he died of old age, a fairly unusual phenomenon for a man who soldiered most of his life, the grateful Florentines gave Hawkwood a huge funeral. They then returned his remains to England, where his tomb is decorated with a hawk in the parish church of Sible Hedingham in Essex.

The arrival of the fifteenth century did not end the conflicts between the Italian cities and regions, but it did influence the mercenary organizations that fought their battles. While soldiers of fortune from throughout Europe continued to pour into Italy, the Italian leaders turned more and more to native-born officers to command their hired legions.

Francesco Sforza proved to be the most successful of the fifteenth-century condottieri. Born in 1401, Sforza had followed his father into mercenary service and as a young man proved himself in battle. He often amazed his fellow mercenaries with his physical strength by bending large metal bars with his bare hands. Sforza advanced in the ranks to become the captain of his company and over the years accepted employment from both Milan and Venice, going to the city that offered the most lucrative contract.

Sforza so impressed the Duke of Milan that the duke arranged for the mercenary leader to marry his daughter. When the duke died in 1450, Sforza and his company took control of Milan, and the mercenary leader declared himself the city's duke. Under Sforza's leadership, Milan became a center of culture and learning, significantly contributing to the Italian Renaissance. In 1454, Sforza arranged for the Peace of Lodi, which negotiated a nonaggression treaty between Milan, Venice, and Florence. This further encouraged the Renaissance and helped unite the Italian powers.

Not all of the notable condottieri served entirely on land. Several naval commanders also offered their leadership and their fleets to the highest bidder. Andrea Doria earned his place as the most successful naval mercenary of the period through his employment by the Papal States and the cities of Genoa and Venice.

Born in about 1468 in Genoa to a family that fought unsuccessfully for the city, Doria spent his youth in the mercenary guards of Pope Innocent VIII. He then served in several other mercenary groups, including as a leader of French troops employed by the kingdom of Naples. In 1503, Doria returned to his Genoa home where he reorganized the city's fleet. He used money earned in previous mercenary efforts to arm eight galleys at his own expense and put to sea as an independent naval power.

From 1507 to 1519, Doria raided Italian and North African ports and merchant vessels. Some called him a pirate, but Doria always returned to Genoa, where he shared part of his booty with the city officials, who considered him a patriot. When internal strife in Genoa brought new leaders who did not approve of Doria, he took his fleet, which now numbered a dozen ships with loyal crews, in search of more approving employers.

Doria soon was sailing the Mediterranean in support of the French and in 1525 assumed command of all of that country's navy. In 1528 he returned to Genoa and took control of the city. He broke up the ruling clans, established new social divisions, and initiated a constitution that encouraged trade and the arts. Over the next two decades he sailed the Mediterranean in the hire of Genoa, France, Austria, and a confederacy composed of the Papal States, Venice, and the Knights of Malta.

Doria retired in 1540 but retained much of his control over Genoa. His subjects erected a colossal statue to him at the church of San Matteo, and he lived in splendor until his death in 1560. Although his statue was destroyed in 1797 by political factions that no longer favored the legacy of the maritime mercenary, he remains today one of Italy's revered military heroes.

Doria was one of hundreds of condottieri captains who influenced all aspects of life on the Italian peninsula for more than a century. These soldiers of fortune, despite their various origins, shared the will and spirit of professional soldiers who had fought for whomever offered the highest payment. They often changed sides—sometimes going back and forth between the highest bidders. Today's friends became tomorrow's enemies, and this produced some interesting aspects of warfare.

Prisoners held for ransom were much more valuable than dead opponents. Although there were ample examples of mercenary companies destroying entire villages, generally battles between opposing condottieri were relatively bloodless. Captains were well aware that hired soldiers would not stay with a leader who readily sacrificed their lives in combat. As a result, opposing mercenary armies often met, put on a show of maneuver and arms, and then decided a battle's outcome with a peaceful meeting of the leaders rather than at the point of sword and pike.

The mercenary leaders and their companies had immense influence on the Italian powers and on the future of Italy itself. The condottieri provided stability where chaos had previously reigned. They also forcefully brought the smaller cities and states under the control of the larger powers. From this turmoil emerged the environment that produced the Renaissance and its revival of the arts, literature, and learning in Italy and Europe from the fourteenth through sixteenth centuries.

The hired armies of the Italian peninsula, however, were not sufficiently strong or dedicated enough to protect their employers from outside invasion. In 1494, France invaded the peninsula and in 1502 became allied with Spain to gain control of much of Italy. Many mercenaries were not willing to engage in the high intensity of the modern battlefield. Italian leaders also realized that they could not depend on hired companies to maintain their independence and began to organize armies from their own citizens who were willing to fight for their state.

By the beginning of the fifteenth century, the condottieri were on the decline. While hired soldiers would continue to fight in Italy as well as elsewhere around the world, the golden age of the great captains and their mercenary companies had come to an end.

Despite their accomplishments and failures, the most lasting—and perhaps accurate—epitaph of the condottieri comes from the Italian military theorist and writer Niccolo Machiavelli. In his masterful *The Prince,* written in 1513, Machiavelli declared:

If any one supports his state by the arms of mercenaries, he will never stand firm or sure, as they are disunited, ambitious, without discipline, faithless, bold amongst friends, cowardly amongst enemies, they have no fear of God, and keep no faith with men. Ruin is only deferred as long as the assault is postponed; in peace you are despoiled by them, and in war by the enemy. The cause of this is that they have no love or other motive to keep them in the field beyond a trifling wage, which is not enough to make them ready to die for you. They are quite willing to be your soldiers as long as you do not make war.

· 6 ·

The Swiss

Switzerland, noted today for its wealth and neutrality, has not always been so known. In the fourteenth century the Swiss began providing soldiers of fortune to the condottieri in Italy, and by the fifteenth century they were sending entire mercenary units to countries throughout Europe. Swiss mercenaries became renowned for their skills and loyalty as special guard units for emperors and military leaders. One of these, the Swiss Guards to the Vatican, formed in 1505, is the longest-existing mercenary unit in history and still protects the pope today.

In 1291 three small cantons (districts)—Uri, Schwyz, and Nidwalden—established the Swiss Federation for their mutual defense and for control of mountain passes along a trade route to their territories. Other Swiss cantons saw the advantages of forming a united front, and over the next century the larger districts of Luzern, Zurich, Bern, and Basel joined the federation. Although most of the warfare of the period took place to the south on the Italian peninsula, the Swiss Federation had to defend against invasion from the Austrians to the east, the Swabians to the north, and the Burgundians to the west.

The federation remained fairly loose until 1394, when the cantons met in response to several minor invasions in which individual districts had been forced to defend themselves without the aid of their neighbors. A unification conference produced the Covenant of Sempach, which assured mutual defense and outlined the federation's military doctrine. It was agreed that each canton would train its own militia; looting was not allowed; holy places, women, and children were to be protected; and deserters were to be punished. The writers of the covenant recognized that some extra benefits would be necessary to keep the troops content, so they amended the agreement to permit pillaging when captains approved and received a percentage of the loot.

The Swiss were able soldiers. During this period several hundred, possibly a thousand or so, Swiss crossed into Italy to join the free companies and later returned home with their gold coins earned as members of the condottieri. Even so, most of the canton members remained satisfied to stay home and engage in farming and commerce.

The Swiss, however, were willing to fight to defend their territory. In 1315 the Austrians invaded Switzerland only to be ambushed and turned back at a narrow pass near Morgarten. Over the next century and a half, the Swiss Federation fought a half dozen invaders, with the Burgundians of southern France causing the most difficulties. The Swiss finally forced the Burgundians, commanded by Charles the Bold, out of their territory at the Battle of Morat in 1476 when they killed eighteen thousand of their enemies with a loss of only five hundred of their own. Morat not only verified the fighting abilities of the Swiss, it also proved that their highly trained infantry fighting with spears and halberds (a combination of a spear and battle-ax) arrayed in in-depth formations could defeat massed cavalry.

Although the Swiss had maintained their freedom through the decades, the price had been costly. Unlike their mercenary brothers who were earning their fortunes soldiering in Italy, the Swiss who had fought at home did not find warfare to be at all profitable. This all changed after the Battle of Morat, when the Swiss pursued the retreating Charles the Bold and his Burgundians into their own homeland. Charles withdrew to Nancy, the capital of Lorraine, where on January 5, 1477, the Swiss Federation attacked. With a frontal assault and an encirclement on the left flank, the Swiss overran the Burgundians and killed Charles and most of his army.

The Swiss victory at the Battle of Nancy was important for three reasons. First, it ended the kingdom of Burgundy, whose remaining territories the king of France annexed. Second, the European powers saw that the Swiss had joined their ranks as an efficient, deadly military force. More important, the battle showed the Swiss that combat could be extremely lucrative.

In the captured Burgundian camp, the Swiss took possession of 420 cannons, 300 tons of gunpowder, 10,000 horses, and 1,500 wagons along with all the food and other supplies of the destroyed army. They also took more than a million florins (gold coins) as well as silver vessels, tapestries, religious icons, jewels, and one of the largest diamonds in Europe.

The Swiss took so much loot that, even after every soldier was granted a share, sufficient treasures remained to fill a room in a Bern museum. Some of the captured items are still on display today as "the booty of Burgundy."

Swiss cantons hired out their armies to whomever paid the price. The cantons provided armies of seven hundred to seven thousand trained and armed men to the highest bidder. Canton leaders required all males from age sixteen to sixty to be available for military service. Swiss units did not stay on active duty between campaigns but did remain armed and trained in the manner of militias while in their home districts. Their ability to mobilize quickly from farm and village proved to be one of their strengths as they could assemble and be on the move within days of receiving orders. Becoming a soldier of fortune and fighting wars for other kings and countries became a way of life for young Swiss men throughout the federation. Most welcomed the opportunity to fight for pay, but for the few who did not care to be soldiers of fortune, the cantons allowed a substitute from another village to be hired.

Like young men before and after, the Swiss found the mercenary life exciting as well as profitable. In one of their marching songs, they asked, "What is there to do at home, suck our fingers and sharpen our fingernails?" They answered, "We have been in the wars as soldiers so faithful that we have won lots of possessions; gold, silver, and lands. The lords have had to give us lots of things in exchange for our precious lives. That's how we have got into habits which we cannot get out of now."

Employers of the Swiss mercenary units—including Spain, Austria, England, Savoy, Holland, and France—appreciated this attitude and their fighting abilities. When the Catholic Rhenish League sent word to a canton that it wanted to hire four hundred Swiss soldiers, the request included the explanation that they were desired "above all for your terrible war cries, and for the reputation you have like your ancestors for spreading terror and panic when you set out on a campaign."

Swiss leaders went to great measures to ensure the future of their most important and profitable export. Although the Swiss were the primary mercenary force in practically every battle fought for a half century after their victory at the Battle of Nancy, they were careful not to fight each other or to engage allies of the federation. Before the cantons sent their mercenaries to fight for Louis XI of France in 1479, they required that the French king agree to terms that the soldiers would not be used against Swiss allies, would be kept together as units and not be parceled out to other armies, and that they would be released immediately if needed for defense of their own homeland.

Louis XI readily agreed, and as his primary intention for the Swiss was for them to be his personal bodyguards, he went a step further. The French king exempted them from routine garrison and guard duties and decreed that they would be punished only by their own officers.

From the time of their victory and looting of the Burgundians in 1477, the Swiss continued to provide personal bodyguards and mercenary units for the next four centuries. As bodyguards, their reputation for loyalty and proficiency remains to this day. However, the regular Swiss infantry mercenary units maintained their distinction of being the best on the battlefield for only about fifty years.

The end of the Swiss reputation as the best infantry in Europe came not from their lack of combat abilities or willingness to fight but rather from disease and a failure to adapt to innovations in weapons and tactics. And although it was not nearly as extreme as the bubonic plague that swept Europe and Asia in the fourteenth century, the spread of syphilis in France and Italy in the latter part of the fifteenth century significantly impacted armies on both sides. One indication is that of the two thousand Swiss mercenaries employed in Naples, only three hundred avoided the disease.

From their very beginnings the Swiss had relied on the cheaply made, readily available pike that dominated warfare for centuries. They also added a combination pike and ax known as the halberd, which gave them the advantage of hacking as well as thrusting.

Using formations of men sometimes dozens of ranks deep, the Swiss had been able to break any enemy defense and withstand any attack. The first indication of the vulnerability of these pike-and-halberd formations came at the 1503 Battle of Cerignola when the Swiss first encountered firearms.

In the latter years of the fifteenth century, France and Spain joined the ongoing warfare on the Italian peninsula so that they could add to their wealth and growing reputations as the most powerful military forces in Europe. After neutralizing the armies of various Italian factions, the French and Spanish began their own war over who would dominate the peninsula.

Early in the conflict the Swiss provided mercenary units to both sides, but by the turn of the century they were primarily in the employment of the French. At the same time, Spain began to depend less upon mercenaries and more upon advancing technology. The two concepts collided in a vineyard in southern Italy when a French army supported by Swiss soldiers of fortune attacked a Spanish force commanded by Gonzalo de Cordoba.

The Spanish had only a brief time to prepare their defenses, but Cordoba integrated a "corps of arquebusmen" into his ranks. Although numbering only several hundred, the Spanish musketmen turned back two assaults of the French and Swiss pikemen before counterattacking and clearing the battlefield.

After their loss at the Battle of Cerignola, the French yielded their claim over Naples to Spain. However, they resisted Spanish control over other parts of Italy and fought against other Swiss, who—no longer barred from opposing their own countrymen by profit-minded canton leaders—were fighting primarily for the Spanish and their allies of Rome, Naples, and other city-states in the northern regions. The French relied less and less on the Swiss and sought mercenaries from other sources while at the same time adding artillery to their arsenal.

The new mercenaries in the French army included Basque, Navarrese, and Gascon infantrymen, but the primary source of combatants came from the provinces that would eventually become Germany. German mercenaries, known as *Landsknecht*—German for "land servants" or "servants of the country"—developed a reputation not only for their fierceness and professionalism but also for their abuses of alcohol, prisoners, and the countryside in general. Despite these excesses, the Germans were extremely loyal to their commanders and employers—as steady, that is, as their paydays. An often-quoted axiom of the time claimed, "*Landsknechts* are as good as the gold you pay them, and last about as long as the beer provided."

The *Landsknechts* had little trouble recruiting replacements, forming companies of volunteers from neighboring villages and farms. *Landsknecht* recruits could earn twice as much in a month as soldiers as they could in a year of tilling crops or herding animals at home. In addition to wages, the German mercenary commanders compensated their men by allowing them to pillage the battlefield and loot the countryside to add to the glory and adventure of the life of a soldier of fortune. They were soon recognized by the colorful clothing they looted from the countryside. While disease and battle often resulted in an average life expectancy of a year or less, those *Landsknechts* who survived three or four years of campaigning returned home to a wealthy retirement.

The greatest clash between the *Landsknechts* and the Swiss mercenaries took place during the French-Spanish contest over northern Italy. At Marignano on September 15, 1515, the Swiss mercenaries fighting for Spain faced the *Landsknechts* fighting for the French. Ultimately the Swiss met the same fate as they had at Cerignola. French cannons and muskets ripped the Swiss ranks that still relied on halberds as their primary weapons. The weakened Swiss survivors then fell to the pikes and swords of the German infantry.

The French victory at Marignano brought a brief ceasefire but no peace to northern Italy. Combat continued between the French and the Spanish, with Swiss mercenaries fighting for whichever side paid their wages. In fact, by 1522 they were again being employed by France.

On April 27, 1522, the forces of France and Spain met again north of Milan at La Bicocca. Once more the French-hired Swiss infantry, armed only with pikes and

halberds, attacked Spanish infantrymen armed with ar-
quebuses. The musket fire left half the Swiss dead or dying in front of the Spanish trenches. The Swiss
mercenaries agreed to attack once again only if their officers led the charge. They did so, only to fall a second time
to a hail of bullets. The third and final attack, supported
by French cavalry, also failed.

On the field of La Bicocca lay more than three thousand
dead soldiers and the reputation of the Swiss halberdmen
as the finest infantry in all of Europe that money could
hire. Switzerland continued to be a source of mercenary
units for various wars after the disaster at La Bicocca, but
the Swiss never again attained their once-exalted reputation. Napoleon hired several Swiss regiments in 1803,
only to lose them along with most of his army in the Russian campaign of 1812.

In 1848, Switzerland formally prohibited its citizens
from serving in foreign armies and focused its efforts on
maintaining neutrality. Swiss leaders learned that the nation could profit even more through banking and trade
while others did the fighting. Their government passed
legislation outlawing fighting for money in 1874 and confirmed the law again in 1927.

While Switzerland prohibited the export of mercenary
units, it did not forbid its citizens from working as bodyguards for princes and kings as well as leaders of the military and the church, a tradition begun in 1481 when King
Louis XI of France hired Swiss mercenaries to serve as his
personal security force. The Swiss guards became such a
fixture of the succession of French kings that they became
a symbol of the monarchy for the next two centuries.

And their loyalty was without reproach. In 1524, when
King Francis I again attempted to achieve French control
of northern Italy, he had one hundred Swiss soldiers as his
personal bodyguards. In early 1525, when the French
army besieged a Spanish force south of Milan at the vil-

lage of Pavia, the Swiss bodyguards defended their employer to the last man; none lived to see Francis meekly
surrender to the counterattacking Spanish infantry.

When the French rebelled against King Louis XVI in
1779, his Swiss guards remained loyal and protected him
through the next three years of attempts to integrate the
people's government with that of the king's. By late summer of 1792 the revolution was in full swing and the six
hundred Swiss bodyguards and an equal number of loyal
French soldiers prepared to defend their king. On the
morning of August 10, Louis spoke to his soldiers, com-
mending their past loyalty and asking for their continued
protection. The Swiss cheered their employer and swore
their allegiance; the French soldiers deserted and joined
the mob of thousands outside the castle.

Louis left his Swiss guards behind as he sneaked off to
a nearby location where the French Assembly was in session. While the king asked for protection, the Swiss prepared to defend a throne that was now vacant. The mob
attacked and the Swiss turned back several assaults. With
casualties mounting and ammunition dwindling, the surviving Swiss fought their way to the Assembly to join
their king. Upon their arrival, Louis demanded that they
surrender in hopes that it would satisfy the mob's blood
lust. Some did so, only to be killed and dismembered by
the revolutionaries. The remaining few Swiss resumed
fighting but were also killed and mutilated. By sacrificing
his mercenaries, Louis survived, but only for five months
until he lost his head to the guillotine.

Except for Napoleon's limited use of Swiss soldiers in
his campaign against Russia, France was finished with
Swiss mercenaries, who the French felt represented royalty rather than the people. The Swiss, however, did not
forget their soldiers who had fought and died in the hire of
foreign kings. In 1821 the city of Lucerne, Switzerland,
dedicated a huge rock sculpture and sanctuary crafted by

Danish artist Bertel Thorvaldsen to the French Swiss guards. Standing at one of the city's gates, hewed on a rock face in relief is a dying lion, transfixed with a broken spear, protecting a shield bearing the fleur-de-lis of France.

The Lion of Lucerne is the largest known monument to the mercenary. American novelist Mark Twain in his 1880 book *A Tramp Abroad* declared the Lion of Lucerne to be "the most mournful and moving piece of stone in the world."

More famous and longer-lasting than the French Swiss Guards are the Swiss mercenaries who have guarded the Catholic popes. In 1505, Pope Julius II signed a treaty with the canons of Zurich and Lucerne, requesting that they provide two hundred soldiers to form his personal bodyguard. The Swiss mercenaries, commanded by Peter von Hertenstein and Caspar von Silenen, marched to Rome where they began their official service on January 21, 1506, after Julius II blessed the force in Saint Peter's Square.

In its early years the Swiss Guards varied in number and even at times briefly ceased to exist with the changes in popes and the numerous invasions of Rome. The most significant combat action by the Swiss Guard occurred on May 6, 1527, when a Spanish army led by Charles V conquered and sacked Rome and the Vatican. Kasper Roist, commander of the Guards, along with 147 Swiss soldiers died defending Pope Clement VII.

Clement survived the battle only to be captured by the Spanish. A year later he made peace with Spain and restored the papal state. Swiss Guards were once again recruited from their home cantons to protect the pope and his successors. Over the years the Guards' responsibilities evolved into ceremonial duties, and they continued to act as the pope's bodyguards and the Vatican's private army. The Swiss Guards and their employers, however, never forgot the sacrifices they made fighting the Spanish invaders. Every year on May 6 the Guards commemorate this historic date with a formation in the Vatican's San Damasco Courtyard. New recruits are sworn into the Guard in German, French, Italian, and Ladino, according to their canton of origin. Each recruit raises three fingers of his right hand—symbolizing the Father, Son, and Holy Spirit—while placing his left hand on the official flag of the Swiss Guards. The flag of the Guards has four sections—mixtures of red, yellow, and blue—divided by the white Swiss Cross. The flag changes with the addition of the coat of arms of each new pope and/or Guards' commander, but the oath remains the same. Each recruit swears to serve "faithfully, loyally, and honorably" and to sacrifice his own life should it become necessary.

Today the Swiss Guard numbers one hundred, including four officers, twenty-three noncommissioned officers, seventy-two enlisted soldiers, and a chaplain. The enlisted men, still known as halberdiers in honor of the weapon they have carried for six centuries, are most often seen standing guard armed only with these ancient weapons. However, today's Guards are qualified with all types of modern arms. These firearms are generally kept hidden at various guard stations, but are readily available if a formidable threat emerges against the pope or the Vatican. One of the few times the Swiss displayed modern weapons at their Guard posts was during the Nazi takeover of Rome in World War II. Although the Germans did not challenge the neutrality of the Vatican, the Swiss Guards stood ready to defend their employer with sandbagged entrances and machine guns.

Although the Swiss Guards today often are in civilian dress when guarding the pope when he ventures outside the Vatican, they normally wear uniforms fashioned after their attire dating back to the sixteenth century. These red, yellow, and blue uniforms are said to be originally designed by Michelangelo, but in reality are more likely an adaptation introduced by the Guards' commanding officer in 1914. Regardless of the origin of their uniforms, the colorfully clad, halberd-armed Swiss Guards closely resemble their forefathers.

Recruits in today's Swiss Guards must be at least sixty-eight inches in height, Catholic, unmarried, and nineteen to twenty-five years of age. They enlist for a period of two years, and with satisfactory service and the permission of their commander may serve for as long as twenty-five years. The majority of the Guards are Swiss nationals, but recently, because of recruitment difficulties, a few French and Italians have been permitted to join. Perhaps the difficulty in finding new Guards is due to the fact that the pay is the equivalent of about a thousand U.S. dollars per month and of course, today's Vatican guards do not have the traditional privilege that attracted soldiers of fortune over the centuries—the right to loot and pillage.

· 7 ·

Wild Geese

Greece and Switzerland were the sources for the majority of mercenaries in Europe and around the Mediterranean. However, Ireland became the first country to provide men-for-hire for causes around the world. Irishmen not only picked up the sword and musket for all the usual reasons of profit, adventure, and employment opportunity, but also for any enemy of their long-term foes, the English.

Many factors combined to produce the personality and spirit of the Irish warrior. The earliest inhabitants of the Irish isles were Bronze Age settlers from the Mediterranean who arrived in about the fourth century B.C. Celts from Gaul came later and by the third century A.D. had established five tribal kingdoms on the island. During the fifth century, Saint Patrick brought Catholicism to Ireland, a religion that soon dominated the population. The Vikings began raiding the Irish coast in the eighth century and established coastal settlements which included Cork, Limerick, and Dublin. In 1014 the Irish, under King Brian Boru, defeated a large Viking force at the Battle of Clontarf near Dublin, which discouraged further attacks against Ireland and focused Norse aggression against England instead.

Still, the Celtic-Catholic traditions of Ireland, influenced by the fighting abilities and spirit of the Vikings, could not withstand the English invasion led by King

Henry II in 1171. Although the English never completely pacified Ireland, they were successful in putting down a succession of rebellions. Their control was sufficiently successful to draft Irish regiments into the English army.

As early as the thirteenth century the English hired Irish cavalry to patrol their border with Scotland. When the Hundred Years' War began with France in 1337, England and its Irish soldiers joined the fight on the Continent. The next three centuries would find Irish soldiers fighting in every conflict and on all sides in the religious wars that swept Europe. Soldiers were Ireland's most numerous and important export and served in countries as varied as England, Spain, and the Netherlands.

With their fighting experience from the Continent and the continuing rebellions at home, the Irish entered the seventeenth century as among the most experienced and proficient soldiers in the world. They distinguished themselves in the battles against the Scots on behalf of the English as well as fighting in the various civil wars that challenged the crown of England.

In 1645, Oliver Cromwell joined the civil war against English King Charles and in four years defeated the Royalists to take control of England. Cromwell then turned his army toward Scotland and Ireland with the intention of ending the various rebellions in these areas and uniting the entire British Isles under his leadership.

Cromwell invaded Ireland in 1649 at Dublin and then stormed the Irish stronghold of Drogheda in September. The English army massacred the surviving defenders as well as civilian residents in what is considered to be the most horrible atrocity in British history.

The massacre at Drogheda brought Ireland briefly under control, but also increased Irish hatred of the English. Over the next three decades the Irish continued to resist the English at home while sending mercenaries to support France, Spain, and the Dutch in their wars against Britain.

In addition to their battles on the Continent, the English also faced continued conflict between Catholics and Protestants over who should occupy the kingdom's throne. By 1689, William III wore the crown as the leader of English Protestants while James II, supported by France, vied to take over for the Catholics. James also received much support from the Irish, who became known as *Jacobites*—the Hebrew word for James.

In March 1689, James and a small French army landed in Ireland, where they were joined by a Jacobian force of forty thousand. Over the next months this combined force pacified Irish Protestant resistance in the northern part of the island and then began preparations to invade the English homeland. William countered by sending his own army, composed of English soldiers as well as mercenaries from throughout the European mainland, to Ireland.

The armies of William and James met at Boyne on July 11, 1690, with the Protestant army sweeping James and his Jacobians from the field. James fled back to France, but his army managed to reorganize and withdraw to the southwest and west of Ireland. On July 12, 1691, a Dutch army in the hire of William attacked and defeated a Jacobite stronghold at Aughrim. The surviving Jacobites withdrew to Limerick, where they prepared to make their last stand.

During this series of battles with William's armies, Patrick Sarsfield, born about 1650 near Dublin, advanced through the ranks to become the overall commander by the time the Jacobites reached Limerick. Sarsfield was the grandson of one of the leaders of the 1641 Irish rebellion and had himself served in various regiments on the Continent both in the employment of the English and their enemies.

Sarsfield and his Jacobites fought bravely in defense of Limerick but were unable to break the English siege of the city. Neither side was able to gain a significant advantage over the following months. Finally, on October 3, 1691, with winter approaching, the two sides agreed to an armistice with two treaties, one military and one civil. The stone on which they signed the agreement is still a major tourist attraction in Limerick's city square.

The civil treaty provided for freedom of religion for the Catholics and an amnesty for past aggressions against the king. Portions of the military treaty offered the Irish pay to serve in the English army and also guaranteed safe passage to France for those who chose not to serve William.

While the English quickly withdrew and reneged on most of the promises in the civil treaty, they did allow Sarsfield and eleven thousand soldiers to sail to France in what became known as "the flight of the wild geese." Some accounts say that the Irish soldiers were manifested on the French ships that evacuated them as "wild geese," but more likely this term came a decade or so later when French ships, delivering brandy and other supplies, recruited new Irish mercenaries to return to the Continent. The ship captains listed these recruits on their manifests as "wild geese" to confuse English customs agents.

Whatever the source, "wild geese" has become synonymous for Irish of every generation who have left the Emerald Isle to serve as hired soldiers in wars around the world. In fact, the term has become so common that all mercenaries, regardless of origin, fighting the numerous conflicts in Africa in the mid-twentieth century were labeled Wild Geese. The widely distributed Hollywood films about mercenaries in Africa used the title *The Wild Geese* in 1978 and *Wild Geese II* in 1985.

Whether known as Wild Geese or simply Irish mercenaries, the army led by Patrick Sarsfield was welcomed in France. James II greeted the army with a message proclaiming he would never forget their loyalty. Although James arranged for the Wild Geese to be paid, he retained a percentage of their fees for his personal expenses.

Sarsfield and his army joined other Irish mercenaries in France to form the Irish Brigade. Soon they were back in combat fighting under the flag of French king Louis XIV against their old enemy King William of England. Sarsfield's defense of Limerick and his continued fight against the Protestant English king gained him fame and the affection of his fellow Irishmen. Many consider him the father of the Irish nation.

With the motto of "Remember Limerick and the English Betrayal," Sarsfield led the Irish Brigade in the service of France. He and his army welcomed the opportunity to fight the English while earning a decent living doing so. By 1692, King Louis had elevated Sarsfield to the rank of marshal of France, but the Irish leader did not have long to enjoy his position. On July 19, 1693, Sarsfield fell to a musket ball while leading the Irish Brigade against the English along a small stream near the village of Neerwinden in the Netherlands. His troops carried him on a stretcher to Huy, about sixty miles south of Brussels, where he died on July 22. According to legend, as Sarsfield lay mortally wounded, he put his hand to his wound and, drawing it back covered in blood, commented that his only regret was that the blood was not shed for Ireland.

Sarsfield's comrades buried him with full military honors in the grounds of St. Martin's Church in Huy. He left behind a nineteen-year-old widow, Honora de Burgo, who, like many of the family members of the Wild Geese, had fled Ireland with her soldier husband. Sarsfield also left behind a three-month-old son. James Francis Edward Sarsfield would follow in his father's footsteps, securing a commission in the Spanish army and earning several decorations for bravery before his death at age twenty-five.

The death of the senior Sarsfield did not disrupt the Irish Brigade. France continued to employ the Irish unit and formed other Irish soldier-of-fortune regiments in times of need to fight their many wars of the eighteenth century. When James II died in 1701, his son James Stuart (James III) continued his father's employment of the Irish Brigade and added five additional regiments.

The Irish units then fought for France in Italy, Flanders, Spain, and Bavaria. They so impressed King Louis XIV with their courage and bravery in the Austrian campaign of 1701–02 that he raised the pay of the new regiments to that of the veteran Irish Brigade.

All Wild Geese mercenary units served with distinction in the employment of France, but the Irish Brigade was the longest-lasting and achieved the most honors. Its finest hour occurred at the Battle of Fontenoy in what is now Belgium on May 10, 1745. A joint English-Dutch army penetrated the initial French defenses early in the battle, but they were turned back when they assaulted the secondary lines anchored by the Irish Brigade. "Remember Fontenoy" became a battle cry within the Irish Brigade as well as in the pubs back home in Ireland. A print of the Irish Brigade displaying captured English and Dutch standards has been reprinted in various Irish periodicals on the battle's anniversary ever since.

Wild Geese not only flocked to France for employment as soldiers to fight against England and anything English but also to Spain where they formed the Hibernia Brigade and Ulster Regiment for King Philip V. When France and England finally agreed to an armistice in the Treaty of Utrecht in 1715, many of the original Wild Geese and other Irish mercenaries serving France joined their comrades in Spain. Others sought employment in Russia and the countries throughout Europe.

Throughout their service as mercenaries in the early decades of the eighteenth century, the Wild Geese constantly sought the means to return to Ireland and free their country from English rule. A lack of ships to transport the

Irish coupled with the strong English navy that blocked the way homeward kept them at bay. Their best chance to return home came in 1746 when most of the Irish Brigade joined the rebellion led by Bonnie Prince Charlie in Scotland. The English, however, defeated the Irish and their Scottish allies at the Battle of Culloden on April 16, 1746.

Some of the survivors returned to France and the life of professional mercenaries. Irishmen continued to serve the French as well as every other country that opposed England. Wild Geese advanced in rank in the regular armies of other countries. Irishman George Brown achieved the rank of marshal while eleven of his countrymen advanced to the rank of general in the Austrian army. Another Irishman, Francis Maurice Lacy, earned the rank of field marshal in the army of the Russian czar. Nineteenth-century poet Emily Lawless later characterized these wandering soldiers of fortune as "Fighters in every clime—Every cause but their own."

The first significant group of Irish mercenaries to arrive in North America joined Louis Montcalm and his French army to oppose the British in the French and Indian War. Part of the Irish Brigade, containing many descendants of the original Wild Geese, fought with Montcalm in their unsuccessful defense of Quebec in September 1759.

While the Irish mercenaries assisted France against the British and their allied American colonists in the French and Indian War, they readily joined the Americans when they rebelled against the British. Irishmen served at every level in the newly formed U.S. Army, Navy, and Marine Corps. Some served to earn citizenship in the new country; others continued their forefathers' tradition of fighting the English wherever and whenever, and still others fought for the small wages in the newly formed American military.

During the extended American Revolution, seventeen Irishmen rose to the level of general or admiral in service to the United States. John Barry, born in County Wexford, Ireland, in 1745, rose from cabin boy to admiral in the U.S. Navy and commanded the frigate *Alliance* against the British fleet in the Revolution's last naval battle. His service earned him the title "Father of the American Navy" for his wartime exploits and later influence on the establishment of the sea arm of the newly independent United States of America.

In addition to individuals who joined the Revolution, regiments of the Irish Brigade still in the employment of France arrived in America to fight the English. The Dillon Regiment, led by its namesake Col. Arthur Dillon, initially sailed to the West Indies to defend French possessions there. In the fall of 1779 about fifteen hundred Irish members of the Dillon Regiment joined other French and American units in the unsuccessful attack against the British at Savannah, Georgia. The Dillon Regiment, reinforced by the Walsh and Berwick Regiments of the Irish Brigade, later assisted in continued French operations against the British in the West Indies.

When Spain joined the French in support of the American Revolution, its Wild Geese also participated in the fight. The Hibernia Regiment fought with other Spanish units against the English at Pensacola, Florida, in 1781.

While many Irish immigrants remained in the United States after the War of Independence, the Irish Brigade regiments returned to France. After nearly a century of faithful service to the crown, they were finally disbanded when the French successfully concluded their own revolution in 1792.

When Napoleon came to power in the early years of the nineteenth century, he remembered the fighting abilities of the Wild Geese and formed his own unit of Irish mercenaries. His Irish Legion contained Irish refugees still in France as well as those fleeing another unsuccessful revolution in Ireland.

The legion did not, however, recruit only Irish soldiers. As the passage of years and battle casualties reduced the numbers in it ranks, the legion recruited English and men of other nationalities who were French prisoners of war. An Irish Legion recruiting document distributed to POWs in 1810 announced, "Any young man of spirit that has an inclination to serve in the First Irish Regiment of Foot, forming at Landau, has only to apply to the Recruiting Officer. The Officer will procure his release immediately. He shall be well fed, well paid, well clothed, receive rapid promotion, and will enjoy more advantage in this Regiment than in any other in France. The engagement is only for four years."

Napoleon's ultimate defeat in 1815 left many Irish mercenaries unemployed, but their fighting skills did not languish for long. Multiple revolutions taking place in South America against Spain and Portugal provided renewed opportunities for soldiers of fortune. While fighting Spain and Portugal may not have been as satisfying as combating the English, the Irish found South America's gold, silver, and other riches a sufficient lure.

In August 1819 the Irish Legion of one thousand men landed on Venezuela's Margarita Island after sailing from Dublin. More than twelve hundred additional Wild Geese, both young recruits and veterans of the Napoleonic Wars, arrived during the next year.

Revolutionary leader Simon Bolivar relied on his Irish Legion in direct combat as well as on his staff. Daniel Florence O'Leary of County Cork became Bolivar's personal aide-de-camp and later rose to the rank of brigadier general as he assisted his commander in plotting political and military strategy. Today a bust of O'Leary overlooks a plaza in Bogotá, and his remains rest in the National Pantheon in Caracas alongside Bolivar and other heroes of the revolution.

The Wild Geese also ventured to Brazil, but they were

not as successful as those who joined Bolivar. More than twenty-five hundred Irishmen, mostly from County Cork, sailed to Rio de Janeiro in 1826 to join the revolution against the Portuguese. The revolution, however, failed and most of the survivors returned home to Ireland. A few remained in Brazil as farmers near the village of Valenca north of Rio.

A few individual Irish mercenaries greatly influenced the future of South America. William Brown, born in 1777 in Mayo County, migrated to Philadelphia as a boy with his parents. He soon joined an American merchant vessel as a cabin boy and over succeeding decades advanced to command his own ship. In the early part of the nineteenth century, Brown sailed into South American waters where he offered his services to Argentina in its revolt against the Spanish. Although seriously wounded in combat with the Spanish fleet in March 1813, Brown stayed at his ship's helm and cleared the Rio Plata of Spain's domination. Argentina awarded Brown the post of governor of Buenos Aires and the unofficial title of "Father of the Argentine Navy."

In nearby Chile another Irishman, Bernardo O'Higgins, was instrumental in yet another revolution. O'Higgins, born in 1777 to a father who had recently arrived from Ireland, entered the Spanish militia as a young man and then joined the Chilean revolutionaries in 1810. During seven years of combat O'Higgins rose to be their commander. Upon his victory over the Spanish in 1817, O'Higgins became the first "supreme director" of the independent Chile.

The first half of the nineteenth century continued to offer employment opportunities for Wild Geese. "Wherever you find war, you find Irishmen" was a common saying with much truth. Events soon occurred, however, that forced the Irish to leave their homeland not just to fight against the British but merely to survive.

The blight that struck the 1846 Irish potato crop left

farmland covered in a black rot. Without their primary crop both for their own consumption and for payment of rent to their English landlords, the Irish farmers faced famine and eviction. Over the next five years the Potato Famine put more than a million Irish men, women, and children in the grave and drove twice that many to foreign shores. During this time all Irish emigrants, whether seeking employment as mercenaries or not, also became known as Wild Geese.

Where Ireland had once sent mercenaries to armies and navies around the globe, it now dispatched entire families who took Irish culture worldwide. Many headed for the United States, a country that had fought two wars against England and promised freedom and opportunity for everyone. There, many Irish immigrants resumed farming or became tradesmen or merchants. Others took up the enlistment promise of the U.S. Army for three hot meals a day, a place to sleep, and a monthly payment. Although these volunteers might not be considered true mercenaries because they sought to serve their newly adopted country, they did meet the standard of out-of-work men willing to fight for money.

When the United States declared war against Mexico on May 13, 1846, Maj. Gen. Zachary Taylor led the U.S. Army across the Rio Grande into Mexican territory. Fully half of his soldiers were born outside the United States, the majority coming from Ireland. Most served bravely, but some of the Irish soldiers found their sympathies and ambitions torn.

Mexico tried to convince Irish soldiers that the war was an American Protestant attack against Mexican Catholics. The Mexican government promised 320 acres of farmland to any American soldier who crossed the lines to join their fellow Catholics on the Mexican side. More than two hundred Irishmen accepted the offer and formed what became known as the San Patricio Brigade. Many died in the following battles; the few survivors were hanged as traitors by the victorious Americans at the conclusion of the war.

The Irish continued to pour into the United States even after the Potato Famine ended. Immigrants sought the freedoms enjoyed by Americans, and many found their first employment, or in previous generations, in their newly adopted country as soldiers in the U.S. Army. During the American Civil War, Irishmen joined the armies of both the North and the South. Many willingly volunteered while others, especially in the North, were literally drafted off the boats that brought them to America.

More than one hundred fifty thousand Irishmen served in the Union forces, mostly in the Irish Brigade of the 1st Division of the II Corps of the Army of the Potomac. Irish-born Union soldiers earned 10 percent of the twelve hundred Medals of Honor awarded in the conflict.

Irishmen also wore the gray of the Confederacy with more than fifty thousand serving the Rebel cause. Several rose to high ranks. Irish-born Patrick Cleburne became a major general in command of what was one of the South's finest divisions. Cleburne and his command participated in many of the war's most influential fights before he died in the Battle of Franklin in Tennessee, on November 10, 1864. General Cleburne thoroughly believed in the responsibilities of a soldier, regardless of the cause. In a letter to his brother shortly before the war began, he wrote, "Life has always been a small matter with me when duty points the way."

Irishmen continued to emigrate to the United States after the Civil War and continued to enlist in the army as their first employment in America. Fully one-fourth of the men who fell with George A. Custer at the Battle of the Little Big Horn in 1876 listed Ireland as their place of birth on their enlistment papers.

With a new century came the chance again for Irishmen to fight their old enemy. When the Dutch "Boers" of Transvaal and the Orange Free State went to war with the British in 1899, hundreds of Irishmen from their home island and from around the world flocked to southern Africa to join the fight.

Most came as individuals, but some found ingenious ways to join the Boers in their war against the English. In April 1900 an ambulance company from Chicago, composed of fifty-three Wild Geese born both in Ireland and the United States, arrived in Pretoria wearing the Red Cross armbands of noncombatants. Once the unit was allowed to land, all but five exchanged their armbands for rifles and marched off to join the Boers.

In 1916, rebellion broke out in Dublin and continued until 1921, when the English finally granted the island its independence as the Irish Free State (but it continued as a dominion of the British Commonwealth). Six counties in Northern Ireland, where Protestants were in the majority, elected to remain a part of the United Kingdom. These developments mostly ended the flight of Wild Geese to armies around the world that had begun after the Treaty of Limerick more than two centuries earlier.

The Irish Free State changed its name to Eire in 1937 and became a republic when it withdrew from the British Commonwealth in 1949. Clashes along the border with Northern Ireland continued until recent years while the terrorist group, the Irish Republican Army, fought the British army in the six counties of the north.

Although Ireland remained neutral during World War II, many of its citizens fought in British regiments. Its own army remained a self-defense force until 1960 when two battalions served with the United Nations in the Congo, marking the first occasion that Irish forces served abroad under their own flag.

All of these activities greatly reduced the numbers of

Irishmen who sought employment as mercenaries. That is not to say, however, that Wild Geese are not still seeking to fight for whomever will pay them for their trouble. In 2001, three Irish citizens were captured by Colombian troops and accused of providing military assistance to the country's narco-guerrillas. The Irishmen, traveling under false passports, were accused by a guerrilla defector of teaching his former comrades how to build pipe bombs and work with other explosives.

The long history of the Wild Geese is mostly over today, but a few young Irishmen still seek the adventure and lure of traveling abroad and joining the armies of other countries. Gerry Corcoran left Ireland to come to America to race bicycles in the mid-1990s. After a few months he used his green card to join the U.S. Army and then served in the 82nd Airborne Division in North Carolina and the 2nd Infantry Division in Korea.

Corcoran recalls, "I was out of a job, broke, and getting hungry. The nice army recruiter promised fun, travel, and adventure as well as 'three hots and a cot' and a regular paycheck." Corcoran later earned an honorable discharge and, in the tradition of Wild Geese before him, went off in search of new adventures.

· 8 ·

Hessians

Conflict between England and France dominated events in Europe as well as in India and North America during most of the eighteenth century. Spain, Russia, Austria, Prussia, Switzerland, Ireland, and the Netherlands allied with first one side and then another in this long period of warfare.

While these various alliances created multinational armies, mercenaries also filled the ranks of the principals. During the eighteenth century soldiers of fortune accounted for half of the English, a third of the French, two-thirds of the Prussian, and a quarter of the Spanish armies. These soldiers of fortune included high-ranking officers as well as ordinary troopers.

Armies met on the field of battle with hired soldiers led by mercenary officers from a multitude of countries. The only common language was that of combat. On occasion, regular soldiers of one country fought their fellow countrymen when one was serving his own flag and another was in the employment of a current enemy, who might very well also have been a former ally.

The Swiss and Irish dominated the mercenary ranks in the latter part of the seventeenth century, many of them joining the Prussian army of Frederick the Great. They served the Prussian general beside hired mercenaries from other countries and under hired officers, many of whom held the army's most senior positions. They received most of their wages in gold that Frederick got from his English ally, but there was no doubt who was in charge of the Prussians. The mercenaries knew they were serving a man who, when he first assumed command of Prussia's army on the death of his father in 1740, announced, "In this kingdom, I am the only person to exercise authority." Over the next quarter century, the hired soldiers as well as the rest of Europe found Frederick to be one of the most able and influential commanders of his age.

When Frederick went home to Prussia in 1763 at the conclusion of the Seven Years' War, his foreign mercenaries either returned to their native countries or sought employment as soldiers elsewhere. The sheer numbers of mercenaries, who came from the nearly three hundred different regions and principalities that composed the Germanic states, caused the princes who controlled these states to realize they had a great income-producing commodity. By creating regiments of veterans from Frederick's army and young men coming of age in the provinces, they could hire out these units at profitable rates. The export of these units would not only provide a steady income but also reduce the number of subjects who would have to be supported at home.

Most members of the numerous German state units had little choice about becoming soldiers because they were drafted. German leaders did not limit forced induction to their own citizens; they also conscripted anyone living or even passing through their states.

A relative, albeit temporary, peace did not readily provide employment opportunities for the German regiments, but a developing revolution in North America soon did. When the American colonists made a stand against the British at the Battles of Lexington and Concord on April 19, 1775, the English thought their army in North America would quickly quell the rebellion. A shocking battle that killed 226 British soldiers, including many officers, and wounded an additional eight hundred troops at Boston's Bunker Hill on June 16 convinced King George that he would need more help to end the uprising.

King George initially turned to his old ally, the queen of Russia. Catherine the Great considered renting her army to Britain, but finally suggested that the English might do better to attempt a peaceful settlement and sent an official reply turning down King George's request to employ her soldiers.

Catherine's formal note also expressed her reservations at using mercenaries to fight the wars of other monarchs. She wrote, "I am just beginning to enjoy peace and Your Majesty knows that my empire has need of repose. There is an impropriety in employing so considerable a body in another hemisphere, under a power almost unknown to it and almost removed in contact with its sovereign. Moreover, I should not be able to prevent myself from reflecting on the consequences which would result for our dignity, for that of the two monarchies and the two nations, from this junction of our forces, simply to calm a rebellion which is not supported by any foreign power."

Catherine's morally superior message omitted the true reason for her refusal—lack of economic necessity. At the time, her majesty and her country were financially well off and, all rhetoric aside, she simply did not need the income produced by risking a good part of her army in foreign combat halfway around the world.

While Catherine might not have needed English gold, other monarchs in Europe were more receptive to the idea. Many German states had veteran regiments sitting idle and costing their princes maintenance money. The German princes in charge of their states needed additional revenue to finance their excesses. One reportedly was charged with the care of seventy-four children and desperately needed new sources of income to maintain his lifestyle.

Prince Frederick II of Hesse-Cassel began negotiations with King George to provide more than sixteen thousand soldiers. The leaders of other German principalities—including Hesse-Hannau, Brunswick, Anspach-Beyreuth, Anhalt Zerbst, and Waldeck—volunteered to provide an additional fourteen thousand. Although each of these states considered itself independent from the others, Hesse-Cassel provided the bulk of the troops, which led to the mercenary army becoming known to both the English and the Americans as Hessians.

On January 15, 1776, the representatives of King George and of Hesse-Cassel signed a lengthy treaty (Appendix A) agreeing to amounts, terms, and payment. The agreement called for specific numbers of battalions, pieces of artillery, and officers. Similar treaties were signed with representatives of the leaders of the other principalities. As happy as King George was to have the reinforcements, the German princes were even happier as they were adding English sterling coins to their treasuries while at the same time sending thousands of men they no longer had to support to America.

Not everyone, however, shared the joy of King George and the German princes. The soldiers themselves, while considered mercenaries because their services were being paid for and they were fighting for a cause that was not theirs, received little of George's sterling. Their pay was minimal, barely exceeding the cost of their food and supplies. Also, as an organized army with permanent officers, they generally were not permitted to participate in the looting and pillaging usually considered a privilege of soldiers of fortune.

Neither was every Englishman convinced. In a House of Commons debate, Governor Johnstone declared, "Shall we despise the history of all those nations from Carthage downwards who have lost their liberty by employing foreign troops and recur to those silly arguments which have always been used as the reason for first introducing them?"

News of the agreement between the British and the Germans met with additional disfavor among the American colonists. Most felt that their dispute with the British was an internal "family" affair and resented the introduction of what they considered barbarous foreigners into the affray.

When the United States issued its Declaration of Independence from Great Britain on July 4, 1776, the document noted, "The history of the present King of Great Britain is a history of repeated injuries and usurpations, all having in direct object the establishment of an absolute tyranny over these states. To prove this, let facts be submitted to a candid world."

The king's employment of the Germans was listed among these candid facts: "[King George] is at this time transporting large armies of foreign mercenaries [Hessians] to complete the works of death, desolation, and tyranny already begun with circumstances of cruelty and perfidy scarcely paralleled in the most barbarous ages, and totally unworthy the head of a civilized nation."

There is little doubt that the Hessians served their British employers fairly well in America, at least initially, helping push the rebellious colonists out of the population and trade centers of New York and Philadelphia during the late fall of 1776. Armies of this period usually went into stationary quarters during the harsh winter months to refit and prepare for offensives in the spring. The British and Hessians settled into fairly comfortable quarters in occupied cities and towns, leaving the rebels to the countryside and smaller villages.

The loss of major cities and the harsh conditions they suffered in their winter garrisons greatly impacted the morale of the rebels. Many of the soldiers as well as their leaders second-guessed the wisdom of the Revolution.

Gen. George Washington, commander of the Continental Army, had other ideas.

After its retreat from New York, the rebel army had marched southwestward through New Jersey and crossed the Delaware River into Pennsylvania. Washington knew that he had to take some significant action to save his army and to recruit additional soldiers as well as acquire needed arms, ammunition, and supplies.

On the night of December 25, 1776, Washington and an army of twenty-four hundred recrossed the ice-clogged Delaware River about nine miles north of the town of Trenton in the midst of a snowstorm. Early the next morning his men rushed past the few Hessian pickets on the west and north of Trenton and attacked the main force of fourteen hundred German mercenaries in the streets and alleys of the town. Many of the Hessians were still feeling the effects of their Christmas celebration the night before. All were greatly surprised to be attacked in their quarters when they thought there would be no more combat until spring.

In a brief fight with musket fire and bayonets, the Hessian commander Col. Johann Rall and twenty-nine of his men died. Some of the German mercenaries escaped to the south, but the Americans took more than nine hundred prisoners and used them through the winter as free labor. Several powder magazines and other stone fortifications, including an impressive structure at Carlisle Barracks, Pennsylvania, still stand today as monuments to these captured soldiers of fortune.

The Hessians again encountered Washington when he executed another surprise attack on a British rearguard detachment at Princeton, New Jersey, on January 2, killing or capturing four hundred Redcoats and mercenaries. Only when Washington did finally take his army into winter quarters at Morristown could the British and Hessians relax for the remainder of the winter in their own garrisons.

The battles of Trenton and Princeton significantly influenced the American Revolutionary War. Recruits and supplies poured into Washington's army as the Americans realized they could successfully defeat the British and their German soldiers of fortune. These events shocked the British at home, who had thought that their army, especially being supported by the Hessians, would quickly put an end to the revolt. Lord George Germaine summarized the thoughts of many British when he said, "All our hopes were blasted by the unhappy affair at Trenton."

Trenton, of course, did not end the war. The Hessians remained employed for another seven years as Washington maneuvered his army in the field. As long as he and his army survived, so did the United States of America. With much of the country supporting him after his victories in New Jersey, Washington thereafter fought mostly a defensive war against the still numerically superior British.

The Hessians, generally well disciplined, continued to perform well, though they had difficulty acquiring replacements for their soldiers lost in battle and to illness. As a result, they welcomed African-American slaves who escaped from their owners. They used most as musicians and support personnel, but a few served as replacements for regular soldiers. Specific accounts are minimal, but Carol Baurmeister, adjutant general of the Hessians, wrote in an official report from New York in 1777 that officers in the Erbprinz Regiments were recruiting black infantrymen to fill vacancies in their units.

One of the few surviving images of Hessians in America is a drawing by J. H. Carl. The print, first published in 1784, shows five members of the Hessian Third Guard armed with muskets or pikes. A black drummer in full uniform accompanies the soldiers.

The Hessians remained in America for about a year after the American victory at the decisive Battle of Yorktown in October 1781. King George still had money, and the German princes were more than willing to continue to be paid for their armies even if they were now serving a lost cause.

After the Americans and British signed the Treaty of Paris in 1783, the Hessians finally sailed home. However, of the thirty thousand German mercenaries who served in America, only seventeen thousand actually returned to their native lands. About one thousand Hessians perished either directly or as a result of their wounds in battle. Another six thousand died of disease or accidents.

The remainder of the Hessians deserted. Nearly a quarter-million German immigrants had preceded the Hessians to America, and most were prospering as farmers and merchants in concentrated areas of eastern Pennsylvania where the Hessians were stationed. These immigrants encouraged the mercenaries to lay down their arms and join their communities. The newly formed U.S. government also encouraged Hessian desertions with the promise of free land. At least five thousand Hessians accepted the offer and remained in America when the war finally ended.

In the two-hundred-year debate on why the world's most powerful country could not put down a rebellion by the American colonists, much of the argument centers on the use of German mercenaries in the conflict. Hessian soldiers, fighting to enrich their monarchs rather than themselves or for any of their own national interest, were reluctant soldiers at best. The English, unable or unwilling to field sufficient numbers of their own soldiers, relied too heavily on their hired troops to roust the Americans who, quite simply, had to fight for their survival.

The American reaction to Hessian mercenaries also served notice to other countries that the once common use of soldiers of fortune was coming to an end. Lord Chatham, speaking to the British Parliament on November 20, 1777, said, "My Lords, you cannot conquer America. In three campaigns we have done nothing and suffered much. You may swell every expense, accumulate every assistance you can buy or borrow, traffic and barter with every pitiful little German prince that sells and sends his subjects to the shambles of a foreign power. Your efforts are forever vain and impotent, doubly so from this mercenary aid on which you rely; for it irritates to an incurable resentment. If I were an American as I am an Englishman, while a foreign troop was in my country, I would never lay down my arms; never, never, never."

As other peoples around the world copied America's example and stood for their own freedoms and independence, most recognized that the best soldiers were the citizens themselves who would enjoy the benefits of that freedom. The tide had turned, and an era of mercenaries was on the decline while the age of the citizen soldier was on the rise.

Edward J. Lowell's 1884 *The Hessians* perhaps sums up best this incongruous band of warriors who found to their detriment that that cause, the cause of the professional soldier, was no longer adequate in a world of liberty:

In spite of the injustice with which the rank and file had been treated, there are signs that many of these involuntary volunteers were not such bad fellows after all. The Germans had their fair share of those virtues which every nation is fond of claiming as its peculiar birthright; honesty, courage, kindliness. The motley mass had been shaped and welded by a rigorous, if often cruel, discipline. They could not wipe out, to American eyes, the shame of their mercenary calling. But the shame fairly belonged to their princes, and not to themselves. In the field, or in captivity, they often deserved and sometimes obtained the respect of their opponents. Many of them became, in the end, citizens of the republic they were sent to destroy.

· 9 ·

French Foreign Legion

Of all the groups of men who have offered themselves as soldiers in exchange for money, perhaps none is better known than the French Foreign Legion. While the Legion achieved its reputation on battlefields around the world—surprisingly . . . often in defeat—it became legendary through a long history of "spin" and good publicity in books, songs, and motion pictures.

The French had themselves long been a primary employer of mercenaries since the Middle Ages. The massacre of King Louis XVI's Swiss Guards during the revolution of 1792 briefly brought an end to the use of mercenaries in France, but within a decade Napoleon added hired armies to assist his efforts to dominate Europe.

Mercenaries stayed on the payrolls in France even after Napoleon's defeat in 1815. Sixteen years after the Battle of Waterloo, Louis Philippe declared himself king of France and began to expand his kingdom. Well aware that the French people were war-weary and less than enthusiastic about sending their sons into still another conflict, Louis Philippe solved his dilemma by hiring foreign mercenaries. He assumed that the mercenaries, if adequately compensated, would not complain about the harsh conditions of their service or the political correctness of their objectives.

Louis Philippe officially organized the French Foreign

Legion on March 10, 1831. It contained seven battalions, each composed of volunteers of similar national origins. Germans made up the 1st, 2nd, and 3rd Battalions while Spaniards dominated the 4th, Italians the 5th, Belgians and Dutch the 6th, and Poles the 7th. Louis Philippe quickly dispatched the Legion to Algeria, which much later modern media would make synonymous with the Legion's exploits.

In truth the Legion's early performance in North Africa was not exemplary. The first volunteers were a mixture of ragged refugees from throughout Europe and appeared to one eyewitness to look more like a circus than an army. Thirty-five legionnaires deserted within twenty-four hours of one battalion's arrival in North Africa. In the same unit, the next day the men in one company became so drunk they attacked their own officers. Two leaders of the minirevolt were executed.

This poor early performance ultimately set the stage for the Legion's reputation for severe discipline. Veteran volunteers from the Swiss and Prussian armies replaced the French officers and instituted the harsh discipline that came to characterize the Legion as a whole.

Despite their reformed performance, Louis Philippe became tired of funding the Foreign Legion and literally sold it to Queen Cristina of Spain, who used it to expand her own interests in North Africa. Cristina then employed the Legion to combat revolutionaries assisted by English mercenaries in her own country. At the Battle of Barbastro, in June 1837, both sides suffered significant casualties in one of the last great battles on the European continent fought primarily by mercenary armies.

Soon after Barbastro, the Spanish disbanded the Legion. It would be nearly a century before Spain organized another unit of foreign soldiers of fortune, this time to fight the rebels in Morocco. The Spanish government was facing increased resistance to the conscription of young men to fight insurgents in their colony of Morocco in North Africa. Following the example of the French nearly a century before, the Spanish authorities determined that hiring foreign professionals would accomplish their mission of ending the rebellion and appeasing the Spanish population at the same time.

Spanish legionnaires, like their French brothers, came from around the world. They fought more than eight hundred engagements in Morocco during their first six years of existence and then served as part of the Nationalist Army against the Republicans in the Spanish Civil War. After the war they continued operations against insurgents in Morocco.

In 1976 the Spanish Foreign Legion returned home after Spain ceded its interests in North Africa. Many Spaniards then volunteered for the elite unit either out of patriotism or a sense of adventure. By 1984, Spanish volunteers were available in sufficient numbers that the Legion stopped recruiting foreign nationals. Two years later a royal decree banned foreigners from joining the Legion, but allowed those currently serving to remain in the unit. Over the years most have left or retired, leaving only a few foreigners on active duty in the Spanish Foreign Legion.

Meanwhile the French established a second Legion on December 16, 1835, in North Africa. Over the next two decades the French Foreign Legion instituted many traditions that continue today. Volunteers were not asked about their pasts, nor were they required to use their real names. To counter any lingering sense of native country loyalty among the troops, commanders organized battalions by mixing all nationalities. Members of the Foreign Legion came to respond to the question about nationality by answering, "Legionnaire, sir."

When France joined Turkey in its fight against Russia in the Crimean War, the Legion left North Africa to participate in the Battle of Sevastopol in 1859 and then ventured briefly into Italy to assist in that country's ongoing civil wars. By 1860, however, peace in Europe threatened to make the Legion unnecessary. With no battles to fight, the French leadership resented the cost of the Legion so they cut back its numbers and forced many veterans into early retirement.

Just when it seemed the Legion was about to be history again, events half-way around the world solidified its future. When the United States became roiled in its own civil war in 1861, it no longer had the assets available to enforce the Monroe Doctrine, its policy of prohibiting foreign intervention in the Western Hemisphere.

The Europeans left the North Americans to determine their own fate and moved into Latin America to take advantage of the turmoil in the United States. Napoleon III, nephew of the great Bonaparte, had ambitions of reviving the greatness of France experienced under his uncle. Using the excuse of unpaid debts and unrest among various revolutionary factions in Mexico, Napoleon allied with Austria and Belgium to expand their influence there.

In 1862 nearly two thousand legionnaires arrived on the eastern coast of Mexico at Vera Cruz. So many of the soldiers became ill with yellow fever along the swampy coast that the Legion officers were forced to move their force sixty miles inland to Cordoba. Securing the lengthy lines of communication between Vera Cruz and Cordoba required that the Legion send security detachments with each supply convoy and patrols to detect enemy activity.

In April 1863, Capt. Jean Danjou, already a Legion hero for his service in Crimea and the loss of his hand in combat in Algeria, took two additional officers and sixty-two legionnaires on a security patrol along the supply route. The captain, who had replaced his destroyed hand with a wooden prosthesis, was about to add to his personal reputation and the legend of the French Foreign Legion.

Early on the morning of April 30, Danjou's patrol was

camped about forty miles southwest of Vera Cruz when his pickets reported a large Mexican force closing in on their position. According to legend, Danjou assembled his men into a fighting square and had them raise their right hands in a solemn oath to fight to the death. The legionnaires broke the initial Mexican charge and then withdrew to the east to more defendable terrain. Danjou repeated the tactic of fighting and withdrawing until he retreated within the walls of a farm known as Hacienda de la Trinidad near the village of Camerone.

Some reports claim that it was not until they reached the fortresslike hacienda that Danjou called upon his men to fight to the death; others doubt that the officer would have bothered to administer such an oath in the midst of battle. Whatever the speculation, their fates were sealed as by early afternoon more than twelve hundred Mexican cavalry and eight hundred infantry prepared to assault Danjou's patrol.

Before they attacked, the Mexican commander sent a messenger to Danjou telling him that they would be treated fairly if they surrendered. Danjou's exact response, other than the single word *Merde,* has been lost to history, but he clearly refused the offer.

Despite his élan, Danjou must have realized that he could not hold off such a numerically superior force. Perhaps he was hoping for a relief column of his fellow legionnaires to arrive, but more likely he preferred to fight, and die, as a soldier than be a prisoner of the Mexicans.

It took several attacks over most of the rest of the day before the Mexicans reduced the legionnaires' numbers to a handful. Throughout the fight Danjou exposed himself to enemy fire as he waved his wooden hand to rally his troops and exalt them to fight on. In the early afternoon a Mexican musket ball finally felled the captain. His surviving lieutenants took charge and continued the fight.

By late afternoon only five legionnaires were left. Down to their last few rounds of ammunition, they fired a last volley, fixed bayonets, and charged into the Mexican ranks. Despite their best efforts to die fighting, two of the legionnaires were spared by a Mexican officer, who again demanded their surrender. The legionnaires responded that they would stop fighting only if they were permitted to keep their weapons and if their wounded lieutenant, who had led their last charge, would be properly treated. In recognition of their bravery, the senior Mexican commander agreed to the terms and eventually returned the men to their own lines. His only recorded statement was, "These are not men; they are demons."

According to Legion history, a relief column arrived several days after the battle and buried the dead. They also recovered the wooden hand of Captain Danjou. Other reports, denied by today's Legion, claim that the hand was taken by a Mexican farmer who later sold it to a French soldier. Whatever its provenance, the relic eventually made its way back to the legionnaire's museum in France. Each year on the anniversary of the Battle of Camerone, the hand is taken to the parade field, where the regiments of legionnaires march by and render a salute to their most sacred artifact.

The Battle of Camerone is also honored in other ways. Its name adorns every Legion flag as a symbol of a mission carried out to its bitter end.

Other legionnaires also died in Mexico from combat and disease; by the time the survivors finally sailed for home in 1866 nearly two thousand were in Mexican graves. Napoleon III erected a monument to the courage of the fallen legionnaires at Camerone.

Back home, the Legion did not have long to wait for its next action. In 1870 it fought in a losing effort against the Germans in the Franco-Prussian War. Then the Legion led France's expansionist objectives to regain international stature by establishing colonies in Indochina.

When Germany attacked France in August 1914, young

men from around the world came forward to join the Legion. Within a month volunteers from fifty countries formed four new Legion regiments.

The Legion units were quickly thrust into the war's fiercest battles, and the mercenaries immediately displayed their bravery and willingness to die for France. The regiments were so decimated by combat that on November 11, 1915, the survivors were reorganized into a single unit called the Foreign Legion Marching Regiment. Over the next three years the regiment participated in most of the war's major battles and earned the honor of being France's most-decorated unit. This accolade, however, came at a high price. A total of 139 officers and more than four thousand enlisted members of the Legion died in the war. Many thousands more were wounded.

Late in the war the Legion, its soldiers already known for bravery, loyalty, and the ability to "die well," added to its reputation for professionalism. In April 1917 the commander of the Legion fell to German fire near the village of Auberive northeast of Rheims. Col. Paul Rollet, a veteran of combat throughout the Western Front as well as in Oran and Morocco, advanced from the ranks to assume command.

Rollet, a small man with a bristling beard who wore his old desert tan uniform, combined tactical expertise with superb command abilities; and with the spirit of the Legion, he produced a unit known for its combat proficiency as well as its bravery. By the end of the war Rollet had earned the title of "Father of the Modern Legion."

Rollet earned the title of father, but an American volunteer garnered the title of poet of the Legion. Alan Seeger, born to privilege in 1888 in New York, traveled the world as a young man, staying for extended periods in Paris, where he wrote poetry. When the war broke out, Seeger was in England, but he quickly returned to France to volunteer his services to the Legion.

By October 20, 1914, Seeger was on his way to the front. Along the way he wrote a postcard to his mother in which he captured the thoughts of many of his fellow legionnaires: "This is the second night's halt of our march to the front. All our way has been one immense battlefield. It was a magnificent victory for the French that the world does not fully realize. I think we are marching to victory too, but whatever we are going to we are going triumphantly."

Over the next two years Seeger experienced sufficient combat to thoroughly understand the dangers along with the triumph. Shortly before his death at the Battle of Belloy-en-Santerre on July 5, 1916, Seeger penned his most famous poem, "I Have a Rendezvous with Death."

The French Foreign Legion had earned its reputation by shedding its blood in the trenches and no-man's-land of the Western Front. The poems of Alan Seeger that were published shortly after his death glorified the unit further. The Legion's image was soon to be greatly enhanced even more by popular novels and motion pictures.

One of those responsible for the Legion's celebrity was Percival Christopher Wren, a distant kin of famed British seventeenth-century architect Christopher Wren. After his graduation from Oxford, Wren traveled the world for five years before joining the British cavalry, where he served in India. Following his discharge, he joined the French Foreign Legion but deserted after a short enlistment. Back in England at the onset of World War I, Wren returned to India, where he served in uniform until he was invalided out of the service with malaria in 1917.

Once more back in England, Wren spent the remainder of his life as a writer, producing about a book a year until his death in 1941. Although his stay with the French Foreign Legion was brief, the experience dominated his literary efforts. Most of his books glorified the Legion. *Beau Geste,* published in 1924, brought myth and legend together and made the Legion the best-known military unit in the world.

Less than two years after release of the book, director Herbert Brenon assembled two thousand actors in the sand dunes outside Yuma, Arizona, to film the movie version of the brave legionnaires. Box office favorite Ronald Coleman played the lead as Beau with Noah Berry in the role of the evil sergeant. Like the book, the motion picture earned the favor of the public and critics alike.

Hollywood filmed Wren's sequels to the novel, with *Beau Sabreur* hitting the screens in 1928 and the first "talkie" in the series, *Beau Ideal,* appearing in 1931. In the interim the legend of the Legion was kept in the forefront with a stage production of the original *Beau Geste* in 1929.

The attraction of Wren's version of the Legion in film led to several adaptations of the soldiers of fortune fighting in the desert. The genre even included comedy with Laurel and Hardy's *Beau Hunks* released in 1931. A more serious story, *Legion of Missing Men,* arrived in the theaters in 1939.

In 1939, Paramount Pictures decided that it was time for a remake of the original *Beau Geste.* They spared no expense, hiring William Wellman as the director and Gary Cooper, Robert Preston, and Ray Milland as the three brothers. Wellman took the company back into the Yuma desert and produced what many think is one of Hollywood's best action adventures of all time.

While the book and movies of *Beau Geste* cover only a small portion of the Legion's history, they have provided the lasting image of the brotherhood of arms. However, for the real Legion, it has not all been fame and glory. Time and time again France has demanded that the Legion perform some of its most dangerous and deadly missions.

World War II was not the finest hour for France or its Foreign Legion. French officials had little trust in the Legion at the time because Germans dominated the junior officer and senior sergeant ranks. In early 1940, Legion units deployed to Norway and Finland to fight the Germans but quickly returned home to oppose the Nazi blitzkrieg across France. After an impotent effort by the French army to stop the Germans, the survivors evacuated Dunkirk for safety in Great Britain, leaving France under the control of the Vichy government that supported the Nazis.

Those French soldiers and legionnaires who escaped declared themselves Free French under the command of Gen. Charles de Gaulle. On June 30, 1940, de Gaulle addressed the legionnaires, who had reorganized into the Thirteenth Demi-Brigade, and asked if they wished to remain loyal to his Free French army or to join Legion units still in North Africa that had sworn allegiance to the Vichy government. About half stayed with de Gaulle, while the others, mostly Germans and Italians, sailed to Morocco.

De Gaulle's legionnaires later joined the British and Americans, also in North Africa, and fought in several battles against their former Legion comrades who were now with the German Africa Corps. After the Allied victory in North Africa, neither the legionnaires fighting with the Allies nor those with the Axis saw much additional action, and generally they were absorbed into the regular armies.

At the end of World War II France reestablished its Foreign Legion in North Africa. The end of the war, however, did not bring peace to the Legion.

France moved to reoccupy Indochina, which had fallen to Japan in the war, and to force an end to armed resistance by the Viet Minh (Vietnamese communists). The Legion was back in combat, and veterans of both sides from World War II now filled its ranks, including former members of the German army and refugees from the Soviet bloc countries.

A new aspect of the Legion was the formation of two

parachute regiments. Some feared this would create "an elite within an elite" that might decrease morale in the other regiments. Such was not the case. The paratroopers were proud of their regiments, but they, like the soldiers of fortune who preceded them, believed themselves to be first and foremost legionnaires.

The Legion in Indochina once more added to its legendary status. Unfortunately, in a manner similar to the Battle of Camerone, the Legion's reputation increased not from victory but rather from defeat. At Coa Bang the 1st Parachute Regiment lost 90 percent of its men, including its commanding officer, to the Viet Minh in 1950. The regiment briefly disbanded but was reorganized in time to participate in the war's final battle.

In 1953, French general Henri Navarre established a series of interlocking bases two hundred miles west of Hanoi in an isolated valley known as Dien Bien Phu (the English translation is "big frontier administrative center"). The bases were close enough together to be able to support one another with fire. Navarre thought that by placing his bases in such remote locations, accessible only by air, he could tempt the Viet Minh to attack. Unfortunately for the French and the Legion, he was correct in his assumption.

Legion paratroopers jumped into the valley in November 1953 to prepare landing strips for planes that would bring in forces to build and occupy the fortified bases. Of the fifteen thousand French troops to arrive, more than half were legionnaires. By early 1954 the valley defenses included nine forts along the eleven miles of mutually supporting defenses.

The mountains that surrounded the valley provided the Viet Minh excellent observation and firing positions, but the French, who did not think the Vietnamese could maneuver heavy guns and artillery through the thick jungle, prepared to fight the Viet Minh with small arms. The enemy had other ideas. The communist soldiers disassem-

bled more than two hundred pieces of artillery and antiaircraft weapons and moved them by manpower and bicy-
cle to the hills overlooking Dien Bien Phu. They also
concentrated more than seventy thousand soldiers around
the French defenses.

On March 13, 1954, the Viet Minh began their attack.
Ground assaults supported by artillery overran the forts
one by one. Their antiaircraft weapons, combined with
bad weather, hindered French air support and resupply.
For nearly two months the battle continued as the French
perimeter shrank under artillery and ground attack. On
May 7 the last fort fell, leaving more than two thousand
defenders dead and ten thousand more ready to surrender.
As Dien Bien Phu joined Camerone on the list of great
battles of the French Foreign Legion, it, like the fight in
Mexico, was glorious in defeat rather than victory.

Despite their losses in Indochina, the Legion played an
important role in France's defense strategy over the next
decades and continues to do so today. In the late 1950s
and early 1960s the Legion again supported French interests in their North African colonies. When France granted
Algeria its independence in 1962, the Legion returned to
France.

Since that time the Legion has remained in southern
France and on Corsica, with detachments on occasional
duty in Djibouti, Madagascar, French Guiana, and Tahiti.
This rather appealing duty has been interrupted with operations in Africa to help stabilize the region. In 1970 the
Legion participated in establishing peace in Chad and in
1978 saved hundreds of Europeans and African civilians
from rebels in Zaire. In 1982 the Legion served under the
United Nations in Lebanon, and it participated in the Gulf
War against Iraq in 1991. In 1992 the Legion assisted in
peacekeeping in the former Yugoslavia provinces, and
during the following three years members of its regiments
served in Kampuchea, Somalia, and Rwanda. They were

back in Central Africa in 1997 and in 2003 helped end the violence in Cote d'Ivoire.

Since the founding of the French Foreign Legion in 1831, the legionnaires—foreigners by birth—have become Frenchmen by blood and sacrifice. Their losses include a total of 902 officers, 3,176 noncommissioned officers, and more than thirty thousand enlisted legionnaires.

Today the Legion of eight thousand stands ready to defend their adopted country. Each legionnaire swears to uphold the Legion's Code of Honor (see Appendix B), which includes the promise that in combat he "will act without relish of [his] tasks, or hatred," and "will respect the vanquished enemy and will never abandon neither [his] wounded nor [his] dead, nor will he under any circumstances surrender [his] arms."

In its own literature the Legion claims to have only one purpose, "To serve France professionally and well." The Legion continues to enlist only foreigners and still follows many of the regulations and traditions developed during its long history.

One such tradition is wearing white kepis with neck protection. The headgear, most useful in desert operations, came to symbolize the unit as much as any other single item. The official red and green colors of the Legion, on the other hand, predate its history as they represent the original Swiss Guards who served the French kings in the seventeenth and eighteenth centuries. Another tradition is that during parades, the Legion marches at the slow, deliberate pace of 88 steps per minute (most units march at 120 steps per minute) to the tune of "Boudin." The song, which translates to "sausage," dates back to 1870 and is derived from the rolled blanket worn across the legionnaires' chests.

The most famous of all the Legion traditions is as important and valid today as it has been for nearly two centuries. Foreigners from around the world are still welcomed in the ranks. The only requirements are that applicants be seventeen to forty years of age and be physically fit, and the volunteers must pay their own way to France from their home country.

Volunteers today can report to one of the seventeen enlistment offices spread across France. They are then transported to Legion headquarters in Aubagne near Marseille, where they undergo rigid medical, physical, and psychological tests. Those who are accepted sign a five-year unconditional contract to serve wherever the Legion desires. Proficiency in French is not required, as the language is taught during basic training.

One option available to volunteers—long a tradition in itself—is to enlist under an assumed name. Although the Legion requires legal names to check for serious criminal histories, it protects the privacy of the volunteer and looks the other way in regard to minor crimes and past legal difficulties.

After three years of satisfactory service, a legionnaire may apply for French citizenship and a resident permit. Upon completion of his enlistment, a legionnaire may reenlist for a period of six months to three years. Those who complete fifteen years of service can retire in France or have their pension payments forwarded to anywhere in the world.

While the French Foreign Legion has always provided challenges and adventures for its volunteers, it does not pay particularly well. Clothing, food, and lodging are provided, but a Legion recruit is paid a little less than a thousand Euros (slightly more than a thousand U.S. dollars) per month. After a few years of honorable service and promotion to chief corporal, this wage increases to about fourteen hundred Euros.

Despite the low pay, harsh discipline, and often dangerous missions, the French Foreign Legion remains today the best known of all the soldier of fortune organizations.

Some of the Legion's reputation is fact, some myth. A statement issued by the embassy of France on February 26, 2001, best summarizes its appeal:

Coming from all over the world, with such different origins, languages, and ideas, it would seem that they have nothing to share. But they have one thing in common; they refuse to be mediocre. Rejecting easy solutions, the legionnaire has bravely broken with his past and his family. Having lost his roots, he is ready to give all he has, even his life. This state of mind binds the legionnaires together and explains their unrivaled cohesion sealed with discipline, solidarity, and respect for traditions. The legionnaire is first and foremost a man of action, brave in combat and eager for change. He disdains idleness and routine.

He is generous to the point of sacrificing both his money and his life, and never loses trust in his leaders. The trust fosters attachment, and the ties between the legionnaire and his leaders include as much respect and admiration as true and sincere affection. Alive he will follow them everywhere, dead, he will never be abandoned. That's why one perceives the Legion as a large family. A man who has left behind his past, his social and family background, transfers to the Legion his need of an ideal, his affection equating the Legion with that of a homeland, to the point of sacrificing everything to it with a generosity which has astonished the world.

· 10 ·

Gurkhas

Mercenaries of the eighteenth and nineteenth centuries came from many regions to fight other people's wars for revenge, money, and adventure. The Irish looked for any cause that opposed England, the Hessians fought so their princes could add to their wealth, and the French Foreign Legion sought to fulfill the daring reputations and myths of legionnaires of the past.

During this same period a new breed of mercenary emerged from the remote mountainous country of Nepal to establish himself as being among the most feared soldiers on the battlefield. Wielding their *kukuri* knives, the tribesmen who would become known as Gurkhas began their mercenary history as enemies of the British. However, a mutual respect developed on both sides that led to an alliance and an employment arrangement that continues today.

In 1757, Lt. Col. Robert Clive led a force of three thousand British and Indian soldiers against a much larger force of French and their Indian allies at the Battle of Plassey, about eighty miles north of Calcutta. By using tarps to keep his powder dry in the heavy monsoon rains and by convincing some of the Indians to betray the French, Clive would win this battle and claim all of India for England and the East India Company.

While the British were solidifying their control of India over the next decade, another power emerged to the north that would limit English claims to the whole region. The city-state of Gorkhali, a term literally translated to "keeper of the cows," located fifty miles west of Kathmandu, initiated operations to consolidate the northern region. Led by King Prithwi Narayan Shah, the Gurkhas, as they would eventually be known, united all of Nepal into one kingdom, joining Rai, Magar, Limbu, Gurung, and Sunwar tribesmen under a central umbrella by 1769.

Early in the nineteenth century, when the British decided to expand their India colony northward into Nepal, they met fierce resistance from the Gurkhas. In 1814 the British governor-general of India declared war on Nepal and dispatched invasion columns to pacify the Gurkhas. This task turned out to be most formidable. At the hill fortress of Kalunga, six hundred Gurkha defenders held off a much larger British force until only eighty remained alive. The Gurkhas so impressed the British with their fierce fighting abilities and their honorable service that the victors erected a stone monument to the defeated. They inscribed on the monument, "They fought in their conflict like men and, in the intervals of actual conflict, showed us a liberal courtesy."

The Gurkhas reciprocated the respect for the British when Lt. Frederick Young led a unit of Indian soldiers into Gurkha territory in 1815. Confronted by a force of Gurkhas flashing their *kukuris* and shouting their war cry *Ayo Gurkhali* [The Gurkhas are here], the Indians fled in panic. The British officers stood their ground until being overwhelmed quickly by the far superior numbers. Instead of slaughtering the British officers, the Gurkhas took them prisoner.

Their leader asked Lieutenant Young why he had not fled with the Indian soldiers. Young replied, "I have not come so far to run away. I came to stay." Young remained a prisoner of the Gurkhas for the remainder of the war.

During that time, he and his captors fostered their mutual respect gained on the battlefield.

After two years of bloody combat, the Gurkhas agreed to a peace treaty signed at Sagauli in 1816. What both sides considered an honorable war led to an honorable peace. Instead of disbanding or punishing the Gurkha army, the British welcomed their regiments into the British force. In the postwar years, Nepal, like so many countries, found that it needed income that could be procured through the export of its young men. Not only did the Nepal government benefit directly from the fees charged, but Gurkhas in service to the British sent most of their wages back home, greatly strengthening the economy of the country, where mountains and snow had impeded agriculture and trade.

Frederick Young went from Gurkha captive to Gurkha leader with the signing of the treaty. Young, who would remain with his beloved Gurkhas for the next twenty-eight years, organized the first four Gurkha battalions to serve under the British flag and had them ready to begin operations in only six months.

Before long the Gurkhas were in combat. In 1817 bands of outlaws and former soldiers from castes and tribes throughout India rose up against their British colonizers in what became known as the Maratha (or Pindari) War. The conflict concluded on January 18, 1826, with the British victory at Bhurtpore, where the Gurkhas earned their first official battle honor for their fierce assault on the town's defenses.

The Gurkhas helped the British defeat the Sikhs in the wars of 1846 and 1848 and proved their loyalty once again during the Indian mutiny of 1857–58, when the 2nd Gurkha Battalion joined the British 60th Rifles to hold a critical position in Delhi during a three-month siege. In the long battle the 2nd Battalion lost 327 of its total strength of 490 men. The battalion's British officers stuck by their Gurkhas in turn, with eight out of nine of their number falling to mutineer bullets.

After the mutiny was suppressed, the British began to use their Gurkha battalions around the world. During the last half of the nineteenth century the Gurkhas served the British in India and defended interests in Burma, Afghanistan, Malta, Cyprus, Malaya, and Tibet. The Gurkhas also saw action in China during the Boxer Rebellion of 1900.

At the outbreak of World War I in 1914, the British added the regular army of Nepal to its ranks and continuously recruited additional Gurkha volunteers from the mountain villages throughout the war. While fifteen thousand Gurkhas replaced British units in India to free those forces to fight on the Western Front, more than a hundred thousand Nepalese saw combat in France, Persia, Mesopotamia, Egypt, Palestine, and Salonika.

The 8th Gurkhas earned great distinction in the Battle of Artois-Loos in the Champagne region of France in 1915. On September 25 the British attacked heavily fortified German positions under the cover of artillery and poison gas. When the advance faltered, the Germans counterattacked. The Gurkhas stood their ground and fought to their last man. In later dispatches their corps commander praised the performance of the Gurkhas, adding that the battalion had "found its Valhalla" in the trenches of France.

Later the same year another Gurkha unit proved itself in an otherwise disastrous campaign in the Dardanelles.

William Joseph Slim served as a young officer with a regular British regiment at Gallipoli and observed the valor and fighting abilities of the Gurkhas. Slim, who joined the Gurkhas in 1920 and attained the rank of field marshal in command of the Burma theater in World War II, later wrote, "I first met the 6th Gurkha Rifles in 1915 at Gallipoli. There I was so struck by their bearing in one of the most desperate battles in history that I resolved, should I have the opportunity come, to try to serve with them. Four years later it came, and I spent many of the happiest, and from a military point of view the most valuable, years of my life in the Regiment." The 6th Gurkhas was the only unit in the entire British invasion force to advance off the beach and capture Turkish positions on the bluffs above the landing sites.

The armistice of 1918 did not bring peace for the Gurkhas. Over the next decade they served in the Third Afghan War and in the almost constant fighting against insurgents on the Northwest Frontier of India.

With the outbreak of World War II, the German blitzkrieg captured France and pushed the English off the Continent. With the Germans bombing the British homeland and the Nazi cross-channel fleet poised for an invasion, England reached its darkest hour. That was when, after more than a century and a half of loyal service to the Crown, the Nepalese provided more than just manpower. In a dramatic reversal of past practices, the Nepalese government sent funds to London in support of England's efforts against the Nazis.

Although it was true that if Britain fell, Nepal would lose its primary source of income from its Gurkhas, friendship and loyalty were nevertheless definitely factors as well. Shortly after the fall of France in 1940, the British minister in Kathmandu approached the prime minister of Nepal to request permission to recruit additional Gurkha battalions for duty. The Nepalese prime minister approved the request and added, "Does a friend desert a friend in time of need? If you win, we win with you. If you lose, we lose with you."

More than 112,000 Gurkhas would serve in forty battalions in support of the British against the Axis powers, fighting in Syria, Italy, Greece, Malaya, Singapore, Borneo, and Burma. Maj. Charles Heyman, a veteran of the Gurkha service in Borneo and later editor of *Jane's World Armies,* noted, "The Japanese were terrified of them."

For a brief period after World War II the Gurkhas served in Palestine, the Dutch East Indies, and Borneo as well as in their traditional service in India. When Britain granted India its independence on August 15, 1947, the two countries met with Nepal to determine the future of the ten active Gurkha regiments stationed there. The three governments signed the Tripartite Agreement on January 1, 1948, which transferred four of the regiments directly to the British army with the others remaining in the service of the new Indian army.

The British organized their four regiments—2nd, 6th, 7th, and 10th—into a brigade and added engineer, signal, logistics, and military police units for support. They also authorized a parachute company to augment the brigade's deployment capabilities.

For the next dozen years the Gurkha Brigade fought what many consider the most successful counteroperation in history when they joined other British units to defeat the communists in Malaya. While the regular British regiments rotated in and out of Malaya every two or three years, the Gurkhas remained for the duration, earning the distinction of being superb, and often ruthless, jungle fighters. From 1962 to 1965, the Gurkhas opposed rebels fighting for independence in the British South Pacific colony of Brunei. After having the Gurkhas protect their interests in Hong Kong during China's Cultural Revolution in 1966, the British army began a reorganization and reduction in strength that trimmed its number of Gurkhas from fourteen thousand to eight thousand and pared the eight battalions (two per regiment) to five. They then further decreased the size of the force by reducing support units and disbanding the military police and parachute companies.

The Gurkhas, however, continued to serve all over the globe. By 1971 they had three battalions stationed in Hong Kong, one in Brunei, and one in the United Kingdom at Church Crookham. In 1974 the battalion in the UK

deployed to Cyprus to protect British interests when
Turkey invaded the island. After returning home it began
a rotation in 1978 to Belize in Central America.

In 1982 the 1st Battalion of the 7th Gurkhas sailed for
the Falkland Islands to take back the British possession
from Argentina. While the Argentina press belittled the
Gurkhas as hybrids of dwarfs and mountain goats, soldiers of the Argentinian army were well aware of the reputation of the knife-wielding fighters from Nepal. When
the Gurkhas attacked near the island village of Stanley
with their war cry *"Ayo Gurkhali,"* the Argentines
dropped their rifles, abandoned their machine guns and
mortars, and ran. A British officer with the 7th Gurkhas
later remarked, "My men were rather disappointed that
the Argies ran away. They looked forward to the fight."

The British continued to use the Gurkhas at the van-
guard of their operations. In the 1990s the Gurkhas served
in Operation Desert Storm to liberate Kuwait and in
peacekeeping missions in Kosovo and East Timor. In
February 2003, Gurkhas deployed to Sierra Leone to advise and train that country's army against a rebel uprising.
Their most recent operations have sent the Gurkhas into
the mountains of Afghanistan.

According to their current press releases, today's
Gurkha Brigade is composed of thirty-five hundred men
who fulfill their assigned role of serving "as an integral
part of the British Army whilst retaining [their] Nepalese
identity and culture, adhering to the terms and conditions
of Gurkha service." The brigade remains flexible in its organization by making frequent changes and adaptations in
its total numbers and in its mixture of infantry, engineers,
and support personnel.

While organizational changes are ongoing, many traditions of the Gurkhas remain much the same as they have
for the past two centuries. They serve and fight under the
simple motto, "It's better to die than be a coward." Every

Gurkha carries the sixteen- to eighteen-inch-long curved *kukuri* that has come to symbolize the soldiers from Nepal. According to legend, a Gurkha never draws his *kukuri* without drawing blood. If an enemy is not handy, then the Gurkha will slice his own hand or finger to satisfy the "blood thirst" of the blade.

If the *kukuri* story is legend, the respect the Gurkhas draw from their British comrades and the fear they instill in their enemies is certainly fact. Their bravery is unparalleled, as demonstrated by the twenty-six Victoria Crosses Gurkha brigades have earned in their nearly two centuries of history.

The British have never had difficulties recruiting Gurkhas. In the Nepal of the past as well as today, for a young man to be selected to join the Gurkha Brigade is an extreme honor—as well as an outstanding source of income for the recruit's family and the country as a whole. Testing takes place at the Gurkha recruiting camp at Pokhara, to which local recruiters (Gurkha veterans) across Nepal send their best candidates each September.

In an average year the brigade accepts 230 to 250 new members from the twenty-eight thousand to thirty thousand applicants who show up at Pokhara, the large majority of whom are the sons and grandsons of Gurkhas. Nepalese villagers as young as seventeen may volunteer, and many of those not accepted in their first attempt return to the recruiting camp again and again until they are accepted or until they realize that they will never pass.

Those volunteers who do pass the rigorous physical and psychological testing at Pokhara are flown to either the United Kingdom or to Brunei, where they undergo ten months of combat training. The selection process is so rigid that it is rare for a recruit to not successfully complete this phase. Upon completion of their training, Gurkha recruits are returned home for leave before joining their battalions. In Nepal they are treated as heroes as well as role models for young men aspiring to join the brigade in the future.

Gurkha recruits initially sign up for five-year tours, but the vast majority reenlist until they reach fifteen years of service, at which time they are eligible for retirement. A few who attain officer rank or become senior noncommissioned officers can remain with the brigade for up to thirty years. Gurkha soldiers receive the same pay and other compensations as other British soldiers of equal rank and length of service. While regular army pay has never been considered generous in any armed force, it is a substantial amount to the mountain villagers of Nepal.

Interestingly, the British government denies that the soldiers from Nepal are mercenaries. The British are careful to note that the 1947 Tripartite Agreement among the United Kingdom, India, and Nepal specifically states that any soldiers subject to the agreement are not mercenaries. They further claim that Protocol 1 of the 1977 Geneva Convention precludes anyone from being declared a mercenary who "is a member of the Armed Forces of a party to the conflict."

So, officially the Gurkhas of Nepal in the hire of the United Kingdom are not mercenaries. Whatever the verisimilitude of this claim, the Gurkhas undoubtedly deserve to be mentioned with their fellow Greek, Swiss, Hessian, Irish, and French warriors who fought for money as well as for causes.

Despite the fact that the British army has reduced its numbers over the past decades with the shrinking of its empire and decreasing worldwide commitments, the Gurkha is in no danger of disappearing. He continues to be a key and inseparable part of the British army. Officers who serve with the Gurkhas, the British army, and the British people look upon the Gurkhas with sincere affection.

Sir Ralph L. Turner, professor of Sanskrit at the University of London and fellow of Christ's College at Cambridge, before his academic career served as adjutant of the 2nd Battalion, 3rd Gurkha Rifles. In 1931 he wrote:

> My thoughts return to you who were my comrades, the stubborn and indomitable peasants of Nepal. Once more I hear the laughter with which you greeted every hardship. Once more I see you in your bivouacs or about your campfires, on forced marches, or in the trenches, now shivering with wet and cold, now scorched by a pitiless and burning sun. Uncomplaining you endure hunger and thirst and wounds; and at the last unwavering lines disappear into the smoke and wrath of battle. Bravest of the brave, most generous of the generous, never had a country more faithful friends than you.

Privateers: Mercenaries at Sea

Over the long span of recorded history, soldiers of fortune have practiced their profession mostly on land. However, their seafaring brothers have also added to the legacy of the mercenary. These mariners, and the vessels they sail, have become known as privateers, defined as "crewmembers of privately owned and manned armed ships commissioned by a belligerent government to attack and capture enemy ships, especially merchant vessels."

Although they have not been employed for more than a century, privateers previously operated under a "letter of marque" (see Appendix C for an example) from a government to a captain authorizing his attacks on and capture of foreign vessels. These letters also provided provisions for how captured ships and their cargos, known as prizes, were to be sold and the proceeds split between the government and the privateer's owner, captain, and crew.

The original purpose of a letter of marque, sometimes known as a letter of reprisal, was to right a private wrong. As early as the thirteenth century, kings issued letters of permission to private citizens authorizing them to capture another country's ships to regain losses. The justification for this act was the belief that a country was responsible for the actions of its individual citizens. For example, if the French took over a Dutch vessel, the victimized captain could approach his king for permission to seek reprisal. With a letter of marque in hand, the Dutch merchant could then dispatch his own ship to capture any French vessel and cover his losses.

These acts of commercial retribution were adapted to times of war under the theory that hostilities damaged or threatened all of a kingdom's residents so they, therefore, had the right to seek reprisals. Kings who had limited resources to build navies saw the advantages of private vessels taking on the enemy. Despite the fact that no country or merchant appreciated losing assets to privateers, the legal operation of such vessels was accepted overall.

Those who crewed privateers closely resembled the crews of regular naval vessels, only their pay came from the sale of prizes rather than as wages. Privateers were, for the most part, respected and honored in their home communities and by the seats of power that issued their letters. Even those who opposed privateers usually referred to them as "gentlemen pirates."

Pirates, on the other hand, were stateless criminals who made their own rules and attacked any ship regardless of the flag it flew. These thieves of the sea were no more mercenaries than were bandits who attacked people or villages on the land. Pirates were generally condemned and pursued by all governments.

The earliest history of privateering began in the thirteenth century when England's King Henry III ordered private vessels from its southeastern ports to attack and capture French merchant ships on the condition he received half of the proceeds. The English throne also became the first to issue a formal letter of marque when it authorized ships to sail against Portugal in 1295.

Over the next two centuries other countries adopted the practice of sanctioning privateers during time of war. Because peace was a rarity during this period, privateers had little difficulty finding work. Some captains owned their own vessels, but many privateers were financed by nobles or wealthy merchants. Contributing to the war effort may have had its own merits, but most of these financial backers looked upon privateering as a sound investment.

No more powerful than armed merchantmen, privateers usually targeted only merchant vessels and avoided enemy warships altogether. While letters of marque were honored by the nation of issue and its allies, they were often not accepted as a legal declaration by any other nation. Hostile nations at times ignored the letters and executed captured privateers as pirates, and legal privateers could become illegal pirates when the war they were authorized to fight ended. In the days of limited communications, a privateer long at sea might be prosecuted when he finally returned home with prizes taken after hostilities had ended.

However, the potential for rewards far outweighed the risks, and privateers were readily available. Governments looked upon privateering as a necessary evil, a means to increase their naval presence at no cost to themselves. With the sharing of money from the sale of captured ships and their cargoes, a government could actually make money from its navy while at the same time eroding the assets and power of its enemies. When the need for privateers exceeded their availability, backing governments could adjust their part of the share to encourage more ships to put to sea. In 1544 during his war with France, King Henry VIII greatly increased his number of privateers by allowing them to keep all, rather than half, the proceeds from the sale of prizes.

In the latter part of the sixteenth century, rich cargoes of silver, gold, and jewels from Mexico and South America significantly added to the coffers of the Spanish colonizers, but England and France also benefited from the riches of the New World delivered by their privateers. The bounty was so attractive that some privateers added additional crew members as marines or foot soldiers so they could sail into enemy ports, loot its stores, and ransom its citizens.

During this period and into the seventeenth century, England was the major source of letters of marque, and its privateers sailed the seven seas in search of prizes. Privateers enriched their sponsors and the English throne, but they were looked upon as expendable when diplomacy required. When Sir Walter Raleigh continued to capture Spanish merchant ships after England and Spain agreed to peace, the highly successful sailor and explorer was executed in 1618.

For England at least, privateering peaked in the eighteenth century. By 1744, a shortage of sailors forced the country to pardon all criminals willing to put to sea.

The seventeenth century and the early decades of the eighteenth saw an increase in privateering to its greatest numbers ever. England was added to the number of potential victims of privateers by declaring that neutrals that traded with France or its colonies were to be considered fair targets. The measure, known as the Rule of 1756, provided significant financial support for the Seven Years' War in Europe and the concurrent French and Indian War in North America. British privateers captured more than one thousand vessels and brought French wartime commerce to a virtual standstill. Not all of the prizes were taken by ships operating out of British ports. The American colonists, especially those from the seafaring coast of New England, readily joined the privateer fleet and accounted for nearly a third of the French losses.

When the United States declared its independence in 1776, its fledgling navy, comprised of vessels commissioned by the individual states, could muster only thirty warships. Funds for building naval vessels were sparse, and volunteers willing to fight against the powerful British armada were few. To give itself a head start, the United States would do what had worked so well for England and issue letters of marque to its merchant fleet.

Other than having possession of a ship and a crew, there

was one additional requirement to securing a letter of marque in the United States. Both the Continental Congress and the state governments required the owners of privateers to post bonds of $5,000 to $10,000 to serve as insurance against possible claims from neutral merchants or other innocent noncombatants who were not subject to the letter of marque.

These bonds were important because privateers did not merely capture a vessel, sail it to a friendly port, and sell the cargo ship itself. Rather, once the captain brought a prize home, he and the owner had to appear before an admiralty court—usually found at seaside ports or along rivers at inland towns where shipyards built many of the privateers—to prove that the captured ship met the requirements as outlined in their letter of marque. Only after the court approved the request and "condemned" the captured ship and cargo could they be sold.

Experienced sailors and landlubbers alike rushed to ports that were outfitting privateers. In a time when slavery was still legal throughout the colonies, captains of privateers became color blind when accepting crew members and hired men based on spirit and experience rather than skin color. Nearly every privateer crew manifest of the period listed several men as "Negro" or "African."

When sufficient volunteers were hard to come by, captains resorted to advertising. In a Boston newspaper, one captain issued "An invitation to all brave seamen and marines who have an inclination to serve their country and make their fortunes."

The advertisement continued, "The grand privateer *Deane,* commanded by Elisha Hinman, Esq.; and proved to be a very capable sailor will sail on a cruise against the enemies of the United States of America, by the 20th instant. The *Deane* mounts thirty carriage guns, and is excellently well calculated for attacks, defense, and pursuit.

This therefore is to invite all those jolly fellows, who love their country, and want to make their fortunes at one stroke, to repair immediately to the rendezvous at the head of his Excellency Governor Hancock's Wharf, where they will be received with a hearty welcome by a number of brave fellows there assembled."

Captain Hinman, after touting patriotism and fortune, added one last inducement. Upon arrival at the ship, he promised that sailors would be "treated with that excellent liquor called grog, which is allowed by all true seamen to be the liquor of life."

Despite such incentives, privateer captains still at times had difficulties filling their manifests. Crews were larger on privateers than on ordinary merchant vessels and even some warships because they had to provide manpower to sail the captured prizes back home. Another deterrent to filling crews was past success. Veterans who had shared in the wealth of prizes were reluctant to return to sea—at least until they had spent their share of the prize money.

Once at sea, privateers relied on speed as their primary asset. Their light ships carried as much sail as possible so that they could overtake slower merchants and outrun enemy warships. Because the privateers' prey were unarmed or lightly armed merchants, they themselves did not need to be heavily armed. Usually a dozen or so 6- or 9-pound guns arrayed on each side of the privateer, with swivel guns fore and aft, provided enough firepower to convince most any captain to surrender.

Privateers also used other tactics to overtake their quarries. Most flew the colors of neutral countries until they neared an enemy vessel, at which time they hoisted the American banner.

Hinman and other privateer captains made no promises as to what the crew might earn. But while some returned home empty-handed, privateers generally could anticipate capturing from one to four vessels during a voyage.

An ordinary seaman who made only about nine dollars per month during peacetime could earn a thousand or more dollars during the same period as a privateer. Officers and gunnery personnel took even larger shares of the rich prizes.

In the early months of the Revolutionary War the American privateers experienced great success. The British, unprepared for the enterprising Yankees, dispatched lone merchant vessels without naval escort from England to the ports they still controlled in the United States and Canada.

A by-product of this success was a boost to the rebel army on land. On November 25, 1775, the privateer *Lee,* operating under a letter of marque issued by George Washington himself, captured the British merchant *Nancy.* Aboard the vessel were two thousand muskets, two thousand bayonets, three thousand rounds of shot for 12-inch cannons, and hundreds of pounds of gunpowder. This latter commodity was in extremely short supply in the colonies, and the bayonets filled a void in the rebel armories.

And arms were not the privateers' only booty. In early 1776 the *Lee,* supported by the privateer *Defense,* captured several transports ferrying more than two hundred soldiers from England to the rebellious colonies. The capture of British troops at sea was not unusual. By the end of the Revolution the U.S. Navy and the privateers accounted for sixteen thousand British prisoners—a thousand more than were captured on land by the Continental Army.

Although the records are far from complete, efforts by privateers certainly contributed to the success of the Americans. During the war the Americans issued about fifteen hundred letters of marque. At any one time about a third of this number were actually on a ship at sea, and these vessels captured at least two thousand enemy merchantmen.

Connecticut kept fairly accurate records of its privateers,

and these accounts provide a good insight into the successes as well as the dangers of privateering. In 1781, Connecticut authorized ninety-six privateers. During the year, seventy-one of these vessels captured eighty prizes while twenty-five proved unsuccessful. British warships captured nine of the Connecticut privateers, and five more sank.

On occasion several privateers sailed as part of a fleet that shared prizes. Both individual privateers and these minifleets avoided British warships, but if they found a man-of-war that was vulnerable due to storm or other damage, they would attack. Fewer than 3 percent of the prizes claimed were warships, but there were advantages to capturing man-of-wars. Although they had little cargo, their guns and the ships themselves were valuable. In addition, the American government added a bounty to the prize money for warships.

As the Revolution progressed, the British initiated efforts to protect merchants sailing for North America by adding warships as escorts. In turn, the privateers expanded their hunting grounds to waters nearer to Great Britain, where they found particular success, especially in the Irish Sea. Some British merchants and their insurance agents became so frustrated by their losses that they hired French merchants to move their goods, as American privateers would not attack a ship flying the colors of France.

After the Treaty of Paris brought an official end to the war on September 3, 1783, the contributions of the privateers during the Revolutionary War were not forgotten with the drafting of the U.S. Constitution in 1789. In Article I, Section VIII, "Powers Granted to Congress," paragraph 11, permits the Congress "To declare war, grant letters of marque and reprisal, and make rules concerning captures on land and water."

While the Americans had a few decades of peace to enjoy their newly won independence, Europe was soon back at war and again issuing letters of marque to privateers. When the French revolted against their king, other European monarchies attempted to take the throne from the French people. France, with few naval vessels, countered with privateers that captured more than two thousand British ships, significantly impacting Britain's sea commerce and ability to resupply troops on the Continent.

The Americans during this period experienced the other side of privateering when their merchants became victims to what they called "Barbary pirates" from North Africa. These so-called pirates sailed under letters of marque from various tribal chiefs and clan leaders little different from those the Americans issued during their Revolution. Eventually the United States was forced to pay ransom for some of their captured ships, but it also took military action to force the signing of treaties that ended the raids against American shipping.

Because Great Britain had never accepted the loss of the American colonies, they ignored the sovereignty of the United States and began measures to regain what they believed was their territory. While the United States was prepared for war neither on land nor at sea, the Americans were fortunate that the British were still fighting Napoleon on the Continent and neighboring waters and could not focus their full power on regaining their colonies. During the brief War of 1812, the United States issued more than five hundred letters of marque to privateers, who captured or sank more than seventeen hundred British ships. The most successful of these privateers, the *Yankee,* made six cruises against the British and captured forty vessels. Proceeds from these prizes enriched the owner and crew of the *Yankee* to the sum of $5 million.

Privateers limited the resupply of British forces in America. By the end of the war many British merchant owners had difficulty even acquiring insurance for their vessels bound for North America because of their previous losses.

Privateering was a necessary evil, but it was a form of warfare that many found repugnant. British naval hero Adm. Horatio Nelson best summed up these feelings in a dispatch shortly before his victory and death at Trafalgar in 1805. According to Nelson, "The conduct of all Privateering is, as far as I have seen, so near piracy, that I only wonder why any civilized nation can allow them."

Nelson and other senior naval and government leaders continued to speak out against privateering in the latter part of the eighteenth century and the early years of the nineteenth. Nelson's death did nothing to end the growing opposition to what many considered legal pirating. Joining military and government leaders in the opposition to privateering were the rich and influential merchants whose ships were being lost and sold as prizes.

The Napoleonic Wars had the effect of augmenting the size of the major naval forces into large fleets capable of both defensive and offensive action. The rise of these powerful navies along with the general antiprivateer movement decreased the number of letters of marque issued during the four decades following Napoleon's final defeat in 1815. Several European countries made agreements to not use privateers against each other during this period, but it was not until 1856 that Great Britain, now the most powerful kingdom with the strongest army and navy in the world, called a conference to abolish the practice.

On April 16 of that year Britain signed the Treaty of Paris along with France, Prussia, Austria, Russia, Sardinia, and Turkey. Included in the treaty was the establishment of a uniform doctrine on "Maritime Law in time of war," which proclaimed that "Privateering is, and remains, abolished."

After the treaty was signed, forty-six additional countries that historically issued letters of marque were invited to accede to the agreement. Most did so almost immediately, and by the end of 1858, forty-two had agreed to end privateering. Only Spain, Mexico, Venezuela, and the United States refused to sign.

Several years before the Paris accord, the Americans had signed treaties with two dozen countries allowing free, unmolested trade among the signers, but none of these agreements specifically banned privateering. The United States was still one of the "have nots" in military power and still favored privateering as a way of augmenting its naval forces.

The United States soon regretted its decision to continue to support privateering when in 1861 its Southern states seceded from the Union. With a navy much larger and more powerful than the all-but-nonexistent sea force of the rebels, the United States now embraced the rationale of demonizing privateering. However, England and France refused a request from the United States to declare the Confederate privateers to be pirates, taking the position that they had already acknowledged the Confederacy as a neutral country. They also noted that the United States was not a signatory to the Paris treaty.

A year after the American Civil War ended, the government of Chile in South America issued letters of marque to privateers in its war against Spain. Over the next decades other countries considered issuing letters of marque, but the general opinion against the practice around the world and the increased strength of modern navies to combat such action brought an end to privateering.

Since 1856 there have been few opportunities for mercenaries to find employment at sea. Piracy still exists, but today's seaborne thieves do not operate with any government sanctions. Some of the modern private military companies advise and provide training for foreign navies, but generally the sailor of fortune has retired into history.

· 12 ·

Mercenaries in the Air

One characteristic common to mercenaries from all ages is their seemingly indiscriminate selection of whom and where to offer their services in exchange for money and plunder. For many centuries their opportunities were limited to employment on land and at sea, but when Orville and Wilbur Wright took aloft a flimsy motorized airplane of canvas and wood at Kitty Hawk, North Carolina, on December 17, 1903, they opened a new world to men willing to fight from the sky for profit. Within a decade of the Wright brothers' twelve-second, 120-foot flight, aviators of fortune were filling the skies, performing reconnaissance for ground troops and fighting air duels with opposing aircraft.

Yet even before the invention of the airplane there were, albeit rare, opportunities for mercenaries riding in lighter-than-air balloons, which were developed as early as the eighteenth century. It was not until shortly after the beginning of the American Civil War, however, that technology made them available for hire. Balloonist James Allen launched a demonstration flight on June 9, 1861, in Washington, D.C., and then later attempted to fly a reconnaissance mission near Falls Church, Virginia, which ended when high winds destroyed his balloon on the ground before he could launch it.

A short time later Thaddeus S. C. Lowe ascended over

Washington in a tethered balloon and communicated his observations to the ground via a telegraph wire. The demonstration so impressed President Abraham Lincoln that he directed the army to hire Lowe at the astronomical wage at the time of $10 per day. Over the next six months Lowe and several other balloonists worked for the Union Army and conducted reconnaissance and artillery-spotting missions. High winds destroyed several balloons, and ground commanders remained mostly unimpressed with the small returns they gained from the balloonists, who required large supply trains to inflate and support their aircraft.

Lowe had some backers among Union generals, but his high wages, compared to the army private's pay of thirteen dollars per month, and grossly padded expense accounts gained him few additional friends. In the true spirit of mercenaries who had gone before him, Lowe ended his flights in May 1863 when his wages were decreased to $6 per day.

The Confederate states also hired several balloonists, with much the same results as their Union opponents. By the middle of 1863, balloons and their mercenary fliers had disappeared from the Civil War battlefields, leaving the carnage of the long war to the soldiers and sailors on the ground and at sea.

During the Spanish-American War the Americans again commissioned balloons within the regular army, but did not hire nonuniformed personnel to fly them. Over the next several decades, other countries, particularly in Europe, added balloons of various sizes to their armed forces, but they, too, kept them within the formal services, excluding possible mercenaries.

Initially most people, including military personnel, looked upon the invention of the Wright brothers as an oddity more fit for carnival amusement than any real military purpose. Early aviation grew not in the armed forces but rather at county fairs and other places where aviators could amuse and astound the paying public.

One of the most successful of these early flying carnivals eventually became the first group to turn mercenary. John Moisant, an Illinois-born adventurer who made a fortune as a plantation owner in El Salvador, became enamored with aviation after a visit in 1909 to Reims, France, where he attended an air show. After only four lessons, Moisant flew across the English Channel. Over the next year he participated in several aerial races and demonstrations before he hired pilots from four countries and organized a flying circus he named the Moisant International Aviators.

After Moisant was killed in a plane crash on December 31, 1910, his circus crews continued barnstorming in the southwestern United States and soon had the opportunity to become soldiers of fortune in the air. Political unrest, revolutionary coups, and uncontrollable banditry plagued Mexico in the second decade of the twentieth century. Less than two months after Moisant was killed, his circus arrived in El Paso, Texas, where Mexican Federal troops, camped just across the Rio Grande, approached the American pilots with an offer of money to fly reconnaissance missions over nearby rebel positions.

Frenchman Rene Simon accepted the offer and flew history's first wartime aerial mission. During the next several days other members of the International Aviators flew for the Mexican army before the fliers moved on to their next scheduled performance. The flights had produced little, but Moisant's aviators had earned the title of "the first aerial mercenaries."

Another Moisant aviator returned to Mexico later in 1911 with the idea that flying for the Mexican government would pay more than doing stunts on the American barnstorming circuit. John Hector Worden, a Cherokee Indian born in 1885, flew reconnaissance for the Mexican government against the rebels until returning home in 1912 to write about his experiences. Worden conveniently overlooked the experiences of his fellow pilots earlier in the year when he claimed in the December 1912 issue of *Aircraft* magazine to be "the first and only aviator up to the present time to participate in actual warfare in the Western Hemisphere."

Other aviators flocked to Mexico upon reading about Worden's exploits and learning that both the Federals and the rebels were seeking aviators. Pilots were always looking for opportunities to fly, and to do so for money made the chance all that more desirable. French aviator Didier Masson, who had come to the United States as a barnstormer several years earlier, met with Mexican rebel recruiters in Los Angeles early in 1913, where he agreed to a salary of $300 a month plus a $50 bonus for each reconnaissance mission he flew and $250 for each bombing run. The Mexicans also agreed to provide an airplane and ground crew.

During his service to the rebels, Masson lived well aboard a plush railroad Pullman car complete with a kitchen and icebox. The mercenary pilot flew many missions for the rebels, including the first bombing attack against ships when he made several attacks against Federal gunboats at Guaymas on the Gulf of California in the summer of 1913. After a couple of crashes, Masson resigned and returned to the United States, but not before he had earned several thousand dollars as an aviator of fortune.

About the same time that Masson was flying the first mercenary bombing missions, another American, Dean Ivan Lamb, joined the rebels as a paid pilot. On one of his first missions, Lamb, flying a Curtiss aircraft, encountered Federal mercenary pilot Phillip Rader at the controls of a Christofferson biplane. The two air soldiers of fortune drew their revolvers, maneuvered their airplanes, and fired away in what was history's first aerial dogfight.

Rader put a bullet through the right wing of Lamb's Curtiss, but despite each man reloading at least once, no further damage was done.

Both the rebels and the Federals continued to hire individual pilots, but each side rarely had more than one airworthy plane in its "fleet" at any one time. In February 1914, American engineer Lester Barlow approached rebel leader Pancho Villa with a plan to deploy an entirely self-supporting air force. With Villa's financial backing, Barlow purchased four planes and acquired a train complete with flatcars to transport his aircraft, boxcars full of supplies and spare parts, and Pullman cars for his pilots and crews. Villa and Barlow painted the entire train a bright green with large letters that spelled out AVIATION DIVISION OF THE ARMY OF THE NORTH. To be sure his hired pilots returned after each mission with his airplanes, Villa often sent along an armed guard in the plane's rear seat.

Barlow's air force, the first airborne mercenary organization, flew reconnaissance for Villa and found the wages good and the dangers few. Although both Federals and rebels intermittently shot at the planes, they did little damage. In fact, during the entire period of more than three years that mercenary pilots flew for the Mexicans, only one aviator was wounded in action. A lucky rifle shot from the ground hit pilot Farnum Fish, entering his leg and then his shoulder. Fish landed safely and made a full recovery to fly again.

Pilots came and went in short order during their employment in Mexico. By the spring of 1916 most of the airmen, especially the Americans, had left the Mexican forces. The primary reason for their departure was Villa's attack on Columbus, New Mexico, on March 9, 1916, and the expedition led by U.S. Army general John Pershing to avenge the invasion. Pershing brought his own airplanes, but at the controls were regular army officers rather than mercenaries.

By this time the Great War in Europe was also opening up opportunities for American aviators, especially with France's vast air force. Some of the first Americans to fly for the tricolored flag came by way of the French Foreign Legion. There, in early 1916, American aviators began arriving from the United States—some had experience in Mexico and other trouble spots around the world. Bert Hall arrived with stories, mostly untrue, of flying in Russia, China, and the Balkans, where he claimed to have been paid $100 a day to fly for the Turks.

On April 20, 1916, the French organized these pilots into the Escadrille Americaine. The squadron, renamed the Escadrille Lafayette in response to complaints from the American State Department, which was trying to keep the nation neutral in the war, flew its first mission on June 13, 1916. Five days later Kiffin Rockwell downed a German reconnaissance aircraft for the squadron's first kill. Didier Masson, who had flown in Mexico, later joined the unit as did Raoul Lufbery, a French-born American, who led the unit in enemy kills.

More than two hundred Americans served with the Escadrille Lafayette over the next two years. Some joined the squadron as veteran pilots. Others brought only the desire to fly.

The pilots of Escadrille Lafayette served on battlefields all along the Western Front, usually assigned in twos and threes to support other units. Their aircraft were unmistakable with the American Indian insignia painted boldly on the fuselage. Ultimately the Americans shot down fifty-seven enemy aircraft with the loss of nine of their own pilots.

Their status as mercenaries ceased in February 1918 when the American Pilots were transferred to the American Expeditionary Force, which had joined the war against Germany the previous year. The Americans took their airplanes with them. This transfer of American pilots meant that a great deal of experience was brought with them to the newly formed U.S. Air Service. Their mentoring of newly arrived aviators from the States undoubtedly saved many lives and airplanes.

Most of the pilots who fought with the Escadrille Lafayette stayed with the squadron when it transferred to U.S. control. A few departed along the way for better financial opportunities. Bert Hall, who claimed previous mercenary duty around the world, proved unpopular with his fellow pilots, who doubted his stories of past adventures. By November 1916, Hall had two enemy kills and claims to several others that were not confirmed.

The paper trail is sparse to nonexistent, but by his own accounts, Hall left France as part of a trade mission to introduce the Spad fighter plane to the Russians. Again, according to Hall's later renditions, he arrived in Petrograd on January 14, 1917, and flew demonstrations with his Spad from Romania to Latvia. Along the way he shot down another German aircraft, bombed an enemy headquarters in Bulgaria, and received a personal decoration from Czar Nicholas II.

Shortly thereafter Hall observed the revolutionary mobs take over Russia and place the czar under arrest. Hall attempted to flee to Scandinavia but found the border closed. He then accepted a contract from a czarist general to assist the officer's mother in escaping the Bolsheviks. Hall took the elderly woman across Russia aboard the Trans-Siberian Railroad to Vladivostok, then by another train to Shanghai, and finally by ship to Yokohama, Japan. With the woman safely in the hands of other Russian refugees, Hall assisted her in selling the family jewels and accepted $38,000 for his services.

Again, most of the details are supplied only by Hall, but he did arrive back in North America with a sizable amount of money. After a brief return to France, he toured the United States as the lead in a play about his own life story titled *A Romance of the Air*.

Hall's former squadron mates in France were soon out of work with the signing of the armistice on November 11, 1918. Some returned to the States to join flying shows that barnstormed the country. Others looked for more exciting flying jobs and quickly found a place for their talents in a brand-new nation.

As a part of the armistice that ended World War I, territory previously held by Germany, Austria, and Russia became Poland. The Poles had not had their own country since 1795 and were anxious to defend their new borders from the Bolsheviks who believed the region to belong to them. The Polish Republic could field ample ground forces but had few qualified aviators to defend their airspace.

In 1919, Merian C. Cooper and Cedric E. Fauntleroy, both veteran American pilots of the recent war, received permission and finances from the Polish government to form an air squadron. The two Americans recruited seventeen of their fellow countrymen into what they named the Kosciuszko Squadron in honor of Tadeusz Kosciuszko, a Polish officer who had assisted George Washington during the Revolutionary War.

The American mercenary squadron proved to be extremely effective in strafing and disrupting Russian cavalry units and in bombing Soviet troop and supply trains. Along with their successes the squadron also experienced difficulties. At times it was difficult to keep their planes, mostly German and French models left over from World War I, in the air because of maintenance problems. Several pilots, including squadron leader Cooper, were also shot down by ground fire.

Fauntleroy appealed to the United States for additional pilots, and twenty-three quickly volunteered. However, the U.S. State Department, not wanting to become further involved in a European war, prevented them from traveling to Poland.

The remainder of the Kosciuszko Squadron continued

to fight for their Polish employers until the Russians and Poles agreed to an armistice on October 18, 1920. The Americans remained in Poland, ready to resume the fighting if necessary, until May 11, 1921, when the squadron was disbanded. The day before the unit broke up, Polish marshal Jozef Pilsudski presented each of the surviving pilots the Polish Cross of Valor. On the same day the squadron also celebrated the safe return of Cooper, who had been held by the Russians as a prisoner of war after being shot down the previous year.

The accomplishment of the Americans who flew in World War I and later for the Poles elevated the airmen into heroes of their time. Still less than two decades old, the concept of manned flight fascinated the public. Air shows and races attracted huge crowds, and many people gladly offered up a full day's wages for a brief ride in one of the flying machines.

This interest in aviation increased even more when Charles Lindbergh became the first to fly solo across the Atlantic in 1927. Lindbergh was well paid for his accomplishment, and the touring barnstormers also earned a decent living as fliers. However, many aviators missed the excitement and monetary advantages of flying in combat as mercenaries. Those who fought in the air did not have to look far to find employment. Revolutionaries and counterrevolutionaries in Latin America and Asia had ample money but few pilots. Aviators, mostly Americans, soon were flying for various governments and causes around the world. Politics mattered little; the amount of pay was the dominant factor in choosing sides.

The popularity of aviation and the reported antics of mercenary pilots around the world combined to catapult these aerial soldiers of fortune into legendary status. In the 1930s this love of flight and interest in adventures of aviators even spread to the comic section of the daily newspapers. "Captain Easy" flew for the Chinese against a mythical invader, "Scorchy Smith" fought against revolutionaries in a South American country, and "Smilin' Jack" saw action in Latin America.

At the end of the 1930s, new opportunities for aviator mercenaries opened in Spain, but, unlike in the funny papers, the rewards and dangers were real. Spain, a world power for centuries, could not maintain a stable government within its own borders by the beginning of the twentieth century. In 1931 the Spanish Republicans ousted King Alfonso XIII and declared the country "a workers' republic." Measures to break up the large estates and separate church and state rallied the general population to the side of the Republicans but created a great number of enemies, including the church, landowners, and the military.

In 1936 the Spanish army in Morocco, led by Francisco Franco, rebelled and returned home with the support of Germany and Italy to free their country from what they considered socialists. The Soviet Union quickly stepped in to help the Republican cause, and the war spread across the country.

Americans, many of them members of the Communist Party or otherwise sympathizers of socialism and workers' movements, joined what became known as the Lincoln Brigade and hurried to Spain to fight the Nationalists. Although these men, who primarily fought as infantrymen, meet the definition of mercenaries, most enlisted out of a sense of justice and commitment to Spanish socialism rather than for the pay. The brigade, actually only the size of a battalion, fought bravely in extremely harsh conditions along with volunteers from more than fifty other countries who joined the Republicans.

Unlike those who fought on the ground, pilots coming to Spain found lucrative pay, bonuses for enemy kills, and a degree of fame. Both the Republicans and Franco's Nationalists received airplanes and pilots from their allies,

Xenophon *(Library of Congress)*

Alexander the Great *(Library of Congress)*

Hannibal *(Library of Congress)*

Roger di Flor *(Library of Congress)*

John Hawkwood
(Library of Congress)

William the Conqueror
(Library of Congress)

Lion of Lucerne
(Library of Congress)

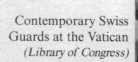

Contemporary Swiss
Guards at the Vatican
(Library of Congress)

The British hire Hessian soldiers *(Library of Congress)*

Hessian Third Guard Regiment with African drummer, from a 1784 print by J. H. Carl *(Five Star Images)*

Headquarters, Irish Brigade, near Washington, D.C., 1865 *(Library of Congress)*

French Foreign Legionnaires from France's African colonies in World War II *(Library of Congress)*

French Foreign Legionnaires and U.S. military personnel train together in Djibouti, 2003 *(Armed Forces Press Service)*

Gurkhas on operations in Iraq, 2003 *(Crown)*

Gurkhas on operations in Kosovo, 1999 *(Crown)*

Gurkhas train in
Scotland, 1999
(Crown)

First Royal Gurkha
Regiment trains in Belize,
2000 *(Crown)*

Claire Chennault
(National Archives)

Claire Chennault with airmen of the
Flying Tigers *(Hoover Institution)*

Montagnard officer and U.S. adviser sample rice wine *(National Archives)*

Montagnard Hmong with U.S. adviser and Viet Cong prisoner *(National Archives)*

Montagnard Hmong on field operations *(National Archives)*

Bob Denard under arrest in the Camores, 1995 *(BBC)*

Mike Hoare *(Library of Congress)*

Tim Spicer *(Tim Spicer)*

An MPRI contractor assists the U.S. First Armored Division in Iraq, 2004 *(MPRI)*

Graduation ceremonies for an Iraqi infantry battalion trained by MPRI, 2004 *(MPRI)*

MPRI radio operator maintains communications while assisting soldiers of the U.S. First Armored Division, 2004 *(MPRI)*

MPRI contractor assisting U.S. Army Recruiting Command *(MPRI)*

but each side actively hired aviators from wherever they could find them.

Early in the war, pilots for the Republicans flew anti-quated planes, including civilian aircraft converted to bombers with the addition of racks attached to the under-carriage, for an average of $375 per week plus a bonus of several hundred dollars for every Nationalist plane destroyed. This generous salary (civilian workers in the United States were fortunate to earn $50 per week during the ongoing Depression) increased as the war dragged on. Experienced aviator Harold Dahl, a native of Champaign, Illinois, negotiated a contract with the Republicans that guaranteed him $1,500 a week and an additional $1,000 for every enemy plane he shot down.

Dahl was not the typical mercenary pilot. Having been convicted of writing bad checks after acquiring gambling debts, his dishonorable discharge from the U.S. Army led him to Spain, where within a year he was shot down, captured, and sentenced to death by firing squad. Dahl's beautiful former-showgirl wife, Edith, sent letters to Franco pleading for her husband's life. Franco canceled the execution but kept the American pilot imprisoned. In the true spirit of the mercenary, Dahl offered to fly for Franco if he were released. Dahl declared, "I don't give a damn about a cause, I'm fighting for money." Franco did not accept the offer, and Dahl remained a prisoner until he was released in 1940 after the Nationalist victory.

Other Americans also flew for the Republicans, but the U.S. government discouraged their participation because it guarded its neutrality and policy of isolationism throughout the 1930s. Not wanting to upset the Germans, Russians, or other European belligerents, the U.S. State Department enforced a 1907 law that took away the citizenship of any American who took an oath of allegiance to any foreign state. The State Department went so far as to stamp passports "not good for travel to Spain," block travel to the war-torn country, and prohibit anyone from leaving the United States with the intent of enlisting in the service of a foreign military force.

American pilots seeking employment in Spain circumvented these restrictions by entering the country from France or by sailing from Mexico. Frank Tinker, a U.S. Naval Academy graduate, went the Mexico route in 1936. In seven months Tinker advanced to command a squadron and earned the privilege of flying the most modern airplanes provided by the Soviet Union. Tinker shot down eight German and Nationalist planes and collected $8,000 in bounty before returning to his home in DeWitt, Arkansas.

Depressed by the surrender of the Republicans to the Nationalists, Tinker committed suicide on July 13, 1939.

Not all the American pilots who arrived in Spain had the experience of Dahl and Tinker. The U.S. Army Air Corps dismissed Albert J. Baumier for "failure to show proper flight proficiency" shortly before he made his way to Spain. His proficiency quickly improved, though, as he shot down five enemy planes to earn himself the title of ace before returning home. Either Baumier kept his exploits secret or he had political and military connections because he rejoined the Army Air Corps, now as a proficient pilot, with no repercussions, shortly after returning home.

Before the Japanese attack on Pearl Harbor in 1941 brought the Americans into the war, one last opportunity arose to fly for money and adventure. In July 1937 the Japanese attacked China and began operations to occupy the entire country. The Chinese leader Chiang Kai-shek had the ground resources to combat the Japanese invasion but not an air force to counter the significant airpower of Japan.

Madame Chiang Kai-shek, assisting her husband as head of China's Aeronautical Commission and the fledgling Chinese air force, negotiated with American officials of the Curtiss-Wright Aircraft Company for planes and technical assistance. Curtiss-Wright executives recommended army captain Claire L. Chennault, who had more than twenty years' experience with the U.S. Air Corps, as Madame Chiang Kai-shek's air force adviser.

Born in 1890 in Commerce, Texas, Chennault had worked as a farmer, schoolteacher, and factory worker before joining the army at the outbreak of World War I. He served as an infantry and Signal Corps officer on the Western Front prior to finally being accepted to flight school a few months after the war ended. Chennault briefly returned to civilian life, but in 1920 rejoined the air corps, where he honed his personal flying skills as well as his instructional abilities at the army's pilot training center.

Promotions were few between the wars, and by the age of forty-three Chennault had advanced only to the rank of captain. Suffering ill health from bronchitis and loss of hearing, he initially turned down the Chinese offer, hoping instead for selection to the Command and General Staff College at Fort Leavenworth, Kansas, an important step to future promotion.

Instead, the army recommended that Chennault retire due to his bad health. On February 25, 1937, he did so and pursued offers from various aircraft manufacturers. Ultimately he contacted the Chinese and was soon on his way east with a three-month contract as an adviser to Madame Chiang. He then was hired full-time at a salary of $12,000 per year, to organize and lead China's fighter pilot instruction.

Chennault's official status in China in his first few years is unclear. The United States supported Chiang Kai-shek's government and apparently took no means to block

Chennault's employment. His only title in the United States was captain, U.S. Army, Retired, while his official position in China listed him as adviser to the Central Bank of China. His passport simply showed his occupation as "farmer."

For two years Chennault worked alone as he established relations with the Chinese leadership, initiated an air-raid warning system, and developed the country's airfields. When the Japanese pressed their offensive against China in 1940, there were too few Chinese fighter pilots to successfully counter the enemy. Generalissimo Chiang Kai-shek sent Chennault back to the United States to seek additional aircraft, and American pilots.

Chennault's first stop back home was at the Curtiss-Wright factory, where workers were busy turning out P-40s for the British RAF. Curtiss-Wright officials accommodated Chennault's need for aircraft by convincing the British to trade their one hundred P-40s on order for an upgraded model. Chennault bought the complete production of the earlier version and shipped the aircraft to China. The U.S. State Department did not participate in the negotiations, nor did they interfere with the shipment of the planes.

Securing pilots and crews proved more difficult than buying airplanes. Both the Army Air Corps and the navy refused to let Chennault talk with their personnel. Fortunately for Chennault and China, they had a friend and supporter in the White House. On April 15, 1941, President Franklin Roosevelt issued an executive order that authorized reserve officers and enlisted men to resign from the Army Air Corps and the Naval and Marine air services for the purpose of joining Chennault in what was now being called the American Volunteer Group (AVG) in China.

In order to continue to maintain U.S. neutrality, Roosevelt released the order unsigned, but the service chiefs understood his intentions and reluctantly complied. Official instructions went out to all military airfields granting Chennault permission to talk with and recruit all interested personnel.

Chennault promised one-year contracts under the guise of the Central Aircraft Manufacturing Company to manufacture, repair, and operate aircraft at salaries of $250 to $750 per month. Although the contracts did not promise that the pilots would be able to rejoin their service after their yearlong employment, this was understood by all. Another unwritten but verbally promised part of the contract was a $500 bonus for every enemy plane shot down. Additional pay for travel, quarters, and rations was also included. With the going price at the time about $600 for a brand-new Ford automobile, the salary and bonus potential appealed to the mercenary instincts of the volunteers as much, or perhaps more than, the opportunity to help China fight the invading Japanese.

The pilots came from varied backgrounds, but most were either just beginning their military careers or were at the end of any advancement opportunities. Difficulties with their commanders, wives, or families prompted many to sign up. One such recruit who became the most famous of the AVG pilots was Gregory Boyington, a twenty-eight-year-old Marine Corps aviator born in South Dakota, who had a reputation as a good flier and a hard drinker. Stuck in a dead-end job as an instructor, harried by creditors, and behind in support payments to his ex-wife, Boyington welcomed the opportunity to leave the United States and make a salary far beyond that of any of his fellow Marines.

The first group of pilots and crews departed San Francisco for China aboard a Dutch-flagged ship on July 10, 1941. Their passports listed their occupations as students, salesmen, entertainers, and even missionaries. Before leaving the States, Chennault received permission from the White House to continue recruiting additional personnel and replacements and left behind an officer to seek additional volunteers.

Chennault coordinated with the British for use of their airfield at Toungoo, Burma, where he began assembling the P-40s and training his pilots. The AVG was almost combat ready when the Japanese bombed Pearl Harbor and the United States entered the war. Chennault divided the AVG into three groups, with one joining the British at Rangoon, Burma, and the other two flying out of Kunming, China.

The AVG flew its first combat mission on December 20, 1941, over the southern Chinese province of Yunnan and shot down nine of ten Japanese bombers with the loss of only one P-40. On December 23 the squadron at Rangoon joined the British to shoot down six Japanese bombers and four fighters at the cost of four P-40s. AVG pilots flew as often as the maintenance crews would allow.

Along with blunting the Japanese attack against China, the AVG was learning new techniques to combat the enemy air force. As the weeks passed, the number of kills increased while the number of losses of their own decreased. Chennault and his staff carefully recorded the lessons learned in air-to-air combat and noted the vulnerabilities of the Japanese aircraft. These facts were sent back to the States, where the services used the information to train their own pilots.

One of the group's best pilots, Eric Shilling, painted shark's teeth on the nose of his P-40, and Chennault soon adopted the practice for the entire group. The AVG made the shark-teeth painting world famous, but they did not originate the practice. Chennault later wrote that some of his pilots had seen pictures in the *India Illustrated Weekly* of Royal Air Force P-40s in the Libyan desert carrying similar nose art. The British, in fact, may have copied the design from early models of German Messerschmitt 110 fighters in the same theater.

Recognized by the shark's teeth, the group became known as the Flying Tigers, though no one is certain where the nickname originated. Chennault wrote that he was surprised by the Flying Tigers moniker in the American media shortly after they began combat operations. Most likely it was a result of the Chinese calling the AVG *fei hou* (flying tigers) after their first successes against the Japanese in December 1941.

Chennault and his Flying Tigers were much more concerned with fighting Japanese than with names. They flew in combat for nearly six months before supporters back in the States approached the Walt Disney studios in Hollywood to design a group insignia. The result was a winged tiger flying through a large V for victory.

Despite the heroic efforts of the Flying Tigers, their numbers were too few to stop the Japanese advance into China and Burma. With the Americans arriving in the theater to join the fight against the Japanese, many U.S. leaders wanted the AVG to be incorporated into the Army Air Corps. Neither Chennault nor his pilots were interested in this idea and, again, like mercenaries of old, agreed to halt operations rather than follow unacceptable terms.

On July 4, 1942, the AVG disbanded. Chennault accepted the rank of brigadier general in the Army Air Corps in command of the China Air Task Force, reorganized in March 1943 as the Fourteenth Air Force. He remained in that position, albeit at a pay reduction compared to his salary as commander of the AVG, until the war's end. He once again retired in October 1945.

A few of the AVG veterans accepted positions as pilots in the Chinese air force. Others took civilian flying positions or jobs with aircraft manufacturers back in the States. Some, like Chennault, returned to U.S. military service and resumed the fight against the Japanese. Among these was Boyington, now known as "Pappy," who would go on to become one of the most successful and decorated pilots of the war. Books, movies, and television series later chronicled, mostly with more fiction than facts, the antics of Pappy Boyington and his Black Sheep Squadron.

Without a doubt the AVG proved itself as the most successful air mercenary unit in history in terms of number of enemy aircraft destroyed and the lessons they passed along to other Allied aviators. Chennault later summarized:

> The group that the military experts predicted would not last three weeks in combat had fought for seven months over Burma, China, Thailand, and French Indo-China, destroying 299 Japanese planes and another 153 probably destroyed. All of this with a loss of 12 P-40s in combat and 61 on the ground including the 22 burned at Loi-Wing. Four pilots were killed in air combat; six were killed by antiaircraft fire, three by enemy bombs on the ground, and three were taken prisoner. Three more died as a result of flying accidents. Although the Japanese promised on their radio broadcasts to shoot AVG prisoners as bandits, they treated our three prisoners as well as regular British and American POWs. I took it as an indication of the enemy's genuine respect for our organization.

In the midst of the war, President Roosevelt added a final tribute to the air-soldiers of fortune. In April 1942 he wrote, "The outstanding gallantry and conspicuous daring that the American Volunteer Group combined with their unbelievable efficiency is a source of tremendous pride throughout the whole of America. The fact that they labored under shortages and difficulties is keenly appreciated."

When World War II finally ended, it left thousands of pilots unemployed. Some left aviation altogether while others found jobs in the expanding commercial air industry. A few continued to seek military flying positions for whoever would pay their way. The increasingly high cost of sophisticated aircraft, however, limited the air capabilities of small governments and guerrilla movements, and few aviators could find employment as mercenaries.

During the half century since the Allied victory over the Axis, conflicts—small and large—have continued on every continent. Small governments as well as modern private military companies actively recruit helicopter pilots and, to a lesser degree, aviators who are qualified to fly fighters and transports. Opportunities are few but the rewards are large, and there is no evidence that air mercenaries are anywhere near becoming completely unemployed or extinct.

· 13 ·

Vietnam

By the late 1950s the region of Southeast Asia known as Vietnam had endured centuries of warfare. After the Vietnamese had defeated the French and their Foreign Legion and gained independence, they were left with a country ravaged by war and torn by political factions at odds.

The Communist North Vietnamese and their Viet Cong allies in the south solicited and received help from the Soviet Union and the People's Republic of China in the form of weapons, ammunition, and other supplies. Overall, however, the communist-supported North Vietnamese and Viet Cong depended upon their own populations for manpower. Soldiers volunteered or were drafted to fight for what they considered a war to liberate the south and reunite it with the north.

The South Vietnamese, on the other hand, received most of their support—both equipment and personnel—from the United States. When the war escalated in the mid-1960s, President Lyndon Johnson sought to increase the numbers of Allied combatants as well as broaden worldwide support for the war. On April 23, 1964, President Johnson issued a public call for additional countries to join the United States in Vietnam. This effort became known as the "more flags" request.

Thirty-nine countries responded to Johnson but most provided only relief support, food, and medical supplies and aid. Australia and New Zealand, close allies of the

United States and in agreement with Johnson's domino theory that if Vietnam fell to the communists, all of Southeast Asia might follow, responded with combat troops. Over the next six years the Australians maintained up to seventy-six hundred combat troops in the war zone. Smaller, less populated New Zealand deployed a force of five hundred men during the same period.

Both Australia and New Zealand bore the entire costs of their forces in Vietnam. Korea, the Philippines, and Thailand also agreed to send troops to Vietnam, but they demanded that the United States pay the costs of deploying the soldiers, an additional per diem payment, an overseas allowance, and a death benefit. It was also understood that the United States would look upon the countries with great favor when it came time to distribute foreign aid. Although not quite as direct as the British employment of the Hessians in the American Revolution, the United States did in fact hire Koreans, Filipinos, and Thais to fight the communists on behalf of South Vietnam. Although they fought under the command of their own officers and wore their national uniforms, they were paid to do so by the United States.

Korea, the Philippines, and Thailand each negotiated their own agreement with the Americans. Korea specifically demanded a promise from the United States that the Americans would not reduce the number of U.S. troops stationed on the Korean peninsula. It also demanded payment and modern equipment for its forces deployed to Vietnam, as well as for those who remained home.

Thailand in turn agreed to provide troops in exchange for a similar modernization of its army and payment of $75 million, while the Filipinos took $36 million for its smaller force. Thai, Filipino, and Korean fighters all received per diem, combat, and death allowances. The Filipinos got a specific per diem reward of $1 per day per soldier and a graduated overseas allowance that provided an additional 10¢ to $6 per day, per man, depending on rank.

The bulk of the payments went to the governments of the three countries. Individual soldiers received only a few dollars a day—poor pay except in comparison to their normal wages. As a result, some critics of the war labeled the troops from Korea, Thailand, and the Philippines as mercenaries, although the United States and their allied three governments preferred to call the payments subsidies to avoid mention of soldiers of fortune. In part, this claim is valid because none of the three countries could afford to bear the entire financial burden of sending their troops to war. It is also noteworthy that the Koreans, Thais, and Filipinos themselves were facing communist threats at home and believed in the domino theory. The opportunity to fight communism on someone else's turf, using someone else's money, certainly had its appeal.

In 1968, at the height of their involvement, more than fifty thousand Koreans were fighting alongside the South Vietnamese and Americans against the communists to earn the reputation as some of the fiercest—and at times most ruthless—soldiers in the war. Thailand provided more than eleven thousand soldiers while the Philippines deployed more than two thousand during their maximum support years. The Thais and Filipinos were known as somewhat reluctant warriors but nevertheless contributed to the defense of South Vietnam.

As the war dragged indecisively on and on, the American people lost interest and their support diminished. Likewise, citizens of Korea, Thailand, and the Philippines tired of the war. When the United States began its pullout from Vietnam in 1969, its "more flags" supporters followed. By 1972 most of the foreign troops were gone, except for Korea's, which maintained more than thirty thousand troops up until the very end of the year.

Although Korea, Thailand, and the Philippines were the

only countries to actually provide "mercenaries," President Johnson and Gen. William C. Westmoreland, commander of U.S. troops in Vietnam, openly looked elsewhere for additional soldiers of fortune during the war. In October 1966, Westmoreland considered hiring the Gurkha Brigade from Great Britain. Rumor had it that the British were about to phase out the Nepalese mercenaries who had served the kingdom for a century and a half.

The idea had some merit. The well-disciplined Gurkhas had extensive experience in counterguerrilla warfare from their operations on the Malay peninsula.

However, no one seemed to know what to do about the British officers who led the brigade—whether or not to replace them with Americans—or if the Gurkhas would even accept U.S. leadership.

All of these issues became moot when the British announced that they were not phasing out the Gurkha Brigade. The Americans and British agreed to review the possibility of using Gurkhas in Vietnam at a later date, but never again discussed the subject.

Westmoreland also considered hiring infantry divisions from Nationalist China. He quickly determined, however, that bringing in troops from Taiwan might provoke the Communist Chinese into providing divisions to the North Vietnamese and dismissed the idea.

While Westmoreland and Johnson sought "more flags" to support the war, they also looked within Vietnam for soldiers to hire. Although about 90 percent of the Vietnamese population resided in the lowlands and shared a degree of common cultural civilization with neighboring countries, in the highlands of Central Vietnam lived about a million and a half additional people in various tribal organizations whom the Vietnamese considered barbarians or *moi* (savages).

By the time the Americans arrived in Southeast Asia, the

numerous highland tribes had become known by the French word *Montagnards,* meaning "mountaineers" or "mountain people." The tribes—composed of peoples with Chinese, Malay, Mongol, and even Polynesian backgrounds—often warred with each other, but they shared one common characteristic. The Montagnards hated all Vietnamese, and few responded when the Viet Cong attempted to recruit them to the communist side. The Yards, as they were later affectionately called by the U.S. Army Special Forces (Green Berets), had little concept of the politics involved except their hatred of the Vietnamese. Although they were not happy to ally with the southerners, they welcomed the opportunity to fight the northerners—especially with the inducement of weapons, supplies, and money.

The many Montagnard tribes varied in their population numbers and their willingness to fight. Tribesmen from the Cham, Tuong, Mien, Jarai, Bahnar, Mnong, Halang, Ragulai, Bong, Ma, Chil, and Durng all joined the Green Berets. The most proficient and numerous Montagnard soldiers of fortune came from the Hre (a tribe of one hundred ten thousand), Rhade (one hundred twenty thousand), Sedang (seventy thousand), Nungs (fifteen thousand), and the Renago (ten thousand).

All of these tribes, except the Rhade, who were Malay-Polynesian, traced their origins to southern China. Rarely did any one tribe provide more than 10 percent of its total population to the mercenary units, but they willingly provided replacements for those killed or wounded.

In 1961 agents of the American Central Intelligence Agency (CIA) and teams of U.S. Army Special Forces moved into the Highlands to recruit the villagers. Ten-man Green Beret "A Teams" organized, armed, and trained the tribesmen into Civilian Irregular Defense Groups (CIDG) and established fortified camps in the interior and along the western border of the South Vietnamese Central Highlands. By 1964 the CIA and Special

Forces had established twenty-one CIDG camps with the mission of blocking North Vietnamese infiltration into the South. That same year, with the arrival of additional A Teams, the CIA withdrew from the program and left it entirely in the hands of the Special Forces.

In 1965 the Green Berets, responding to complaints from the Montagnards that their villages were vulnerable to attack and looting by the Viet Cong when their warriors departed to join the CIDGs, supplied weapons and training to natives who stayed behind to protect their own homes and villages. Payment for these "Regional Forces" also came from the Americans.

The Green Berets and the Montagnards worked well together and developed a mutual respect and a sincere bond of loyalty. Mountain warrior tribesmen came to quickly learn how to use modern weapons and implement counterguerrilla tactics. They became excellent scouts, and a select company was even trained as paratroopers. One adviser later remarked, "The Yards were tough little bastards. They had little fear of death and seemed to enjoy fighting—especially against the hated Vietnamese."

In 1964 and 1965 the United States attempted to transfer some of the CIDG camps over to control of the South Vietnamese Special Forces. The Yards objected and several of the camps rebelled. Only after the Green Berets agreed to stay with the CIDGs and the South Vietnamese promised a degree of self-autonomy for the Montagnards once the war was over did the mountain tribesmen resume their operations against the communists.

Several of the more belligerent CIDG camps were closed during the unrest, but after the sides came to an agreement the number of camps of Yard mercenaries increased to sixty-two. During this period the Special Forces added quick reaction units called Mobile Strike Forces to respond to CIDG camps under attack or to reinforce other Allied operations in trouble all across Vietnam. Nungs made up most of these "Mike Forces" and these ethnic Chinese tribesmen earned the reputation as the most loyal and fiercest of the Special Forces Yards.

When a large force of Viet Cong attacked a camp at Polei Krong in the Highland province of Kontum on July 4, 1964, many of the South Vietnamese soldiers who shared the camp either refused to fight or joined the communist attackers. The Nungs stood their ground, organized an orderly retreat, and withdrew along with the other survivors.

Two nights later the Viet Cong attacked the Nam Dong Camp in Thua Thien Province. Although the camp was lightly defended by a Special Forces A Team commanded by Capt. Roger Donlon and a company of Nungs, they held out despite repeated assaults by a large number of Viet Cong. At daybreak the communists withdrew in defeat. The reputation of the fighting abilities of the Nungs grew from their actions at Nam Dong, and Donlon received the Medal of Honor for his leadership of the camp's defense.

The Green Berets regarded the Nungs so highly that they organized a special security platoon of them in 1964 to serve as guards for the 5th Special Forces headquarters in Nha Trang. This platoon was later expanded into a force of three companies that guarded approaches to the entire city.

In their efforts to counter the communists, the Americans also employed mercenaries in Cambodia and Laos. More than six thousand Cambodian Khmer Kror—primarily advised, armed, and paid by the United States—joined the fight against communism in their own country and opposed the North Vietnamese who were using their country to invade South Vietnam.

The Americans also hired the Montagnards of Laos. The Hmong comprised about 20 percent of that country's population and, like their fellow tribesmen in Vietnam, shared the reputation of being savages. As early as 1961 the United States deployed Special Forces advisers into Laos to hire and train the Hmong to combat Laotian communists as well as troops from North Vietnam. Ultimately about a thousand Green Berets led a force of thirty thousand Hmong soldiers of fortune.

Cambodian and Laotian mercenaries joined fellow mountain tribesmen from Vietnam to form a sizable and effective army. By 1965 more than sixty thousand Montagnards were serving in CIDG, Regional Forces, and Mike Force units—the equivalent of about five infantry divisions. This number remained fairly steady until their numbers declined with the U.S. withdrawal from Vietnam that began in 1969. During most of the period, the United States secured this large number of allies with the deployment of only about two thousand Green Berets.

The costs of employing the mountain mercenaries were relatively small. Some payment was in gold, but these remote tribesmen had little experience with or use for hard cash. They preferred food, clothing, and other goods in exchange for their military service. As the war progressed and the years passed, the Special Forces began to pay the Montagnards in Vietnamese piasters, which they used to purchase items from traveling merchants. Ethnic Chinese traders along with South Vietnamese went to the camps and villages to exchange their goods for the mercenaries' money. Undoubtedly some of the merchants had to pay the Viet Cong in order to safely cross communist-controlled areas to reach their customers; it can be assumed that at least some of the mercenaries' income ended up in the pockets of their enemies.

People who had for centuries lived off the land did not expect or require much in the way of salary, nor did they require as much logistical support as the American infantry. On average, ten Montagnards could be sent into battle for what it cost to have one U.S. soldier take the field. Even at their low wages, about $60 a month, most of the Montagnards were making more than soldiers in the South Vietnamese Army—a fact they sincerely appreciated.

When the United States began its withdrawal from Vietnam, it ended its support for the Regional Forces and reduced the numbers of CIDGs and Mike Forces. Control of the remaining units passed to the South Vietnamese—but their pay, routed through local officials, continued to come from the Americans. Despite resentments on both sides, the Montagnards served the South Vietnamese well and continued to fight bravely after the departure of their Green Beret advisers. During the Easter Offensive of 1972 the Montagnards anchored the defense of the Central Highlands, and they held the communists out of Pleiku and Kontum during the North Vietnamese offensives of 1973 and 1974.

The Montagnards remained loyal to the South Vietnamese and their former American advisers until almost the bitter end. In an action not uncommon to many mercenaries of centuries past, the Montagnards finally received what they thought was a better offer from the North Vietnamese. Before the final offensive in 1975 against the South, agents from North Vietnam approached key Montagnard leaders with cash payments and promises of increased independence if they would change sides.

The South Vietnamese responded by promising the tribes local autonomy for their continued loyalty, but the offer came too late. To the Montagnards, and indeed the world, the ultimate demise of South Vietnam was already apparent. There is no evidence that the mountain mercenaries turned their weapons against the South Vietnamese, but they did agree to stop fighting. When the North Vietnamese made their final assaults into the South, the Montagnards provided little resistance.

After the fall of Saigon, the communists quickly forgot

any promises made to the Montagnards. Instead they began a campaign of retribution. As mercenaries on the losing side have always suffered the consequences of the vanquished, Montagnards would be no different. The communists murdered some of the Montagnard leaders and sentenced others to long terms in "reeducation camps." Vietnamese from the lowlands were moved into traditional Montagnard territory, leaving the Montagnards without land or a means of survival.

During the three decades since the fall of Saigon, the exact toll on the Montagnards for their service to the Americans is unknown. It is apparent, however, that their prewar numbers and lifestyle no longer exist. Their enemies are many, their friends few. They are fortunate, however, that their former Green Beret employers are among these few. For years Green Beret veterans have worked with the governments of the United States and Vietnam to bring Montagnards to America. They have been successful in relocating several thousand to the States, where the former Green Berets have arranged housing, food, job training, and adjustment to the tremendous cultural shock of moving from the mountains and jungles of Vietnam to American suburbia.

· 14 ·

Africa

As we have seen, the continent of Africa spawned some of history's first mercenaries, from Egypt, and later from Carthage. However, in the last half century, various African nations have been the major employers of mercenaries from around the world. By the mid-twentieth century, much of Africa was demanding, and getting, independence from its European colonial masters.

Unfortunately for the long-suffering Africans, the new nations assumed the borders of the previous colonies, which were rarely based on tribal territory. The basic question of who should assume power once the white colonizers departed usually led to civil warfare. War, wealth from gold, diamonds, and other natural resources, and a good supply of unemployed veterans from World War II, made for a conducive atmosphere for the mercenary in Africa.

In the Congo in the late 1950s, Belgium began planning for country-wide elections and transfer of power back to the Congolese people. But by early 1960 the impatient Congolese demanded immediate independence and riots swept the country. Belgium didn't need much convincing and quickly turned the country over to Prime Minister Patrice Lumumba and President Joseph Kasavubu, who declared the independent Congo Republic on June 30, 1960.

Fighting among rival factions, mostly based on tribal

and regional differences, broke out immediately. The Congolese army mutinied, and Belgium flew in paratroopers in response to attacks on the one hundred thousand or so Europeans still in the country. At about the same time Moise Tshombe, a provincial tribal leader, declared the copper, uranium, and diamond rich southern province of Katanga independent from the Congo.

Lumumba turned to the United Nations as well as the Soviet Union for help in expelling the Belgians, ending the riots, and regaining Katanga. The Soviets provided weapons and supplies; the UN sent troops and airpower. The casual observer needed a score card to know who was fighting who for what. Teenage rebels, often of undetermined allegiances, looted and murdered at will. Accounts of cannibalism and the raping of Catholic nuns further fanned the flames of world interest.

Fighting among the many factions continued throughout 1960 and into 1961, spreading death and destruction across the country. Before the United Nations finally successfully brokered a National Conciliation Plan in January 1963, Prime Minister Lumumba fell to unknown assassins, likely mercenaries, on February 13, 1961, and UN Director Dag Hammarskjold died in a mysterious plane crash in nearby northern Rhodesia on September 18 of the same year.

During the long struggle, Tshombe saw that his enemies in Katanga outnumbered his allies. He had the advantage, however, of financial reserves and the backing of several European mining companies that wanted to protect their interests. With only a small army of his own and no chance of reinforcements from other countries, Tshombe turned to employing soldiers of fortune.

Tshombe hired his mercenaries by sending longtime adviser Charles Huyghe to South Africa and other countries to solicit soldiers. By August 1961, Tshombe had more than five hundred foreign, mostly white, mercenaries in his employment. These men came from varied countries and backgrounds, including many former members of the French Foreign Legion. The demeanor and ruthlessness of the mercenaries in the service of Tshombe earned them the title of Les Affreux (the dreadful ones) during their short stay in the Congo.

United Nations forces moved into Katanga and, after a brief and mostly bloodless fight, forced most of the hired soldiers to leave the country. Many of the mercenaries accepted free flights on UN planes back to their homes, where they vacationed briefly before returning to the Congo and further employment by Tshombe.

After several battles, numerous atrocities committed by both sides, and yearlong negotiations, the UN finally convinced Tshombe to leave the Congo so that Katanga could reunite with the rest of the country. The remaining mercenaries accepted UN transportation out of the country or arranged their own escapes.

Many of the soldiers of fortune who served in Katanga, including Frenchman Bob Denard and Irishman "Mad" Mike Hoare, would over the next two decades become the most widely known mercenaries of the twentieth century.

Hoare's first tour of duty in the Congo was brief. He arrived in either late 1960 or early 1961 and for several months led a mixed group of mercenaries loosely organized into what he called 4 Commando. On at least one occasion 4 Commando engaged in a firefight with UN forces and several other times prevented the killing of Belgian nationals by rebel bands. All in all, these actions were not particularly noteworthy, but they did set the stage for a career that would make Mike Hoare's name synonymous with the word *mercenary*.

Thomas Michael Bernard Hoare was born in Rush, Ireland, just north of Dublin, on March 17, 1919. His entering the world as an Irishman on St. Partick's Day would seem an omen for his pursuing the profession of arms.

That, however, was not the way his career began. Hoare attended school in England, where he enjoyed the study of the classics. He did consider becoming an army officer and applied to Sandhurst in 1935, but his father died, requiring him to seek paid employment. The future famous soldier of fortune accepted a position as an apprentice in a London accounting firm.

After four years of fighting numbers and balancing books, Hoare welcomed the opportunity to enter the military when war broke out with Germany in 1939. Hoare joined the London Irish Rifles, a part of the Royal Ulster Rifles. He later recalled that he and the other recruits took their enlistment oath on an *Oxford Dictionary* rather than a Holy Bible because his garrison was under blackout and in the darkness his commander grabbed the wrong book for the ceremony.

Whatever book upon which the young Hoare swore his oath, he took it seriously and discovered he adapted readily to military life. In an interview conducted by his son Chris in 1985 for the magazine *Soldier of Fortune,* Hoare recalled the day of his enlistment. "It was the happiest day of my life. I knew we'd get three square meals a day . . . it was the perfect situation."

In December 1940, Hoare attended Officers Training School and upon graduation deployed to India. There he served in units that assisted in maintaining order and in putting down riots against the British colonial government. From there he joined the fight against the Japanese in Burma with the Chindit irregular guerrilla forces. Promotion to major brought Hoare back to Edinburgh, Scotland, where he assisted in the repatriation of Poles during the final months of World War II.

Hoare considered remaining in the military but accepted a discharge in 1946. He later recalled, "I might have stayed on, as I had enjoyed the war. It suited me in every way. But there was at that time an upsurge in all forms of learning and culture. I got caught up in it and went to London."

For a brief period Hoare studied the classics and resumed his work as an accountant. Not surprisingly, this soon proved far too dull for the combat veteran, who became "fed up with going down to the city in striped trousers."

Remembering a week spent in Cape Town while sailing to India during the war combined with his reading about the region convinced him that South Africa offered an environment of opportunity and adventure.

Upon arrival, the former British officer explored much of Africa as he traveled throughout the continent by motorcycle. He then organized a tourist company and led the first safaris across the Kalahari Desert and to Victoria Falls. He also headed expeditions that sought to capture previously unknown species of wildlife and blazed jeep trails into uncharted territory.

During these adventures, Hoare became acquainted with the landscape and people of Africa, meeting many individuals who would become important in his future. When unrest broke out in the Congo in 1960, Hoare had the knowledge, connections, and, more important, the adventurous spirit to begin the life of a soldier for hire.

When the United Nations pushed the mercenaries out of Katanga in 1961, Hoare along with several of his men from 4 Commando returned to South Africa and immediately resumed his safari business. Unrest continued in the Congo, but the United Nations managed to maintain a degree of peace for several years. In 1964 the United Nations decided the country was sufficiently stable to leave it in the hands of the Congolese. It was not a wise decision.

The United Nations departed on June 30, 1964, and in a scenario that could take place only in an action novel or in the Congo, Moise Tshombe, via political pressure and the support of various armed groups, returned from exile in

Spain to assume the position of prime minister. The former rebel leader now was in charge of the entire country, but he faced rebel forces, composed mostly of teenagers supported by the Soviet Union and other communist regimes. Known as "Simbas" (lions), the rebels began a campaign of murder, looting, and rape against Congolese loyal to Tshombe and whites of any cause or country. The Simbas practiced various types of witchcraft that united their ranks and spread terror among their opponents.

Within weeks after assuming power, Tshombe hired white mercenaries to defend himself and end the Simba reign of terror. Among the first to answer the call for soldiers of fortune was Mike Hoare. The South African mercenary met with Tshombe, who offered him the impressive sounding title of commander of land forces.

Hoare later recalled for *Soldier of Fortune* magazine, "I was still politically naïve and saw it as a great adventure. The thought of commanding a very big force . . . He was talking about a division of 1,000 white mercenaries and 14,000 blacks. I would have complete autonomy and an air force. It was going to be a very big show."

The mercenary leader also noted that although Tshombe awarded him a commission as a colonel, the job did not pay particularly well. According to Hoare, "Money played very little part in it. The most I earned in a month was 500 pounds and half of that was in Congolese francs, which you could do nothing with."

Hoare designated his army 5 Commando, but also unofficially referred to his unit as the Wild Geese in honor of his Irish ancestry and its mercenary lineage. He sought recruits through the grapevine and took out discreet advertisements in English, Belgian, and South African newspapers seeking "any fit young man looking for employment."

Many of Hoare's old comrades joined him in the Congo as did veteran mercenaries from the early days of that country's civil war. Hoare did not care about his subordinates' backgrounds as long as they could and would follow orders and fight. Among the officers he hired was Capt. Siegfried Muller, who often wore the German Iron Cross he had earned in World War II.

Hoare had little difficulty assembling adequate leaders, but finding enlisted men to fill the ranks proved to be more challenging. In his memoirs Hoare wrote about the young men who flocked to the Congo seeking employment as soldiers of fortune. "The general standard was alarmingly low. There was too high a proportion of alcoholics, drunks, booze artists, bums, and layabouts, who were finding it difficult to get a job anywhere else and thought this was a heaven-sent opportunity to make some easy money. I discovered to my horror that there was a fair sprinkling of dagga smokers and dope addicts, many of whom were beyond recall. Perhaps the greatest surprise of all, and it was to remain so right through the three six-month contracts we served, was the incidence of homosexuals."

Hoare accepted the best of this odd lot of volunteers, organized them into eight subcommando units numbered 51 through 58, and began a training program that emphasized physical endurance and weapons proficiency. Even though he accepted men with questionable backgrounds and abilities, Hoare was never able to assemble more than three hundred mercenaries.

Despite their numbers, 5 Commando was well armed, adequately led, and effectively transported, having various military vehicles to assist in their fast-attack tactics. Their Simba opponents closely resembled a gang rather than an organized military force, and their troops were mostly equipped with ancient rifles and spears. Hoare and his mercenaries had the advantage of being portrayed as the "good guys" by the world press that converged on the Congo. Their freeing of white hostages from the Simba rebels and their efforts to reopen roads for commerce gained them praise from the media.

The Eastern press was not so kind and downplayed the atrocities committed by the Soviet-supported rebels while portraying Hoare and his men as the savages. An East German radio reporter referred to the mercenary leader as "that mad bloodhound Hoare." According to other accounts, reporters often said, "That bloke's mad." Whatever the exact source, from that time on "Mad Mike" became the name made both famous and infamous by the Irish soldier of fortune.

Mad Mike and his 5 Commando hit the world's front pages in late 1964 with their efforts to liberate more than three hundred white hostages being held in Stanleyville. As 5 Commando pushed toward the city, grim stories of Simba atrocities grew more horrific. The Simbas paraded the Stanleyville mayor, Sylvere Bondekwe, naked through the streets. Then in front of a huge crowd a teenage warrior cut the liver from the man's body while others held him upright. The young warrior took a bite of the bloody organ and passed the remaining liver to his comrades, who tore it apart and devoured it in front of the dying mayor.

On November 24, Belgian paratroopers jumped onto the Stanleyville airfield while 5 Commando entered the city by roadway. The Simbas massacred more than fifty of their hostages, but Hoare was credited with saving the others.

From Stanleyville the mercenaries began operations back into the countryside to rescue missionaries, traders, and others who had been taken hostage by the Simbas. Again the superior organization and arms of the mercenaries easily defeated the communist-supported rebels. All the while, the media continued to praise Mad Mike and his commandos for their rescue of hundreds of white civilians.

Hoare later wrote, "What I saw tore out my heart" after he liberated the village of Yangambi. "The room was full of nuns and priests so badly bruised and beaten that some were difficult to recognize as human beings. Nuns lay stripped of their clothing, their bodies black and blue with bruises, and red with marks of the lash, teeth broken and lips swollen. Priests lay naked and ashamed, their bodies tortured beyond human endurance. A young nun in strips of clothing stumbled to the door, and with tears in her eyes, flung her arms around my neck and kissed me on the cheek. She may have been beautiful once. 'God has answered our prayers,' she cried out over and over again."

Repeated rescues of whites, particularly missionaries, continued to gain fame for Hoare and 5 Commando. Some reporters occasionally questioned the idea of white mercenaries fighting black natives, but the atrocities committed by the Simbas justified the actions of the soldiers of fortune to most of the world.

Overall the men of 5 Commando were sufficiently armed and proficient in their duties that their casualties remained light. Their pay, about twice the normal middle-class wages of the time, arrived regularly, and there was ample opportunity for acquiring additional wealth. When 5 Commando freed towns and villages, they also liberated local banks and other financial institutions. The exact amount of gold, currency, and other valuables sent back to the homes of the soldiers is unknown but was likely considerable. One veteran of 5 Commando later recalled that on one occasion they shipped kitchen appliances, air conditioners, and other household goods out of the country via a captured aircraft.

Hoare's last campaign in the Congo took place in the Fizi-Baraka area near Lake Tanganyika. The Simba rebels had now been reinforced by Cuban advisers and supplied with more up-to-date weapons. Unbeknownst to the participants at the time, the world's most famous mercenary—

Mike Hoare—was fighting the world's most notorious communist guerrilla leader—Che Guevara.

Che Guevara had yet to make his reputation, but he shared many attributes with Hoare. About the time Hoare was touring Africa by motorcycle, Che had traveled throughout South America also on a motorized two-wheeler. Now the two met in the Congo with Hoare coming out the victor, though he later admitted that it was his toughest fight.

By November 1965, Hoare had completed three six-month contracts. The Congolese government again changed hands and the support of the media for white mercenaries fighting an African country's war began to erode. Hoare turned over leadership of 5 Commando to British mercenary John Peters and returned home to South Africa, where he began work on his memoirs. He also kept his ears open for further opportunities as a hired soldier.

Other mercenary units served in the Congo alongside 5 Commando. The best known of these, 6 Commando, joined the fighting in late 1964 under the leadership of Bob Denard. Born in Bordeaux, France, in 1929, Denard served in the French army in Indochina and Morocco before leaving the formal service for the life of a soldier of fortune. Denard's history is clouded at best but it can be confirmed that, in addition to employment with 6 Commando in the Congo, he participated in at least a half dozen other conflicts in Africa over the next three decades. There is also evidence that during some of these operations he had the quiet backing of the French government and drew pay from that country's intelligence organizations as well as from his mercenary employers.

Denard formed 6 Commando with Belgian, French, and Spanish mercenaries about six months after Hoare organized his unit. Although Denard did not achieve the international fame of his fellow mercenary Hoare, he ultimately remained in the Congo for a longer period of time.

For several years after Hoare departed in 1965, the Congo continued to be ripped by revolutions, counterrevolutions, coups, and countercoups. World observers often did not know who was in control and few, even those in the country, had a clear view of just who were the good guys and who were the bad. Apparently, however, Denard and the other mercenaries continued to get paid because they remained in the country and were often the only stabilizing force that kept anarchy from taking hold. Even then the atrocities and butchery continued with few prolonged periods of peace.

By 1967 the Congo had become so unstable that the mercenaries themselves turned against their former employers and attempted to take over the country. The takeover soon fell into chaos with both the rebels and the government forces fighting against them. Beginning in July the mercenaries fought several engagements but soon found themselves outnumbered and outgunned. With their pay no longer coming from the Congolese government and the dangers increasing, many of the mercenaries melted away across the borders to return home.

By November 1967 fewer than two hundred soldiers of fortune remained in the Congo and their enemies were closing on their positions. Denard and most of the mercenary leaders escaped into Rwanda, but at least thirty of their men were captured and executed while about one hundred twenty were kept prisoner until their release in April 1968. Congolese leaders continued to kill each other and their supporters during the following years before the country became stabilized in 1971 when the Congo changed its name to Zaire.

Today the Democratic Republic of the Congo (formerly Zaire) remains one of the poorest nations in Africa, and unrest is always just below the surface. Conflicts between tribal factions continue, often resulting in bloodshed, but the Congolese seem to now keep the fighting among their own. The time of Hoare and Denard is past, and the nation has no desire to see their return.

Other parts of Africa were also fertile ground for the mercenary and his trade. When Nigeria gained its independence from Great Britain in 1960, internal conflicts began there immediately among tribal and regional factions as well as between Christians and Muslims.

Political arguments and sporadic fighting took place until full-scale civil war broke out when the country's Biafra region declared its own independence in May 1967. Both sides quickly advertised for soldiers of fortune to defend and expand their claims.

The Nigerian federal government's greatest need was for pilots to fly its small air force of Soviet-supplied MiG-15s that originally came with Czech and Egyptian pilots. These proved inadequate both as pilots and fighters, so the Nigerian government contacted John Peters, recently of the Congo, to recruit mercenaries. Peters's men, mostly from England and South Africa, were soon flying the majority of the missions. Despite their reputation as hard drinkers—the Nigerians called them "whiskey pilots"— they performed well.

The Biafran rebels also sought mercenaries, particularly experienced infantrymen. They initially contacted Mike Hoare in South Africa, but he turned down the request. Some accounts state that Hoare simply wanted too much money while others claim that Peters, his old subordinate in the Congo, went to him and asked him to stay out of the conflict. Whatever the real reason, Hoare decided to sit out this war.

Bob Denard and his fellow French soldiers of fortune were not so reluctant to fight against their old ally Peters and arrived in Biafra shortly after retreating from the Congo. Several hundred mercenaries served under Denard, but many quit when they discovered the limited number of weapons and supplies available to the rebels. The Biafrans attempted to bring in additional supplies by air, with two Americans, Henry Warton and Lucien Pickett, competing for the contracts that paid $12,000 for each aerial delivery.

Aviators hired by the Americans rivaled their "whiskey pilot" opponents. These pilots from many countries brought varied degrees of experience to the conflict. Pickett's executive officer was Col. Otto Skorzeny, the extremely proficient Nazi unconventional war expert who had masterminded the rescue of Italian leader Mussolini during World War II.

During the two-year Nigerian civil war, mercenaries participated but were not pivotal. Their numbers were never large and, unlike in the Congo, neither the federal government nor the Biafrans allowed them to operate independently. Most of the mercenaries grabbed their pay and disappeared from the country. At least one air soldier of fortune was said to have taken off with a quarter million U.S. dollars marked by the Biafrans for the purchase of weapons.

The mercenaries may not have made any great impact on the civil war, but that is not to say that it was not a bloody affair. Federal and rebel native troops brutalized and killed each other in masses, and the long war so disrupted the country's agricultural production that famine killed many of the noncombatants. By the time the war finally ended, more than a million and a half of the country's total population of 50 million had fallen to combat or starvation.

Peace did not bring prosperity or freedom for the now united Nigerians. Despite vast resources, most of its population lives in poverty. In the world arena today, Nigeria has the reputation of being one of the most corrupt countries in history.

Independence movements continued to sweep across Africa. Portugal made little effort to maintain its African colonies and granted independence to Mozambique and Angola in 1975. Both erupted into internal fighting between communist and nationalist forces. The Soviet Union and Western countries provided some military and other aid, but generally the bloodletting was left to the natives with no employment opportunities for soldiers of fortune.

Those looking for work as mercenaries would not have to wait long, however. Great Britain had colonized a region in southeastern Africa in the last decade of the nineteenth century to exploit its vast natural resources. The British named the colony Rhodesia in honor of the colonist leader Cecil Rhodes. Rhodesia gained self-rule in 1923 and for the next half century was a country composed of a black majority totally ruled by a white minority.

In the mid-1960s black guerrillas supported by the Soviet Union and other communists began an independence movement against the white Rhodesian government. Despite diplomatic pressure from other African countries as well as Western nations, the country's prime minister, Ian Smith, swore to defend white rule in Rhodesia and advertised for additional soldiers for his army. Unlike in the Congo and Nigeria, white mercenaries were recruited to fight as members of all-white units against black revolutionaries. Whereas in earlier African wars, white mercenaries joined whichever side they chose, usually based on the salary offered, in Rhodesia they signed on for what was basically a white-against-black conflict.

Ian Smith, who discovered that the sons of rich white landowners did not care to risk the rigors and dangers of warfare, openly solicited soldiers of fortune from around the world with ads that promised "fun" in the Rhodesian army. Few South Africans answered his call. The descendants of that country's original white German settlers, known as Boers, did not want to fight alongside their longtime British enemies, even against black rebels.

Instead, Smith drew most of his paid volunteers from what remained of the British Empire, including Australia and Canada.

Shortly after the civil war began to spread all across Rhodesia, another event occurred that assisted Smith in his recruiting. In 1975, American Vietnam veteran Bob Brown published the first issue of *Soldier of Fortune* from his home in Boulder, Colorado. One of the articles detailed Brown's visit to Rhodesia the previous year and his observations of the whites fighting there. The American press quickly condemned Brown's magazine for recruiting mercenaries, but the tenacious former Green Beret was able to fight the press and lawsuits to keep his magazine going. Despite ups and downs, including legal battles both lost and won, *Soldier of Fortune* remained in print to become the most widely read periodical on a subject popular with both real and "wannabe" mercenaries who wished to stay abreast of developments in weapons, guerrilla warfare, and conflicts around the globe.

Smith was able to field an army of about six thousand, with at least two thousand of these soldiers of fortune coming from Great Britain, Australia, New Zealand, Canada, Germany, Holland, Sweden, and Greece. About two hundred Americans, or perhaps as many as four hundred, accepted Smith's offer. Most of these American men were recently discharged veterans of the Vietnam War who wanted to continue the life of combat soldiers. Because salaries ranged from only $4,000 to $7,000 per year, few Americans joined the Rhodesian army for any reasons of profit.

Rhodesia paid all expenses for volunteers to come to their country and then processed them through the immigration department to make it appear that the future soldiers desired to become Rhodesian citizens. Sufficient numbers arrived for the recruiting officers to be particular about whom they accepted. In an interview with Bob

Brown for *Soldier of Fortune,* a recruiting officer reported, "Volunteers must be fit, tough, and capable of operating on their own or in small groups. We also prefer volunteers who will accept a three-year tour of duty; who will make good Rhodesians."

Volunteers also had to pass an interview with a selection board. Those who failed the interview were given an airline ticket back to their country of origin.

Most of the foreign mercenaries joined units of the Special Air Service (SAS), modeled after the British unit of the same name, or the Selous Scouts of the Rhodesian Light Infantry (RLI), which resembled the American Long Range Reconnaissance (LRP) and Force Reconnaissance units used in the Vietnam War. White Rhodesians made up most of Smith's regular army. Blacks loyal to Smith also served in the regular units and acted as guides for the SAS and Selous Scouts, but all of the leadership and most of the troops were white.

Soviet bloc news media and at times the Western press referred to the SAS and Selous Scouts as mercenaries. Rhodesia claimed otherwise. In a 1976 interview with the *International Herald Tribune* (Paris), the chief of recruiting for the Rhodesian army denied that any of the foreigners in his army were soldiers of fortune. Instead, he claimed that they had enlisted because they had an "enthusiasm about fighting communism—they don't want to see a repeat of what happened in Vietnam."

Whatever their reasons for joining the Rhodesian army, these foreigners met any and all definitions of mercenary and proved to be the most proficient warriors in the Rhodesian army. For several years they were instrumental in maintaining Smith's control of the country's government. However, time, increasing numbers of rebels, and general opposition to continued white rule over a black country forced Smith to make concessions in 1978. During these final years most white Rhodesians exited the country, and eventually Smith turned over all power to the newly declared independent nation of Zimbabwe in 1980.

The mercenaries moved on to other endeavors. Some traveled to Angola to fight for three different organizations attempting to take over that country. There they found only treachery—first from their employers, who withheld their wages, and second from enemy firing squads for those unfortunate enough to be captured.

Mercenaries again failed to significantly influence the war's outcome in Angola. That failure, along with increased dangers of the job and mounting opposition to soldiers of fortune, had by the late 1970s generally brought an end to fighting for money in Africa. Mercenaries, however, led by the old veterans Denard and Hoare, were to mount two more significant operations—with greatly differing results.

Bob Denard hired out his services in nearly all the conflicts in Africa from the Congo to Nigeria. Nicknamed "The Terrible," he earned the reputation of being an able soldier of fortune. Denard helped leaders of greatly divergent causes, but in the late 1970s he began operations to help himself.

Denard's target was four islands between the African mainland and Madagascar known as the Comoros, an archipelago few people in the world cared about or even knew existed. The mostly Muslim Comoros, taken as a colony by the French in 1912 as a part of Madagascar, produced nothing for export except the rare ylang-ylang flower used in aromatic oils in the French perfume industry.

Even though most of the income in the Comoros came from handouts from France, the islanders nevertheless joined the African independence movement in the 1970s. Through negotiations with the French and a general election, the islands declared their independence on July 6, 1975, with Ahmed Abdallah as their leader.

During this period Comoroan Marxist Ali Soilih hired

Denard and fellow mercenaries to train his small army. Within a few days of Abdallah's election victory, Soilih executed a coup and took over the islands' leadership. Abdallah fled to exile in Paris. Denard accepted his pay and left the islands to look for further employment as a mercenary.

Soilih's ideas were far from ordinary. He burned all government records to ensure a fresh start and appointed a fifteen-year-old boy as head of his police department. Soilih, believing in various types of magic, was quite disturbed when a local witch doctor spoke of a vision in which a white man accompanied by a black dog killed the leader.

Meanwhile, back in Paris the ousted Abdallah contacted Denard with an offer rumored to total $6 million if the mercenary would turn against Soilih and help him return to power. Denard, who later claimed to be concerned by Soilih's neosocialist dictatorship, accepted the contract and began recruiting. He carefully selected his followers, using the standard he had established in earlier conflicts. His guidance to his subordinates stated, "Absolute secrecy, and conquered fear, are the key words to your success. To them is attached a fidelity. Without your comrades you are nothing and they are nothing without you. You must choose them well, prepare them for their missions, and always prove to them you are their chief."

On May 13, 1978, the forty-nine-year-old Denard landed in the Comoros aboard a converted trawler with forty-six handpicked mercenaries, and soon after Soilih was found shot in his bed. Knowing of the witch doctor's vision and wanting to impress upon the islands' residents that he was in charge, Denard draped Soilih's body on the hood of a jeep and drove through town. At Denard's side was a black Alsatian canine.

The crowds cheered Denard and welcomed the return of Abdallah. This time Denard did not take his money and run in search of other mercenary missions. Instead, he made Abdallah the country's puppet leader while he remained in overall charge of the islands with the official title of head of the palace guard. For the next eleven years Denard and a select group of a dozen other mercenaries lived the life of kings. Denard converted to Islam, married for at least his seventh time, and changed his name to Said Mustapha Madjoub (Staff of Life).

During his more than a decade in power, Denard added to his personal fortune by allowing South Africa to use his ports to ship arms to Iraq and by providing training grounds for various African revolutionary groups. He also maintained close ties with France, which apparently preferred to have its own mercenary in charge of the country over a local Marxist.

Denard's tenure began to unravel in 1989 when Abdallah was executed. The exact reason for his death remains unknown, but apparently Abdallah wanted to remove Denard and become more than just a figurehead. Complaining about the killing and resenting a white man's running the Comoros, other African leaders pressured France, which had over the years either overtly or covertly supported Denard, to force the mercenary out of the islands.

Denard peacefully departed the Comoros in late 1989. Just how much money he took with him or had already secreted away in overseas banks is unknown. The aging Denard lived for a few years in quiet retirement, but despite his wealth he became bored and restless.

On October 4, 1995, the old soldier of fortune, accompanied by thirty-three subordinates, once again invaded the Comoros from the sea. They quickly took over the islands' two airports, the radio station, and the police barracks. By morning Denard had complete control of the islands, but his new reign of paradise was brief. Two days later six hundred French paratroopers landed on the island, causing Denard and his mercenaries to surrender after offering only limited resistance.

In 1999, France finally brought Denard to trial for his role in the 1995 invasion of the Comoros and for the execution of Abdallah. When the court asked Denard his profession, he replied, "First I was a soldier, then I was a consultant, and then I went to Africa to serve in foreign armies. I have led a particular lifestyle. I have always followed my own path, which I never betrayed."

Denard did not like the court's reference to him as a soldier of fortune but accepted the label "mercenary." He added to this, however, by saying that in Biafra in 1968, he and his men had been referred to as "mercenaries of charity." When asked about his long reign in the Comoros, Denard replied, "I built more than I destroyed." He made no mention of financial gain and told the court that he was currently living on social security because, he explained, he deserved it. "I paid my dues," he said.

Many French officials testified on behalf of Denard during the trial. The prosecution failed to prove any of the charges against the mercenary, and on May 17, 1999, he was acquitted and set free to enjoy the rewards of the mercenary life and the well-earned reputation as the most financially successful soldier of fortune in modern history.

While Denard was living like a king in the Comoros, his old mercenary comrade Mike Hoare was living a quiet retirement in the village of Hilton near Durban, South Africa. He had established a successful business brokerage and investment company that provided ample income for his hobby of sailing. Hoare also found time in 1978 to act as military adviser to the motion picture about mercenaries entitled *The Wild Geese* and then toured the United States for three weeks to promote the film.

Despite his financial well-being and advancing age, the old mercenary still yearned for excitement and adventure.

Undoubtedly influenced by Denard's power and wealth in the Comoros, Hoare resumed the life of a mercenary under the guise of deterring the spread of communism across Africa.

Whatever the real reason, Hoare welcomed the opportunity to resume his old life when James Mancham approached him, wishing to hire him to assist Mancham in regaining his former position as president of the Seychelles, a group of eighty-nine islands north of Madagascar where tourism and fishing provided the primary income and Catholicism laid claim to about 90 percent of the population.

Mancham had become the country's first president when it gained its independence from Great Britain on June 29, 1976. A year later, while he was in London attending a conference, France-Albert Rene, supported by Tanzanian soldiers, took over the government. Rene announced that he was an "Indian Ocean Socialist" and that Mancham had been too pro-Western.

Mancham believed that he had strong support in the Seychelles and that he could easily regain power in a bloodless coup if he could find the right man to lead it. After approaching several other mercenaries, Mancham found Hoare. Hoare understood the dangers that a coup presented, but still believed in what he had written in 1966, "Literally, 30 or 40 well-armed ruthless men can overthrow a stable government."

The old mercenary gathered his small group of "ruthless men" from those who had served with him in the Congo and other conflicts across Africa. Many of those he selected had fought in Rhodesia, including two Americans. One, Charles W. Dukes, had served in Vietnam and then in the Rhodesian SAS before working as a bouncer in the bar of Durban's Palm Beach Hotel, from where Hoare recruited him. The soldiers of fortune were paid 1,000 South African rand up front and promised

$10,000 U.S. upon successful completion of the mission.

Hoare's plan was simple. An advance party of five men was to go into the Seychelles capital of Victoria on reconnaissance. When the main party arrived, the advance group would lead them to Rene's office and to the city's police headquarters. Then in a quick show of force they would take over the country without firing a shot.

Hoare planned to fly his forty-seven men into the country on a chartered Royal Swazi flight. The more experienced mercenaries thought it would be safer to land by ship, but Hoare believed that flying in would be faster and was worth the risk. His idea of minimizing the risk was to disguise the men as a rugby team and members of a drinking club called the Ancient Order of Frothblowers who were coming to the islands to distribute toys and gifts to needy children.

The reconnaissance team reported that airport customs was extremely lax, so Hoare decided to bring in his arms and ammunition in his men's luggage and "toy boxes." The mercenaries landed at Point Larue Airport on November 25, 1981, and the plan immediately began to fall apart. Customs officials observed some of the "rugby players" acting suspiciously and demanded to check their bags. The mercenaries pulled their weapons from their luggage and a firefight broke out with customs officials and airport police. Seychelles military, including light armored vehicles, soon joined the fight.

Hoare and his men secured part of the airport, where the battle continued sporadically through the night and into the next morning. At midmorning a regularly scheduled Air India Boeing 707 landed. According to Hoare, he negotiated with the pilot to fly him and his men to South Africa along with the body of his only casualty. The Seychelles government and most others called the action a hijacking, but Hoare later claimed that the Indian pilot willingly provided the transportation and even served them champagne to celebrate their escape.

Upon landing in South Africa, Hoare and his men were arrested—not on charges of having attempted to organize a coup in a foreign country but rather for violating specific parts of the Civil Aviation Offenses Act of 1972. After much debate, all but Hoare and five of his chief lieutenants were released. Meanwhile in the Seychelles, the police arrested the original reconnaissance group. They were tried, convicted, and sentenced to hang; however, negotiations between the South Africans and President Rene, along with payment of $3 million, secured their release and return to Durban.

The trial of Hoare and his lieutenants in South Africa drew worldwide attention. Many sympathized with the most famous mercenary in modern history while others damned him and his entire profession. The judge agreed with this latter opinion and declared that Hoare was "an unscrupulous man with a highly cavalier attitude to the truth." He then sentenced Hoare to ten years in prison and his subordinates from one- to five-year terms.

During his prison time Hoare received more than thirty-five hundred letters of support from around the world. Letter-writing campaigns and actions by many of Hoare's former employers pressured the South African government to release the mercenary. On May 6, 1985, Hoare walked out of jail. Awaiting him were international reporters to whom Hoare, now sixty-five years of age, replied, "It has been a grim experience. Even so, thirty-three months of imprisonment did something for me. It revitalized my soul, refreshed my liver and regulated my bowels. Beyond that, I cannot recommend it."

The press also reported that Hoare claimed to have "hung up his guns," but in an interview with *Soldier of Fortune* magazine the following December he denied the statement. He added that he had made no decision about retirement and that he felt that age was irrelevant in his profession.

Whatever Hoare really felt ended up being inconsequential as no further job offers were forthcoming. His reputation had been greatly diminished on his last operations and even *Soldier of Fortune* in March 1982 led its story about the affair with the headline "Seychelles Fiasco: 'Mad' Mike Hoare's Mercs Muck Up."

Denard's final failure in the Comoros and Hoare's disaster in the Seychelles mostly brought an end to the days of independent mercenaries who could turn the tides of war and decide the future of countries. A swashbuckling chapter in the history of soldiers of fortune had come to an end; however, the future of mercenaries was far from over. Conflicts big and small continued in Africa and indeed continued to rage around the world. As long as people and governments were willing to pay others to fight their wars, mercenaries would continue to find ample employment opportunities—but in new ways and with more formal organization.

· 15 ·

Executive Outcomes

The latter years of the twentieth century brought great changes to the world's balance of power and in the use of soldiers of fortune. The fall of the Soviet Union and the end of the Cold War greatly altered the conduct of warfare and the source of combatants. With the Soviets no longer competitors for the hearts and minds of Third World countries and the threat of annihilation from nuclear warfare mostly ended, the apparent need for huge conventional armies came to an end.

During the years between 1987 and 1994 the total number of active military personnel worldwide decreased more than 17 percent—from 28 million to 23 million. The conclusion of the Cold War, however, did not mean an end to conflict. Border wars, political rivalries, and ethnic conflict still existed, but terror groups, usually acting in the name of religion, were beginning campaigns to spread or support their agendas throughout the world.

Privatization—contracting out government jobs to civilian enterprises—now has a military application. Instead of individual or small groups of soldiers of fortune, modern mercenaries have united into private military companies (PMCs). PMCs, or private military firms (PMFs) as they are sometimes called, are not the mercenaries of the past, spoken of in hushed tones, and never in polite company, but rather groups of specialists recognized, supported, and at times even appreciated by major nations. This includes the United States, which in 2003 spent more than $30 billion (8 percent of its total defense budget) for the services of PMCs. With the expansion of America's war against terrorism, this figure continues to increase.

Today's PMCs claim they can provide combat, peacekeeping, and country-building assets at lower costs and with fewer political entanglements than national or allied armed forces. PMCs can also provide training as well as support services for regular military units. Although they prefer to be called contractors or operatives, these modern hired soldiers have clear links and a close resemblance to mercenaries who for centuries have fought other people's wars.

The first private military company to make a significant impact on world events fielded its hired soldiers even before the conclusion of the Cold War. In 1989, Eeben Barlow incorporated Executive Outcomes (EO) as a private security company and registered it in South Africa and later in Great Britain. Much of Barlow's background— his first name is spelled either *Eben* or *Eeben,* depending on the source—as well as the history of EO is shrouded in secrecy. Information on him and his organization, like many mercenary organizations of the past, is often conflicting, but certain facts are generally accepted.

Barlow, with his most recognizable physical feature of having one green eye and one blue one, was born in Northern Rhodesia but moved to South Africa as a boy. In 1974 he entered the South African Defense Force (SADF) and in 1980 joined the 32nd Battalion and moved up the ranks to become second in command of South Africa's most elite, and often most ruthless, unit. Deployed along the country's borders and into neighboring countries to protect South African interests, the 32nd's most important role was enforcing the policy of apartheid.

Barlow and the 32nd Battalion assisted the anti-Marxist

UNITA (Union for the Total Independence of Angola). There in Angola and in other conflicts along the South African border, the 32nd Battalion gained the nickname of "the terrible ones"—the same moniker bestowed on Belgian mercenaries nearly two decades earlier. The 32nd earned the reputation of being the most proficient unit in the SADF with the highest kill ratio, but it was also accused by its enemies and later by its own government of committing human rights violations.

In the mid-eighties, Barlow, then a lieutenant colonel, transferred to the South African Civil Cooperation Bureau (CCB). This rather peaceful-sounding organization was anything but. The CCB was responsible for importing sensitive technology for South Africa's nuclear weapons program. It also contained a covert unit responsible for worldwide espionage and, from some accounts, the assassinations of opponents to the continued policy of apartheid.

Barlow would have likely remained in the SADF and the CCB for the remainder of his military career if South Africa's apartheid government remained in power. However, when Nelson Mandela was freed after years of imprisonment for his anti-apartheid beliefs and became the country's leader, one of his first actions was to disband the 32nd Battalion and similar special forces units as well as the CCB. Faced with discharge from the army as well as the end of his elite unit and lifestyle, Barlow went looking for new opportunities.

As a lifetime resident of Africa and a participant in several of its conflicts, Barlow was well versed in the successes and failures of mercenaries in the continent's history. He also understood that the old swashbuckling days of Hoare, Denard, and others were over and that the current powers would not accept the traditional mercenary format. After some study, Barlow came upon the idea of adopting the mercenary craft into a respectable, businesslike profession. He would call his organization Executive Outcomes (EO).

Barlow had little difficulty finding recruits for his new enterprise. Many of his old comrades from the 32nd and other special forces units were unemployed, their only marketable skills being military specialists. Although nearly all his officers were white, more than 70 percent of the EO soldiers were blacks, coming mostly from Namibia and Angola, having served in the SADF. These black Africans were already essentially mercenaries as they had hired out to the SADF army to enforce apartheid against their fellow Africans.

With wages equivalent to $2,700 per month for basic infantrymen regardless of color and $13,000 per month for senior officers and experienced pilots, Executive Outcomes quickly formed an army and air force of about two thousand men. Barlow promised payment in U.S. dollars and provided full medical coverage and life insurance for all his employees—a mercenary first. Because nearly all of EO recruits were veterans of the SADF, they were already trained and accustomed to the organization's command and control system.

Funding for recruits, weapons, ammunition, equipment, and other supplies for the independent army came from other organizations associated with EO. Overall, EO was a subsidiary of Strategic Resources Corporation (SRC), a large South African holding company and venture capital firm based in Pretoria. In addition to EO, SRC owned or controlled at least twenty additional companies, including Lifeguard and Teleservices, which provided security for various mining interests in Angola and Uganda. These subcompanies also worked for and with another SRC firm, Branch-Heritage, a major mining and mineral exploration company. EO officers, including Barlow, sat on SRC's board of directors, but the definitive lines of control and intercompany relations are difficult if not impossible to track.

Ibis Air was another company closely associated with EO and its allied organization. This private air force owned four transport planes, including two 727 passenger jets, and about a dozen Soviet-made cargo and attack helicopters. Several MiG-23 fighter-bombers rounded out the air fleet. In addition to possessing these aircraft, Ibis also had connections in place to lease additional aircraft of all types as needed.

Barlow selected the horse-head paladin as EO's corporate symbol. In addition to its maneuverability as a chess piece, the dictionary definition of *paladin* as "the outstanding protagonist of a cause" fit Barlow's vision of the company.

Executive Outcomes initially marketed itself as assisting regional stability. Its services included direct infantry and light armor participation; combat air patrols; battle planning and advisory operations; and training assistance in medical support, logistics, and marksmanship. In its promotional literature and on its website, EO proclaimed itself as a "world leader in security services." The promo explained, "Protecting the lives and assets of persons in a world of increased violence and crime is an incalculable science. It requires professionals who strive for the highest excellence. We at Executive Outcomes believe that excellence is achieved not merely through our repeated actions, but from the irrefutable habits that we form. At Executive Outcomes we start from the beginning to form the habits that will provide the highest quality of service and protection for our clients."

Potential employers for EO contacted the company. The first offers came from Sudanese rebels and Algerian religious factions, but the EO leadership turned these down, explaining that they would work only for legitimate governments recognized by the United Nations. EO did not want to threaten its claim of legitimacy as an army-for-hire by working for what it thought to be illegitimate causes and there is no evidence that EO formally accepted any offers to practice its trade during its first few years.

Executive Outcomes did not acquire its first significant contract until 1992 when Sonangol, the state oil company of Angola, hired the organization to protect its Gulf Chevron oil fields from rebel forces. Angola had been in a state of turmoil since gaining independence from Portugal in 1975. Support from the Soviet Union had provided a degree of stability against the anti-Marxist UNITA rebels, but with the departure of Russian troops from Angola after the collapse of the Soviet Union, the rebels had begun to steadily take over the country.

When the rebels captured the oil fields around the coastal town of Soyo in March 1993, the government of Angola asked EO for assistance. Despite the fact that many EO soldiers had previously fought with the rebels against the formal Angolan forces, the company now readily accepted a contract to support the country's government. Its reasons for doing so were both direct and indirect. From a direct standpoint, EO needed a revenue-producing contract, and the sitting Angolan government met EO's stated requirement of assisting only those recognized by the United Nations. An indirect reason may have been that part of the Soyo oil field was owned by EO's senior organization, Branch-Heritage.

Exact details of the contract, which has been disclosed, show that the Angolan government paid EO about $30 million for two months of work. Whatever the costs, Angola got its money's worth. Within days after signing the contract, fifty to eighty EO soldiers accompanied by regular Angolan army forces conducted a surprise attack and freed the oil fields from the rebels after a fierce battle.

The Soyo operations proved the value of hiring a modern, independent mercenary company. For a minimum cost the Angolan government acquired an effective army without having to solicit help from reluctant neighbors, who might want something in return, or approaching the bureaucratic, slow-moving, and politically minded United Nations.

With the income from the regained oil fields, the Angolan government quickly recovered its costs for EO's assistance. Additional profits from the oil fields went to more contracts with EO. During the remainder of 1993 and on into 1994, Angola hired EO to train about five thousand infantrymen, including counterguerrilla specialists, and thirty pilots. EO also continued to provide security for the oil fields and other national resources, such as diamond mines.

Estimates suggest that during this two-year period the Angolans paid EO more than $100 million. Some of this money went toward the salaries of employees and into the bank accounts of Barlow, his officers, and their sponsors. A portion of the funds paid for arms and equipment was procured from overstocked manufacturers around the world, particularly in the former Soviet bloc, that were actively seeking new customers in the post–Cold War era.

EO units, along with the Angolan army they trained, continued their success against UNITA. By November 1995 the rebels appeared defeated and agreed to a peace accord. One of UNITA's few demands accepted by the Angolan government was a provision for the exit of EO from the country. Despite the demand, EO remained in-country for another month before outside pressures, including lobbying by U.S. President Bill Clinton to end what was considered mercenary activity in Angola, finally forced their return to South Africa.

With the exit of EO, the UNITA rebels resumed their attempt to take over the country. A UN peacekeeping operation failed to stop the fighting. Within months the rebels had again captured the Soyo oil fields and unrest swept across the country. Many directly credited this resumed rebel success to the absence of the EO contractors. Other countries in need of assistance recognized that EO had brought victory and peace, which neither the Angolans nor the United Nations could preserve after their departure.

The next employment opportunity for Executive Outcomes came in the western African country of Sierra Leone. The British had begun trade in the country as early as the seventeenth century and, after their failure to put down the American Revolution, had begun to use the territory as a resettlement area for former slaves from North America and the Western Indies. Sierra Leone became an official British colony in 1808, but the former slaves from the Americas and the African natives of the colony never got along. The British maintained a semblance of order over the next century and a half before granting the country its independence in 1961.

Coups, countercoups, and rebellions brought a series of leaders to head the country over the next decades, but unrest dominated. Despite having rich diamond deposits and other natural resources, the country and its citizens remained poor as a result of the constant turmoil and series of corrupt leaders.

In March 1991 guerrillas under the leadership of Foday Sankoh began operations as the Revolutionary United Front (RUF) to take over the government. Sankoh united the rural residents against the city dwellers and recruited teenagers and even preteens to bolster his army. The sitting Sierra Leone government enlisted criminals and young teens of their own to counter the guerrillas. Soon both sides were murdering and pillaging across the country.

In early 1995 the rebels gained the upper hand, forcing the sitting government to seek outside help. First to be

hired was the Gurkha Security Group (GSG), a newly
formed private military company of retired Nepalese and
other mercenaries based in the Isle of Man in the United
Kingdom. Members of the GSG had some previous experience as contractors guarding corporate assets in Angola
and Mozambique, but they were not prepared for the fero-
ciousness of the RUF.

Shortly after their arrival in February 1995, the GSG
contingent was ambushed by a superior number of rebels.
Among the casualties was the contractor's leader, Bob
Mckenzie, an American veteran of the Vietnam War and a
mercenary with experience in Rhodesia and Croatia. The
rebels emasculated Mckenzie's body and then ate the remains. GSG decided the risks were not worth the rewards,
evacuated its survivors, and canceled its contract with the
Sierra Leone government.

By April the RUF was threatening the capital city of
Freetown. Foreign embassies and residents alike evacuated the city. Requests to the United States, the United
Kingdom, and the United Nations for assistance were all
turned down. Sierra Leone turned to a private military
company and found Executive Outcomes willing to stop
the rebel advance for a contract of $15 million.

Valentine Strasser, a twenty-six-year-old army captain
who had assumed the leadership of Sierra Leone in its
most recent coup, later explained that he had learned of
Executive Outcomes by reading *Newsweek* and *Soldier of
Fortune* magazines. It is also likely that EO was recommended by officials of the Branch-Heritage mining company, which had extensive operations in the country.
Apparently Branch-Heritage agreed to finance the EO
contract for cash-poor Sierra Leone in exchange for future diamond mining concessions.

Using only 170 soldiers and six aircraft, EO quieted the
rebellion and in just nine days pushed the rebels back
more than eighty miles into the jungle. Much of the dam-

age by the mercenaries was accomplished with helicopter gunships, which had not been used in the conflict until that time. EO lost only two dead while killing at least two hundred rebels and encouraging an additional thousand to desert their cause.

During the remainder of the year—under additional contracts that brought the value of their services to $35 million—EO trained the government's army. By the end of 1995 the RUF was pushed back to the country's borders and willing to negotiate a cease-fire. By February 1996, Sierra Leone was stable enough to hold its first democratic elections in twenty-eight years, although another coup soon took place that replaced Strasser with Gen. Julius Bio.

Military and civilian officials from around the world observed the impact of Executive Outcomes in bringing peace to Sierra Leone. In a report to the United Nations about the actions in the country, Canadian brigadier general Ian Douglas stated, "I think there's a place for these companies. You have to stop violence before you can start negotiations. Executive Outcomes did that in nine days. They literally stopped the war."

Not everyone, however, shared General Douglas's opinions. In Africa and elsewhere people still equated the private military company negatively with South African apartheid and mercenaries in general. Outsiders wanted the United Nations to keep the peace and officials in Sierra Leone agreed. In January 1997 they did not renew EO's contract and the soldiers departed the country.

The United Nations once again changed its mind and did not send peacekeepers. Within months another coup toppled the government and rebel groups once again began terrorizing the countryside. Lifeline and other private military companies provided security for major mining operations and other industries, but the war between the government and the rebels continued and peace has yet to return to Sierra Leone.

During the latter years of the 1990s, Mozambique, Uganda, and Kenya all turned to EO for help. In February 1997 Eeben Barlow, still in command of EO, explained his success, "I'm a professional soldier. It's not about politics. I have a job to do. I do it."

Despite its successes and claims that the company was strictly apolitical, Executive Outcomes had its detractors. Critics noted that peace lasted only as long as the EO operatives remained in-country and that war had broken out in Angola and Sierra Leone soon after their departure. The United Nations also objected to the use of any "hired armies" and drafted resolutions outlawing mercenary organizations of all types.

Executive Outcomes' host country also began to question the existence of the enterprise. Not only could the country do without the negative publicity generated by EO, but black South African officials were also very much aware that EO owners and executives were for the most part former members of the apartheid government or had served in enforcement units that maintained the separation between the races. EO was therefore seen by many as a dark legacy of South Africa's past that was not only alive but flourishing.

In 1998, South Africa passed legislation that prohibited the contracting of armed conflict for profit and on January 1, 1999, Executive Outcomes officially closed their Pretoria office and disbanded the company. In a final press release the company stated that it was disbanding because of "the consolidation of law and order across the African continent."

EO ceased to exist and faded into obscurity, but it had earned the honor of being the first modern private military company. Many more would follow.

· 16 ·

Sandline International

With the demise of Executive Outcomes, other private military companies quickly stepped forward to fill the void. Anthony Buckingham, a veteran of the British Special Air Service (SAS) and currently senior director of the Branch-Heritage Group, had been instrumental in Executive Outcomes' securing contracts in Angola. Anticipating that South Africa would eventually force the breakup of EO, Buckingham organized a new private military company.

In 1993, Buckingham formed a company called Plaza 170 Limited in the same building that housed the headquarters of Branch-Heritage. For several years Plaza 170 was little more than an idea, with no permanent director or proposed mission. Its organization was so loose that on at least one occasion Plaza 170 used the Branch-Heritage letterhead on correspondence by mistake.

After years of success, and the possibility of Executive Outcomes being banned by the South African government, Buckingham and other Branch-Heritage officers decided to reform Plaza 170 as a fully operational private military company. Buckingham contacted Timothy Spicer, a former lieutenant colonel in the Scots Guards. Spicer later wrote about his meeting with Buckingham in his 1999 biography *An Unorthodox Soldier:* "I had not met him, but he was an entrepreneur and former soldier, a man with his fingers in many pies, especially the oil industry, and a man who has an insight into the military mind. We met for lunch, at Alvaro's excellent La Famiglia restaurant in Chelsea. We hit it off at once and he told me what was on his mind. What that was eventually became Sandline International, a private military company."

Spicer came from the right background to lead Great Britain's first major PMC, having been born at the army hospital in Aldershot in 1952 to a career officer in the Dorset Regiment. His mother, the former owner of a motorcycle garage, enjoyed riding two-wheelers fast and driving automobiles even faster. After graduating from secondary school, Spicer spent a year in the United States before returning to London to study law.

Spicer did not last long in law school and none of his friends were surprised when he decided to follow in his father's footsteps and join the army. He earned his commission at Sandhurst, where he was honored as the most promising cadet. Upon graduation he attempted to join the SAS but was turned down. Instead he joined the Scots Guards and over the next two decades served in the Falklands War, Northern Ireland, the Gulf War, and Bosnia.

Spicer's career was nothing but successful; however, he did have his critics. Some of his fellow officers described him as arrogant and often irritable. Others said he was a maverick prone to Walter Mitty–like dreams who still resented not being accepted into the SAS. Spicer simply explains that he's always had a bit of a rebellious streak.

By the time he met Buckingham, Spicer was a lieutenant colonel with battalion command behind him and few prospects in his army future except boring staff jobs. Still longing for adventure—and desiring to make more money than his meager army salary provided—Spicer welcomed the opportunity to join Plaza 170. It was a match that would benefit all concerned.

Spicer took over Plaza 170 in February 1996 and began to make plans, solidify contacts, and establish the company's overview and mission statements. He soon renamed the company Sandline International and, in order to avoid difficulties with the British government, registered the company as a corporation in the Bahama Islands. Spicer, however, maintained the primary Sandline office in London and hired former U.S. Army Special Forces colonel Bernard McCabe to open an American branch in Washington, D.C.

Rumors have been rampant about the company. The parties involved have always denied that Buckingham was, or is, a director of Plaza 170 or Sandline. Spicer and Sandline also have denied that Executive Outcomes have ever owned or controlled the company. Also, although many of the operatives for EO ended up working for Sandline, neither Eeben Barlow nor the other EO owners played a role in establishing Sandline.

In its own promotional literature, Sandline is rather nonspecific about its ownership. According to official statements, "Sandline is privately managed by a number of senior ex-military personnel from the UK and U.S. armed forces. The management team is supported by access to a pool of consultants with extensive international commercial and legal expertise. Sandline personnel are highly professional, often former military, police, and government employees, recruited from a number of countries."

In its mission statement Sandline notes that its clients "must have international recognition and preferably democratically elected governments. The organization prefers to support causes backed by the United Nations as well as genuine, internationally recognized and supported liberation movements."

Spicer and Sandline officials defined these "genuine . . . liberation movements" as those they consider legal and moral, that meet the standards of First World military forces, fall broadly within the policies of key Western governments, and take place exclusively within the national borders of the client country. Simply put, Sandline undertakes only those missions that are directly or indirectly approved by the United States, Great Britain, or their allies and assists only in internal conflicts rather than international disputes. Even more simply, Sandline declares they are on "the side of the good guys."

The policy statement also clearly delineates that Sandline will not accept contracts from terrorist organizations, drug or crime cartels, or any group that does not recognize the basic Laws of Armed Conflict as outlined in the Geneva Convention of 1949. Furthermore, Sandline will not become involved with the proliferation of nuclear, biological, or chemical weapons or participate in illegal arms trading.

What Sandline offers is a full line of what it calls "core skills." These include basic advisory, training, and intelligence support. Humanitarian operational services add medical support and training, disaster relief, water purification, and land mine clearance. Communications assistance focuses not only on battlefield systems but also covers public relations, international lobbying, and political analysis.

Although some of this assistance, especially the latter, is more "suit and tie" than "camouflage and combat," Sandline emphasizes its abilities to get down into the trenches. To directly influence the outcome of armed conflicts, Sandline offers command and control teams as well as special forces units, heliborne reaction forces, special warfare maritime units, pilots and engineers, and artillery and air support coordination teams.

Sandline also advertises its abilities to enforce law and order. Specific missions the company seeks are counterdrug operations, antiterrorism, organized crime opposition, natural resources and key installations protection, antipoaching operations, and fisheries security and maritime surveillance.

In all its literature and sales briefings, Sandline reiterates that its project approach encompasses all aspects of a mission—including a withdrawal plan for its operatives upon achieving success. Although they do not note it in their operational statements, Sandline enters each contract with an exit plan in case they are not achieving success and the dangers begin to exceed the rewards.

Sandline declares up front that they are interested only in receiving the agreed-upon payment and harbors no desire to be rewarded with mineral concessions or other natural resources or indigenous assets. They promise to fight and leave, declaring that "all Sandline contracts have addressed the issue of remuneration in an exclusive monetary form."

Sandline concludes its promotions for contracts with the statement, "We seek to provide training for local forces, generating a transfer of our skills which enables client governments to become self-supporting after the withdrawal of the company's personnel on the conclusion of the contract. We are capable of very rapid deployment and operate in a cost effective manner. We are confident that the cost to a client of deploying a Sandline project team is invariably cheaper than the cost of sourcing alternate forms of external assistance."

Early in Sandline's development, Tim Spicer summarized, "We would like to conduct ourselves in the way most people would expect a First World army to conduct itself."

Sandline's seemingly professional and certainly honorable objectives may be in effect today, but the company has not always been so high-minded. Its earliest operation took place in 1997 when President Julius Chan of Papua New Guinea (PNG) contracted Sandline for $36 million (complete contract is in Appendix D) to recapture a rich copper mine occupied by separatists on Bougainville Island. The contract, approved by Chan's National Security

Council but not submitted to the PNG Parliament, was not released to the public.

Spicer assembled a force of seventy operatives, mostly South Africans, who stopped en route to Bougainville to refuel their airplane at Port Moresby. An Australian official noticed the contractors and began to ask questions, attracting members of the press. News of the mercenaries appeared in Australia and then around the world.

The Australian prime minister declared the Sandline mission as "absolutely and completely unacceptable" and initiated measures to prevent his country's further participation. Spicer and his men nevertheless made their way to Bougainville and while there kept a low profile while they awaited the arrival of their weapons (and for the media storm to calm a bit).

The turmoil, however, did not subside. The mission began to disintegrate amid military, political, and economic conflicts. Australia, already contributing more than $200 million in annual aid to Papua New Guinea, refused to have the aid go to bankrolling the mercenaries. When the press revealed that the contested copper mines were half-owned by a British corporation, further questions arose about Sandline's motivation and purpose.

The situation then became explosive when members of the PNG army learned that members of the Sandline forces were reportedly each receiving more than $35,000 per month in salary. Gen. Jerry Singirok, commander of the PNG defense force, publicly condemned Chan's contract with Sandline. The people of PNG agreed and unrest swept the island nation. Full-scale civil war was avoided only by the resignation of Chan and his government.

After Chan resigned, the Sandline force flew out of the country for home. Spicer was held by PNG police for three weeks before he, too, was released and allowed to return to London. After the departure of the Sandline group, the arms and ammunition it had purchased for the operation arrived in PNG, where the PNG army had neither the skills to use the equipment nor the funds to maintain it. They sold some of it to other countries; the rest was left at the ports to rust. Fortunately for the people of PNG, because the rebels and their new government negotiated a cease-fire and a sharing of power, international observers would maintain the peace.

Sandline failed miserably in its first operation, but the effort was not unprofitable. Spicer lobbied an international tribunal that forced PNG to pay the mercenaries the remainder of their original fee—about $18 million. Although defeated by politics and world opinion, Sandline again proved that war can be profitable, and all the better when the risks are few.

Sandline's next action was in Africa. The peace and democracy brought to Sierra Leone by Executive Outcomes in 1996 had lasted only weeks after Barlow and his company departed in early 1997. Fueled by long-term tribal hatred, the Revolutionary United Front (RUF) that had been nearly destroyed by EO reconstituted itself and resumed its bloody campaign across the country.

On May 25, 1997, a military coup led by Maj. Johnny Koroma deposed Ahmed Tejan Kabbah, who had been elected president a year earlier. Kabbah and most of his government fled to neighboring Guinea, where they sought assistance to regain their country. Once more, brutal warfare swept across Sierra Leone, and with it, atrocities against civilians on a gargantuan scale. As the country wallowed in a bloodbath of murders, rape, and mutilation, a U.S. naval task force appeared off shore to protect the evacuation of U.S. embassy staff and other Westerners.

Because of his election by a democratic vote, Kabbah had the support of the United Nations, the United Kingdom, and most African countries. Their efforts to help, however, were fairly weak and inept.

The United Nations, in its usual practice of believing that paper is stronger than arms and ammunition, finally issued Security Council Resolution (SCR) 1132 on October 8, 1997, condemning the coup that deposed Kabbah. The resolution would support actions by the Economic Community of West Africa States (ECOWAS) to restore Kabbah to power and placed an injunction on the supply of arms or other support to the rebels.

On the suggestion of President Kabbah, Sandline was contracted to provide weapons, equipment, and training for those in-country still loyal to him and to the armies of neighboring countries who were providing assistance to his cause. In early 1998, Sandline and Kabbah agreed to a contract for $10 million for training and operational support of the army from ECOWAS as well as delivery of $35 million of arms and equipment, reportedly mostly from Bulgaria.

Within two months the army, trained and supplied by Sandline, stabilized the Sierra Leone government and elections were again held in 2002. The rebels remain undefeated.

Spicer and his employees—Sandline later claimed to never have had more than twenty men in-country at any time—returned to London with their $10 million but quickly discovered that their actions in Sierra Leone were not appreciated by all. Members of the United Nations and several agencies in Britain claimed that Spicer's delivery of the arms and equipment from Bulgaria violated the terms of SCR 1132. Members of the House of Lords supported an investigation by the British Customs Agency, which included a search of Sandline's headquarters and files.

The investigation expanded into what became known as the Sandline Affair and over the next months occupied the halls of government and the front pages of the daily newspapers. The British Foreign Ministry initially denied having any communications with Sandline, but admitted their error when Spicer and his staff showed memos and other materials proving they had proceeded with the knowledge, if not the permission, of the ministry.

The Sandline Affair, which almost led to the resignation of British foreign minister Robin Cook, forced the country to establish better regulations on the control and oversight of private military companies and arms trafficking. Sandline, except for legal expenses, came out of the investigations fairly unscathed. In his autobiography, Spicer later wrote, "We were fortunate in that the truth prevailed in the end, but I would not pretend that this wasn't a difficult time for Sandline."

Spicer left Sandline in 2000 but is still involved in security and training activities with his new company Strategic Consulting International (SCI). Perhaps the greatest lesson learned by Sandline in Papua New Guinea and Sierra Leone was to maintain a low profile. During the first years of the twenty-first century, Sandline has continued to provide training and support on a small scale in Africa and the Mideast. It apparently has avoided direct combat or combat support, but Sandline remains extremely secretive about its activities.

Queries to Sandline about current operations and contracts are always met with the same response: "It is company policy that we never discuss client projects for confidentiality reasons."

Military Professional Resources Incorporated (MPRI)

Executive Outcomes led the way in introducing the concept of private military companies, but quickly concluded operations because of internal problems in South Africa and general widespread opposition to its officers, many of whom were former supporters of apartheid. Sandline International advanced the concept of PMCs, but its debacle in Papua New Guinea and the continued veil of secrecy concerning its operations have relegated it to the status of a minor player in the field of modern mercenaries.

Both Executive Outcomes and Sandline International influenced the growth of private military companies, but it is an American firm that has refined the concept and shown the world the future of the mercenary. In 1987, Maj. Gen. Vernon B. Lewis Jr. along with a group of other retired U.S. Army officers formed Military Professional Resources Incorporated (MPRI) and opened its first office in Alexandria, Virginia, only minutes from the Pentagon.

Lewis, a native Texan who served a combat tour in Korea and three in Vietnam, had extensive experience with the army's operations office. After retirement, he organized and briefly led Cypress International, a firm that handled the supply of war materials. From their experience in the Pentagon, Lewis and his fellow officers saw that in the post–Cold War reduction of military forces, many needed functions in the army could be performed more cheaply and efficiently by contractors than by regular uniformed personnel. The term *outsourcing* was not yet in vogue, but it is exactly what Lewis and MPRI proposed.

Lewis was well aware of a large labor pool available to his organization. Most military personnel retired after only twenty years, still in their prime, and had a massive amount of experience to offer. Too old to be of interest to civilian employers yet desiring a higher income than that provided by their retiree benefits, these professionals were a natural fit for a PMC.

Lewis and the founders of MPRI knew from personal experience that combat is "a young man's game." The average age of the combat soldier was twenty-six in World War II and not quite twenty in the long Vietnam conflict. "Old retirees" might not make good "on the ground and in the mud" infantrymen, but they could offer significant contributions as instructors and advisers. Furthermore, MPRI knew that contracted combat soldiers, such as those deployed by Executive Outcomes and Sandline, were viewed unfavorably as mercenaries. MPRI always prefers the term *contractor,* but, whatever they call themselves, they are indeed the progeny of more than two thousand years of mercenary history.

MPRI's first contract with the U.S. Army was to provide training for the regular and reserve forces on new weapons systems, including the M-2 and M-3 Bradley fighting vehicles. The company also began providing instructors and other support personnel for the army staff and war colleges. Both the army and MPRI quickly understood that a "contractor" could replace a regular soldier at a lower cost because of the expense of recruiting, training, moving, and maintaining uniformed personnel. More important, in an army of decreasing size, every man freed from training and support duties provided an additional combat soldier. Today "Rosie the Riveter" of

World War II is a PMC employee—a civilian contractor releasing a soldier for combat.

MPRI makes every effort to remain in good stead with the government of the United States as well as the United Nations. From its beginnings, MPRI has been careful to maintain a close relationship with the U.S. State Department and the Department of Defense, refusing to accept any contract without their approval. The company readily claims that it is dedicated to supporting good causes and spreading the traditions of freedom and democracy.

Unlike Executive Outcomes, some of whose personnel had supported a racist government, and Sandline, which was led by midlevel officers supported by secretive business connections, MPRI maintains the integrity that is assumed of retired general officers. Furthermore, it is easily discerned that the senior officers associated with MPRI would not risk their professional reputations—and especially their retirement salaries and benefits—on contracts that might be illegal or even questionable.

Whereas it was said in the nineteenth century the sun never set on the British Empire, it may be stated that in the twenty-first, the sun never sets on employees of MPRI. Today, MPRI contractors can be found on every continent in the world with the exception of Antarctica, and that frozen land may very well be a future source of contracts.

During its first several years of existence MPRI focused on the U.S. market and expanded its contracts with the Department of Defense in weapons training. Their first international contracts came at the conclusion of the Gulf War in 1991 when MPRI put together a package of briefings on lessons learned in the conflict and presented them to the senior military leadership of Sweden and Nationalist China. MPRI then provided teams to train Nigerian peacekeeping forces in Liberia how to use and maintain military vehicles supplied by the United States. About this same time MPRI secured a five-year contract with the U.S. State Department to ship and distribute more than $900 million in donated food, medical, and other supplies to the former states of the Soviet Union.

Despite these lucrative contracts, MPRI continued to operate primarily within the United States until early 1994, when the State Department awarded MPRI a contract to provide forty-five border monitors to observe the UN sanctions against Bosnia. In September 1994 the Republic of Croatia hired MPRI to modernize and train its national army and the following June issued another contract for classroom instruction in democratic ideas and civil-military relations for its officer corps.

Prior to the arrival of MPRI, the Croatian National Army was structured according to the Soviet military model and aptly described as "ragtag" and inefficient. The Croatians quickly took to the U.S. model of military organization and warfare and in the summer of 1995 began operations to eliminate Serb-supported militias within their borders.

Critics of the action complained that the offensive created more than a hundred thousand refugees and accused Croatian soldiers of murdering unarmed Serb civilians. The International War Crimes Tribunal has since indicted several Croatian commanders for the operation that, in fact, did violate a UN cease-fire. Some observers have accused MPRI advisers and the U.S. Defense Department of being duplicitous in the alleged crimes, but no evidence has been offered to support these claims.

But few could argue that in less than a year MPRI contractors converted an ill trained, undermotivated, ineffective army into an efficient fighting force. It was also evident that the MPRI military training, based on the U.S. Army's Air-Land Battle Doctrine, provided tremendous results for the money spent.

On that basis, MPRI's success in Croatia elevated it from a moderately successful private military firm into a

worldwide influence on modern soldiers of fortune.
Shortly after Operation Storm in Croatia, the government
of Bosnia hired MPRI in May 1996 to reorganize, arm,
and train its armed forces. The contract differed from that
with Croatia in that this one specifically contained provisions for MPRI to provide combat training.

MPRI and Bosnian officials agreed to a contract amount-
ing to $50 million for the first year with provisions for an-
nual renewals. Another $100 to $300 million was
authorized for the purchase of arms and equipment. Although the U.S. State Department had to approve the MPRI
portions of the contract and maintain some oversight of the
entire operation, the U.S. government did not finance the
program. Instead, the money came from a coalition of mod-
erate Islamic countries, including Saudi Arabia, the United
Arab Emirates, Kuwait, Brunei, and Malaysia, which
hoped that the improved Bosnian army could protect the
country's Muslim majority from its non-Muslim neighbors.

Arms for Bosnia included forty-six thousand rifles, one
thousand machine guns, sixty-six hundred radios and tactical telephones, eighty armored personnel carriers, forty-
five tanks, eight hundred forty light antitank weapons, and
fifteen utility helicopters. Generally the Bosnian Defense
Ministry was happy with the arms package but complained that they were receiving thirty-year-old U.S.
M-60 tanks rather than the more modern M-1 Abrams
models. To introduce the weapons into the Bosnian army
and to train the force, MPRI sent retired U.S. Army Maj.
Gen. William Boice, recently commander of the U.S. 1st
Armored Division, and a team of 163 veteran U.S. military personnel.

MPRI's successes in Croatia and Bosnia increased the
firm's visibility and its reputation for efficiency and professionalism. Contracts began to roll in at an ever-increasing
pace, and soon MPRI personnel were working around the
world. From one contract and a few dozen employees in

1987, the company had expanded to a dozen projects in the early 1990s with hundreds of workers. By 2002, MPRI had seven hundred employees working in several states and foreign countries. By mid-2004 the number of employees had more than doubled to fifteen hundred.

As of this writing, MPRI has five divisions—the National, International, Support, Alexandria (Virginia), and Ship Analysis groups, all headed by retired generals and Department of Defense officials.

MPRI's National Group provides support and training for the Department of Defense and other government agencies within the United States. These services include the original MPRI contracts to introduce new vehicles and weapons systems and to provide assistance to the various service schools. This group has recently expanded its services to replace many of the active duty officers in the college Reserve Officer Training Corps (ROTC) programs and develop training materials for the Civil Air Patrol. To support these activities, MPRI maintains offices at Fort Leavenworth, Kansas; Fort Knox, Kentucky; Fort Sill, Oklahoma; and Fort Bliss, Texas.

MPRI's International Group has conducted successful programs in virtually every region of the world. Contractors from MPRI are currently assisting various foreign defense departments in establishing policies, procedures, and strategic plans, and in providing humanitarian assistance. MPRI also provides management training, education, leadership development, emergency management, and the use of computer simulators to its international employers.

Successful contracts to modernize the armies of Croatia and Bosnia led to a similar effort in Bulgaria, which included equipment modernization and rearmament and an evaluation of force plans and structure. MPRI also has long-term contracts with Kuwait for the continued modernization and training of that country's army. Force-on-force training exercises for the Kuwaitis and the U.S. forces there are planned and conducted by MPRI. The firm is also deeply involved in the war on terrorism with training in Afghanistan.

MPRI employees in Iraq are actively training that country's new army as well as providing equipment orientation and other services for the U.S. and other allied forces serving there. One of MPRI's primary contracts in Iraq is at the Kirkush Military Training Base, where a ninety-man team organizes and trains thousand-man Iraqi battalions. After two months of training, a formal graduation ceremony is held and the battalions join the Coalition Forces in maintaining the country's peace.

Since 1999, MPRI has assisted the U.S. Department of Defense in the establishment and operations of the African Center for Strategic Studies. This program provides African senior military and civilian leaders seminars and symposia where they study and share ideas on a wide range of topics. More than fifty African countries participate in these activities that promote peace and strengthening ties with the United States.

The U.S. State Department negotiated with MPRI to conduct the African Contingency Operations and Assistance Program (ACOTA), an effort that hopefully promotes cooperation among African countries and will lead to collective security for the continent. MPRI also provides the military training necessary to achieve these goals.

MPRI has executed agreements with Nigeria to conduct leadership development seminars and to study and recommend ways to improve its armed forces. A similar contract with Equatorial Guinea includes a National Security Enhancement Plan that involves assistance in securing its seashore along with implementing improvements in its army. And in an ironic turn, MPRI is providing assistance in a range of training analysis programs to the Republic of South Africa, the home of the first private military company.

The International Group of MPRI is also busy in Asia. In the Republic of China, MPRI teams are training the Taiwanese to use advanced communications systems and teaching local instructors how to prepare future generations. Similar operations are ongoing in the Republic of Korea.

In South America, MPRI has provided support to the Center for Hemispheric Studies since 2000. This includes analytical support as well as conference and seminar planning and presentation.

MPRI's rapid growth in size and influence eventually became a cause for concern within the American government as well as among Defense officials. In 1997 the army determined that it needed guidance on the conduct and regulation of private military companies and directed its Training and Doctrine Command (TRADOC) to prepare the regulations. So what did TRADOC do? It hired MPRI to develop and write the regulations, of course. The results, as approved by TRADOC and the Department of the Army, produced Field Manual (FM) 100-10-2, *Contracting Support on the Battlefield,* released in April 1999, and FM 100-121, *Contractors on the Battlefield,* the following September.

Since its initial formation, MPRI has focused on land warfare, but it recently acquired the Ship Analytics company to assist in naval matters. Founded in 1972, Ship Analytics currently provides maritime training simulations for a major contract in Indonesia. The MPRI Ship Analytics Group also markets programs for managing responses to man-made or natural disasters, including oil spills, toxic chemical releases, nuclear radiation, hurricanes, fires, earthquakes, and terrorist attacks.

MPRI has also assumed law enforcement training through their Homeland and Corporate Security division.

This includes risk assessment, security planning, and leadership training.

MPRI has advanced the status of private military companies to respectability and professionalism. As one of the company's contractors stated in 2004 prior to deployment to assist in training the Iraqi army, "We aren't your daddy's brand of mercenaries anymore."

In addition to bringing respectability to the profession of soldiers of fortune, MPRI has also made the profits of the modern mercenaries available to the general public. In mid-2000, L3 Communications, a former part of the Loral and Lockheed defense aviation and communications company, purchased MPRI. L3 Communications is publicly owned and traded on the New York Stock Exchange. Now everyone can own a piece of the modern mercenary company.

The CEO of L3 Communications, Frank Lanza, discussed the acquisition in an interview with *Business Wire* on July 18, 2000. According to Lanza, "MPRI is a growth company with good profit margins and competitive advantages that no other training business can match, and its services are complementary to our products. In addition, the company is at the forefront of two positive defense industry dynamics. The U.S. military is privatizing many functions to reduce its increasing operations and maintenance budget and to compensate for its expanding national security commitments and declining manpower. MPRI is also active on the international front, as changing political climates have led to increased demand for certain services. These programs tend to expand and to lead to other opportunities."

· 18 ·

Expansion of Private Military Companies

Over the past decade private military companies have proliferated and thrived. Companies large and small, old and new, have assumed profitable roles in military contracting. Some of the private military companies incorporated to service a single contract while others are in the business for the long haul. A few frequently change their names or combine with other companies. Any list of current private military companies would be good for only a day or two in this rapidly changing business.

Defining *modern military companies* is not all that simple. Corporations that build and manufacture weapons, vehicles, and other armaments and supplies are part of the "military-industrial complex," but their workers are not soldiers of fortune. Other companies have been supporting various armies for decades in the construction of buildings, roads, and airfields; they likewise cannot be considered mercenaries.

Private military companies that do meet the definition of *mercenaries* are those that provide direct support to combat operations by either providing the warriors themselves or performing duties that free others to fight. Some of these PMCs provide armed security for high-ranking civilian and military leaders and sensitive buildings and other sites. Others specialize in training and maintenance to increase the proficiency of the armed forces of their clients. Still others offer behind-the-scenes support in areas such as food preparation, water purification, and waste removal.

The numbers and types of PMCs are, of course, dependent on need. The post-9/11 war on terror and the ongoing efforts to halt drug trafficking have greatly increased the demand for the services of PMCs. During the Gulf War in 1991 there was only one contract employee for every hundred uniformed military personnel supporting the conflict. In Operation Iraqi Freedom, the number of contractors has increased to one per every ten soldiers.

By mid-2004 the best estimate on the number of private military companies providing direct combat services to various governments and causes is more than two hundred. There are still a dozen or more PMCs in Africa that filled the vacancy left by Executive Outcomes. Several more are based in western European countries. Many more, and some of the most secretive, are based in Russia and other countries once part of the Soviet Union.

The vast majority of the modern private military companies, however, are in the United Kingdom and the United States. Reasons for this concentration are fairly simple. First, the United Kingdom, and especially the United States; are the largest employers of PMCs, and their leaders prefer to work with contractors they know and understand. The downsizing of the American and British militaries as a "peace dividend" has limited the capabilities of the active forces, requiring additional resources for them to meet their worldwide commitments.

Other countries also actively seek the support of the U.S. contractors. Since World War II, and specifically after the end of the Cold War, the United States has been the single most powerful economic and military force in the world. For the past several decades the entire world has wanted American hamburgers, fried chicken, and blue jeans. They listen to American music and watch American television and movies. Little wonder that when these foreign nations search for military support and innovation, they look to the United States of America.

Corporate executives of U.S. private military companies observed this need as an excellent chance to increase profits. Skilled military personnel leaving the armed forces saw the PMCs as sources of strong salaries, excellent benefits, and continued service to their country.

While Military Professional Resources Incorporated (MPRI) continues to set the standard for PMCs in the United States and Sandline continues its mostly successful history in Great Britain, other PMCs are winning contracts. Among the leading PMCs in the United States are firms that are subsidiaries of some of the country's largest corporations. In the war in Iraq and Afghanistan, contractors from Halliburton, ITT, General Dynamics, and others provide a variety of services and support for the combat troops, ranging from food service to vehicle and weapons maintenance and communications. Other companies, large and small, provide armed security guards for officials, government sites, and transportation resources.

One of the largest PMCs in the world today is a division of Halliburton, a company well known for extinguishing the more than three hundred burning oil wells in Kuwait at the end of the Gulf War.

During the post–Gulf War period, when Halliburton's oil and petroleum support revenues decreased, it began to broaden its field of services. In 1995 former defense secretary Dick Cheney joined Halliburton as its president and chief executive officer. Halliburton immediately began to bid on military contracts and in only twelve months secured a billion dollars in work.

Today Halliburton contracts with the U.S. armed forces under its own name and as Kellogg, Brown & Root, with KBR handling most of its military work. In 2004 in Iraq, KBR provided more than $9 billion in services to U.S. and allied troops, including food preparation, laundry service, and mail delivery. Its construction workers build command centers and living quarters with showers, latrines, and even Internet connections for communication with families back home. KBR also has contracts to repair and maintain Iraqi oil facilities and to deliver gasoline and other petroleum products to the combat units. Although Halliburton's contractors are supposedly in support rather than in direct combat roles, they share many of the dangers with the regular uniformed forces. On April 9, 2004, Iraqi gunmen attacked a fuel convoy operated by Halliburton. The attackers killed three contractors and took another prisoner.

Another major U.S. company, the Vinnell Corporation of Fairfax, Virginia, has been providing training and support of international military forces for the past quarter century. Vinnell began in 1975 with contracts to assist in the training, logistical support, and modernization of the Saudi Arabian National Guard. Since that time Vinnell contractors have trained that country's soldiers, noncommissioned officers, and officers. When the Royal Saudi Land Forces decided to buy Bradley fighting vehicles from the United States, they engaged Vinnell to prepare the vehicles, train their operators, and demonstrate their use on the battlefield to its command structure.

In 1980 the Vinnell Corporation signed a contract with the Royal Saudi Air Force to provide everything from logistics to systems analysis and aeronautical engineering. Vinnell also provides similar support for the Royal Air Force of Malaysia.

Vinnell, a subsidiary of the major defense firm Northrop Grumman, is not the only U.S. contractor in Saudi Arabia. General Dynamics, a leading U.S. Fortune 500 company, has also sought a portion of the lucrative PMC market. General Dynamics proudly claims in its advertisements and promotional material that "it takes pride in producing products that help defend the freedom and security of this and other nations."

But General Dynamics does far more than just provide "products." Through its General Dynamics Land Systems (GDLS), the company provides contractors to train soldiers in the capabilities and maintenance of modern weapons. In 2004, GDLS deployed instructors and technicians to train Saudi troops on the M-1 and M-60 main battle tanks as well as self-propelled artillery. Other GDLS personnel train Saudi army battalion and brigade commanders how to integrate these weapons into their battle plans.

Another major U.S. company, ITT Industries, has assumed a role in the proliferation of private military companies. According to its literature, its ITT Systems Division branch "provides select government, commercial, and international customers value-added, total worldwide systems solutions for their air and missile defense, air traffic control, communications, command and control, range, and force protection needs, as well as full logistics support services for facilities and equipment."

From its headquarters in Colorado Springs, Colorado, ITT Systems is ITT's fastest-growing division with operations in 120 locations within the United States and in forty-one foreign countries. In early 2003, ITT Systems secured a $95 million contract with the U.S. Air Force to support Operation Enduring Freedom in Southwest Asia. In 2004 it began logistical support in the Balkans with work sites in Bosnia, Croatia, Macedonia, Hungary, Slovenia, Romania, and Greece. An interesting aspect of this recent contract is that American soldiers of fortune are now providing military support in the homeland of the great mercenaries of the ancient world.

On the other side of the globe, Pacific Architects and Engineers (PAE) has been the leading American contractor for nearly a half century. Established in 1955, PAE was the major builder and maintainer of American and allied facilities during the long Vietnam War. PAE continues to work in the Pacific with specific operations in Japan and New Zealand.

Private military companies are also significantly involved in American counterdrug operations. South America had proven to be an excellent market for the PMCs because of limitations placed by the U.S. Congress on regular forces serving there. Long before the media worried about "Iraq becoming another Vietnam," the same sentiments were being expressed about Colombia. When Colombia, Peru, and neighboring countries requested help from the United States to fight their drug cartels, the State and Defense Departments faced public and congressional demands to keep the number of regular troops sent there to a minimum. As a result, the Defense Department deployed only about two hundred regular soldiers—but they issued or approved contracts to several PMCs for support.

One of the first contracts went to DynCorp of Reston, Virginia. Some reports claimed that part of the contract went to DynCorp's subcontractor Eagle Aviation Services and Technology, Inc., in nearby Chantilly, Virginia, which had been accused of running guns and ammo to the Nicaraguan rebels for Lt. Col. Oliver North and the National Security Council in the late 1980s. Both the State Department and DynCorp denied these allegations.

The State Department did admit that DynCorp was hired to fly eradication missions over Colombian coca and poppy fields. In February 2001 the supposedly unarmed DynCorp helicopters became engaged in a firefight with left-wing guerrillas on the ground.

Another one of the initial contracts quickly produced a political and public relations nightmare. An Alabama-based company, Aviation Development Corporation, flew airplanes with sophisticated detection and tracking equipment over Peru. On April 20, 2001, the contractors spotted a Cessna aircraft they thought to be carrying drugs and reported it to the Peruvian air force. The Peruvians shot down the Cessna, killing an American missionary and her child. No drugs were on board.

Still another incident occurred on February 13, 2003, when rebels shot down a surveillance aircraft over the Colombian jungle. One contractor was killed and three American contractors were taken prisoner. As of this writing in mid-2004 all three are still being held prisoner by the Revolutionary Armed Forces of Colombia (FARC). FARC, which has financed its revolution through the drug trade and kidnappings, claims they will free the hostages only in exchange for fellow rebels held by the Colombian government.

In addition to revealing the widening use of contractors in South America, the capture of the Americans has also given insight into the secrecy and complicated relations between and among the PMCs. Initial reports stated the captured contractors were flying for AirScan International of Rockledge, Florida, while other reports said they worked for DynCorp or for Computer Systems Corporation (CSC). This latter confusion evolved from the fact that CSC purchased DynCorp on May 7, 2003, and absorbed it into their company. Apparently, however, none of these reports proved to be correct. Most recent reports state that they were operating as contractors of California Microwave Systems, another subsidiary of Northrop Grumman.

MPRI also provides services to U.S. support efforts to combat drug trafficking in South America. Other contractors work either for the United States or directly for the South American governments.

Not all the private military companies are part of large corporations or based in major metropolitan areas. The Confederated Native American Salish and Kootenai Tribes, based in St. Ignatius, Montana, own S&K Technologies. Like most PMCs, S&K actively recruits former military officers and noncommissioned officers for their engineering, telecommunications, and computer projects. S&K proudly advertises that they have an advantage over other PMCs in that, as an Indian tribal-owned business, they receive special consideration from the U.S. government in negotiations and "are not limited by dollar thresholds on sole source contracts."

The vast majority of the modern soldiers of fortune working as contractors for the PMCs operate under much better and safer conditions than the mercenaries of old. Although they do face some dangers, as proven by the capture of the aviators in Colombia and the deaths of the convoy drivers in Iraq, most contractors are employed in relatively secure rear-area jobs.

There are some exceptions, however. Whereas many contractors are hired because of their skills in training, logistics, and communications, some men are recruited because they are experts with weapons. The PMCs that specialize in security operations seek men with combat experience and actively recruit outprocessing veteran SEALs, Rangers, Green Berets, and Special Operations Unit veterans. According to one security PMC recruiter, "SEALs and Rangers earn the big bucks; guys that served with Delta Force can almost name their own price."

Some companies like Omniplex World Services Corporation in Alexandria, Virginia, primarily provide security personnel for the Department of the Interior and other U.S. agencies. The Steele Foundation based in San Francisco provided security for Haitian president Jean-Bertrand Aristide and accompanied him into exile in 2004.

The vast majority of security companies, however, are currently employed in Iraq and Afghanistan. Custer Battles Incorporated of Fairfax, Virginia, provides security personnel for the Baghdad International Airport. Dyn-

Corp trains the Iraqi police and provides bodyguards for Afghan president Hamid Karzai. Global Risk of Great Britain guards the new civil administration, and Pilgrims, Incorporated of the Seychelles Islands offers security for many of the international journalists and news media.

PMCs that specialize in security are even more secretive than those in more supportive roles. Blackwater USA in 1998 was founded by two former U.S. Navy SEALs. Headquartered at Moyock, North Carolina, the security firm has maintained a low profile from its inception. Even the Sheriff of Currituck County, the home of Blackwater, admits to knowing little of its operations. In an April 1, 2004, interview with the *Virginia Pilot,* Sheriff Susan Johnson stated, "Nobody knows anything about Blackwater. They don't bring a lot of attention to themselves."

Despite Blackwater's efforts to remain anonymous, the company—and PMCs in general—came to the forefront of world news after a group of their contractors was ambushed in Fallujah, Iraq, in April 2004. The attackers killed four Blackwater employees—one a former Navy SEAL—and then dragged their burned bodies through the streets before hanging the remains from nearby bridge girders.

Pictures of the atrocities were seen around the world, exposing the barbarity of the Iraqi rebels—but also increasing the awareness of the PMCs and the dangers they faced. For the first time, many international news media began to refer to the contractors as mercenaries.

In less than two decades since Executive Outcomes became the first modern PMC, other companies have joined the business to provide all types of military support just short of direct combat to governments around the world. Generally they have hired out their services to legitimate governments and, despite an apparent increase in public awareness, they are becoming more and more acceptable. From huge, publicly owned firms to small independent companies, the corporate world has learned that war is indeed good business, and business is good and getting better.

· 19 ·

United States of America

The U.S. government has grown to be the largest employer of private military companies because they provide a means for an overextended American military to perform the missions asked of it around the world. It is axiomatic that politicians first and foremost want to satisfy their contingents, and expanding the size of the military to meet increasing needs has never been a popular stance. Hiring private contractors to perform or support certain military duties has not only proven efficient and economical, but also it keeps the voters back home happy and the incumbents reelected.

While modern soldiers of fortune work in the employment of the PMCs, mercenaries of sorts have served in the American armed services from the beginning. Thousands of young men arriving as immigrants on American shores have donned the uniform of their adopted country since the days of George Washington. During the Civil War, army recruiters signed up battalions of Irish immigrants literally off the boat; some were on the battlefront within days of their arrival.

In the decades following the Civil War the U.S. military greatly decreased its numbers but still faced formidable Native American tribes on the Western plains. Recruiters continued to meet immigrant ships to sign up men for the infantry and cavalry. Irish, Italians, Poles, and other Europeans volunteered to wear the blue uniform in order to gain their citizenship—and to have a job. At the Little Big Horn in 1876, fully a third of George Custer's 7th Cavalry who fell were foreign-born.

The United States has traditionally filled its military ranks during time of war and often in peace with draftees. The services have encouraged volunteers with promises of branch of service and job specialty selections rather than arbitrary assignments forced upon draftees. By the mid-twentieth century, the draft supplied men for the infantry, artillery, and other combat arms while volunteers had the choice of safe duties in support and rear-echelon areas. During World War II, many young men became familiar with the phrase, "Volunteer for the navy, or get drafted for the infantry."

After the fall of Germany and Japan in World War II, the majority of the U.S. military personnel accepted their discharges and returned to civilian life. Volunteers and a limited number of draftees remained in the smaller peacetime forces. During these postwar years some U.S. leaders investigated alternative means of continuing to meet enlistment quotas without extending the draft.

In 1950, Sen. Henry Cabot Lodge Jr., the Republican senator from Massachusetts, introduced a bill to the Senate to enlist displaced Europeans into the U.S. Army. World War II created more than 14 million European refugees, and in response the United States and its allies had initiated various programs to rebuild Europe and to provide food, homes, and jobs for these displaced persons. One of these programs offered the displaced enlistment in the U.S. Army and citizenship for those who served honorably.

The Eighty-first Congress passed Public Law 597, better known as the "Lodge Act" or the "alien enlistment program," in June 1950. Its first enlistees began arriving at the 7720th Replacement Depot at Sonthofen, Germany, in early 1951.

Despite the good intentions of the Lodge Act, it produced few soldiers. The opportunity was poorly advertised in the refugee community, and several levels of bureaucracy both within the United States and in European governments limited the number of volunteers. Ultimately only about twenty-three hundred candidates came forward, and fewer than four hundred met the physical and mental qualifications to complete their basic training at Fort Dix, New Jersey.

Lodge and his supporters envisioned Public Law 597 as an initial step to eventually replace many U.S. troops in Germany with battalions of displaced Europeans in what they called a Volunteer Freedom Corps. Little mention was made of the fact that these former refugees would in essence be mercenaries paid by the U.S. government if the program had been successful. Although never formally stated, this is likely one of the primary reasons the European countries never supported the plan and allowed it to fail.

The United States maintained the Lodge Act, at least on paper, until 1960 when it finally abandoned the idea. Although the plan was far from successful, it did have its positive points. More than thirty of the refugees who completed their training transferred to the 10th Special Forces Group when it formed at Fort Bragg, North Carolina, in 1953. Their language skills—which included fluency in Czech, Hungarian, Russian, Polish, German, and others—combined with their hatred of the occupation of their homelands by the Soviet Union did much to make the first European Green Beret unit a success when it moved to Bad Tolz, Germany.

During the Korean War the United States relied on the draft to fill its ranks. The patriotic feelings left over from the victory in World War II generally limited complaints about compulsory military service.

It was not until the long Vietnam War that American opinion of the draft began to sour. Now, the thought of dying in an unpopular war replaced the patriotic fervor of the previous generation.

Further objections against the draft came when the public, especially the economically disadvantaged, realized that the sons of the wealthy and affluent were avoiding conscription. College deferments were automatic, and those who left school could easily find a sympathetic doctor who would send draft boards reports of physical or mental maladies that would exempt them from induction. Sons of the rich and of elected officials were often granted coveted slots in National Guard and Reserve units that had little chance of being called to active duty and sent to the war zone.

A resort to the lottery system in the war's final years did little to quell protest against conscription. In 1973, with nearly all American troops withdrawn from Southeast Asia and the numbers in the armed forces significantly reduced, the United States ended the draft and went to an all-volunteer military. Higher pay, enlistment bonuses, postservice education plans, and other benefits lured enough volunteers for the most part. And when enlistment goals fell short, especially in the army, more career fields were opened to women to encourage their enlistment. During the 1970s the U.S. Army received praise from women's groups as well as the public in general for its progressive stance on equal opportunity, although it was less than clear that the army was all that happy with the concept of the female soldier.

Overall the American public welcomed the end of the draft and accepted the all-volunteer force. The wealthy no longer had to dodge the draft; protestors no longer needed to march in the streets. And those who needed it saw the military as a job opportunity and a chance to better themselves. Everyone was happy, at least for a while.

The minor conflicts in Grenada and Panama in the 1980s created few casualties and proved that the all-volunteer force could fight and fight well. The Gulf War of 1991, again with few casualties, showed the world that the all-volunteer force, with American superiority in weapons and support systems, could rule the battlefield. A few of the old antimilitary guard joined by new zealots coming of age in the peace movement protested that the all-volunteer armed forces more closely resembled a mercenary horde than that of a national army. Some even chanted, "Who fights your wars, the minorities and the poor."

Generally, however, the antimilitary crowd took a back-seat to renewal of patriotism and respect for those in uniform after the quick liberation of Kuwait from Iraq. The men and women of the armed forces had proven that they could and would fight well and that they were as dedicated and loyal as any other Americans committed to the battlefield in previous wars.

Shortly after the Gulf War, victory parades welcomed the soldiers, sailors, airmen, and Marines home, and just as the yellow ribbons tied to trees and picket fences began to fade, additional information about the relationship between the all-volunteer force and mercenaries came to light. Many of the U.S. veterans and casualties of the Gulf War were not U.S. citizens. Recruiters, always anxious to meet their goals, actively sought newly arrived legal immigrants. Anyone who held a "green card" was a legitimate candidate for the armed forces; in fact, during the Vietnam War era, legal immigrants had been just as eligible for the draft as regular citizens.

Attracted to the promised full-time job, training, and future education benefits, the ultimate inducement up the recruiters' sleeve was the promise of U.S. citizenship after an honorable discharge.

In the aftermath of the Gulf War, supporters of immigrant causes saw the moral issue of immigrants being allowed to fight and possibly die for the United States without enjoying the benefits of citizenship. Some even questioned if these foreigners might be more soldiers of fortune than patriots. In response, President Bill Clinton issued an executive order on November 22, 1995, that allowed the 14,713 immigrant soldiers who had served in the Gulf War to apply for expedited citizenship.

During the decade after the Gulf War, which followed the collapse of the Soviet Union, the American public experienced a booming economy and the realization that the United States was now the single world power. Except for a few who wanted defense funds diverted to social programs, most Americans ignored the military. The rich and influential continued to send their sons and daughters to universities and left manning of the services to the poor and minorities.

By early 2002 women comprised 15 percent of the U.S. Army, and minorities, both male and female, made up 42 percent of the total force. Similar numbers of women and minorities filled the ranks of the other services. Recruiters continued to actively recruit legal immigrants. The U.S. Immigration and Naturalization Service (INS) continued its policy of requiring immigrants in uniform to wait three years for their citizenship—a slight advantage over the five-year wait for those not in the military. Between 1990 and 2000 the INS granted 8,430 military personnel their citizenship after the three-year waiting period.

The serenity and security of the great victory in the Gulf War and the end of the communist threat from the Soviet Union did not last long. When Muslim terrorists attacked the World Trade Center and the Pentagon on September 11, 2001, a new threat emerged. President George Bush dispatched forces to end Taliban rule in Afghanistan and find Osama bin Laden, the mastermind of the attacks. The war against terror expanded into Iraq to eliminate Saddam Hussein in 2003 and continues on to the time of this writing.

More than any other conflict, the war in Iraq showed how much the United States relies on private military companies. It also has revealed that the armed forces, even with the call-up of reserve forces, have difficulties meeting all their worldwide commitments. Extensions of overseas tours and quick turnaround of units rotated home are further symptoms of a growing problem.

Not coincidentally, on July 3, 2002, President Bush signed an executive order announcing that service members fighting the war against terror no longer had to wait three years to apply for citizenship.

But the problem remains. The conflicts in Afghanistan and Iraq combined with other continual U.S. military commitments around the world are stretching the armed forces almost beyond their capabilities. Even the call-up of National Guard and Reserve units is providing only short-term solutions. The military simply needs more men and women, and some members of Congress are even proposing a renewal of a limited draft.

Sen. Joe Biden, a Democrat from Delaware, said in early 2004, "Our standing army is not large enough" to handle the wide-ranging jobs it has been given.

Chuck Hagel, a Republican senator from Nebraska, at the same time stated that the commitments to the war against terror required additional resources. Hagel explained, "I'm not proposing a draft, but I think some kind of mandatory service should be something we take seriously." He concluded that if some type of draft does return, it should apply to all families equally including "the privileged, the rich, and those who have a lot."

The increased commitments overseas and the resulting extended periods away from families combined with the dangers of combat have decreased the number of service members staying in uniform beyond their initial enlistment. The answer proposed by the politicians and some military leaders is to "buy a solution."

The Department of Defense is seeking an increase in hardship pay for those in combat zones from $300 to $750 per month. David S. C. Chu, undersecretary of defense for personnel and readiness, spoke before a Senate subcommittee on March 2, 2004. Chu admitted that the extended combat operations in Iraq were a test for the all-volunteer concept and encouraged additional pay to keep men and women in uniform. Chu concluded, "Because we are at war and will be for the foreseeable future, our goal is to continue to recruit soldiers who have the warrior ethos and those who seek to serve our nation fully in these very difficult times."

Soldiers serving in units that are rotating in and out of Afghanistan and Iraq can receive bonuses of $5,000 to $10,000 by volunteering to extend their tours, and lest one only dismiss the importance of a secure Korean Peninsula, U.S. soldiers, who reenlist for a second tour of duty in South Korea, can receive a bonus of as much as $20,000.

It would be unfair to the many brave men and women, both citizen and noncitizen, who accept the bonuses to question their patriotism or their commitment to their country. However, it would not be unfair to note that increased pay, citizenship, and other benefits in exchange for enlistment are not all that different from the reasons soldiers of fortune have fought since the beginnings of time.

· 20 ·

Opposition and Legislation

As is true of the world's other oldest profession, sooner or later one is forced to confront the moral stance of the mercenary. Certainly in the ideal world, diplomacy rather than force resolves conflicts, and when combat is necessary, patriotic citizens dedicated to their country and cause fight the battles. Unfortunately, diplomacy and willing warriors are often in short supply in time of war, and morality is the first casualty.

Since the dawn of civilization, soldiers who are paid to fight other people's battles have played an important role in warfare and the resulting balance of power. Kings hired mercenaries to maintain their kingdoms, the church to defend their cathedrals and beliefs, dictators and despots to preserve their rule. Now democracies use contractors to do a good share of soldiery so that much of the citizenry need not.

Throughout recorded history mercenaries have provided their skills in return for pay. Generally their employers have praised their service while their enemies have condemned their presence. It was not until the twentieth century and its two world wars that mercenaries began to lose their jobs to large conscripted armies. By the end of World War II only the Gurkhas and the French Foreign Legion carried on the banner of soldiers of fortune. The African unrest of the 1960s brought a renewal of mercenaries with the emergence of Hoare, Denard, and their like. Few world leaders expressed support for the new mercenaries, and the Western powers, including the United States, mostly ignored their presence—or covertly supported them, due to their stance against communist-supported regimes and rebels.

The Geneva Convention of August 12, 1949, made brief mention of the control of mercenaries. It was not, however, until June 8, 1977, with the addition of Protocol I on the Protection of Victims of Armed Conflict, that the convention specifically defined *mercenaries* and outlined their rights on the battlefield.

In Part III, Section II, Article 47 of the protocol (the complete article is in Appendix E), the convention stated that mercenaries "shall not have the right to be a combatant or a prisoner of war." The article then defines what the convention considered to be mercenaries. Although the 1977 Geneva Convention Protocol provided a definition for mercenaries and limited their rights, it did not declare the employment of soldiers of fortune to be unlawful under international law.

In 1979 the United Nations began discussions to outlaw mercenaries altogether. As with everything in the United Nations, the process moved slowly. It took a year after the representative of Nigeria brought the topic before the assembly for the United Nations to appoint a thirty-five-member ad hoc committee to draft an International Convention against the Recruitment, Use, Financing and Training of Mercenaries.

Between 1981 and 1989 the committee held eight sessions to perfect the antimercenary document. After nine years of negotiations the committee submitted the convention to the UN General Assembly, which adopted it without a vote on December 4, 1989. The presiding officer of the session that adopted the convention, Joseph N. Garba of Nigeria, announced that the document symbolized "the political will of the international community, despite initial differences, to outlaw once and for all the activities of these soldiers of fortune, who have not only contributed to the destabilization of the affected States but also plundered and looted villages and farms in Africa, Latin America and Asia."

For the convention to become international law under the provisions of the United Nations, it required the signature of merely 22 of its 185 members. Over the next nine years only 16 members approved the convention. This included Italy and Poland, but most of the signers were small nations with little influence such as Togo, Barbados, and Morocco. In late 1998 the international media described the convention as "gathering dust" and criticized the United Nations for its failure to ratify the document. The pressure from the press and a renewed effort on the part of UN officials finally produced the twenty-second signature in October 2001.

The United Nations for the first time had an official law, supposedly recognized by most of the world, against soldiers of fortune. The convention provided high-sounding and moralistic words on the definition, proposed limitations, and punishment for mercenaries and their employers. Although the document itself is not without merit, the United Nations has had neither the means nor the will to enforce its provisions.

During the last few years the United Nations was seeking the final signatory nations to ratify the antimercenary convention, it began to realize that private military companies were assuming many of the jobs performed by soldiers of fortune. Again, in its usual way, the United Nations studied the situation and wrote a report rather than take direct action.

A lengthy report on the use of mercenaries published on January 13, 1999, by the United Nations's Economic and Social Council's Commission on Human Rights included several pages devoted to "Private Security and Military

Assistance Companies." The report's primary author, Enrique Bernales Ballesteros of Peru, wrote, "These companies are developing their offers more and more aggressively, putting forward arguments for legitimacy based on military efficiency, cheaper operations, their personnel's proven experience and an alleged comparative advantage that would make it feasible or desirable to hire them for peace-building or peacekeeping operations."

The report further stated that, "National States are showing no sign of a reaction that focuses on these companies' international expansion and the dangers it entails for State sovereignty and objectives." He noted, however, that South Africa was the country that had declared the clearest position on these companies and mentioned the legislation that led to the end of Executive Outcomes.

The report outlined the proliferation of private military companies and warned, "These companies would like to be regarded as an alternative to the conduct to United Nations peace operations."

Ballesteros included additional warnings in his report that PMCs apparently intended to take over many of the responsibilities of the United Nations. He wrote, "Mercenary activities continue to exist in many parts of the world and to take on new forms. The recruitment and hiring of mercenaries by private companies providing security services and military assistance and advice and, in turn, the hiring of these companies by Governments which entrust them with responsibility for security, maintaining public order and safety and even armed combat against rebel forces and organized crime are a serious challenge to the international human rights protection system currently in force."

The report concludes, "Although mercenaries pose as technicians and military experts hired as such by private companies providing security services and military assistance and advice, or by Governments, this changes neither the nature nor the status of those who hire themselves out to meddle and cause destruction and death in foreign conflicts and countries."

While the United Nations has been aware of the expansion of companies that supply contract soldiers and has finally adopted an official convention against mercenaries, it has done nothing to enforce its provisions. In fact, the United Nations itself is under pressure from some sources to employ soldiers of fortune of its own because internal politics and the bureaucracy of the huge organization prevents it from taking timely action. By the time the United Nations can agree on anything, the situation with which it is concerned is usually already over or has expanded beyond a quick solution.

In 1994, opposing tribesmen in Rwanda began murdering innocent women and children in addition to each other. The most common weapons were knives and machetes. The United Nations debated, wrung its collective hands, and did nothing as more than a half million Rwandans died. If the United Nations had hired a private military unit, perhaps as small as only a few hundred well-armed and trained men, it could have quickly deployed the unit to Rwanda to stop the slaughter.

A similar genocide is ongoing today in Sudan, where opposing groups, mostly based on religion, have driven more than a million civilians from their homes. Villages are being burned, men tortured, women raped, and children starved. The United Nations talks about the problem but has done nothing to stop the violence. Again, a small, professional force of contractors could stabilize the region and reduce, if not end, the killing.

On May 6, 2004, the New York–based Human Rights Organization issued a seventy-seven-page report on Sudan. It stated, "Ten years after Rwandan genocide and despite years of soul-searching, the response of the international community to the events in Sudan has been nothing short of shameful."

Neither the United States nor Great Britain have joined the United Nations in any great efforts to condemn or outlaw mercenaries, but they have made limited attempts to at least identify the problems private military companies have presented. After the "Sandline Affair" in Sierra Leone came to light, the British government began a study in 1999 to determine legislative options for the control of PMCs. Originally the plan called for the investigation to last eighteen months, but it took twice that long because of what the study committee called "the complexity of the issues it considers."

The "green paper" that finally resulted from the study concluded "that the lack of centrally held information on contracts between Government Departments and private military companies is unacceptable." It recommended that immediate steps be taken to collect and update such information, but no measures were actually taken to control the activities of British PMCs.

In the United States the principal legal basis for the uniformed military is established in Title 10 of the U.S. Code, which ignores the private military company issue. The services themselves have defined the roles of "battlefield contractors" only in contracts with PMCs, but there is as yet no government framework for their regulation and control.

The news of captured and murdered contractors working in Iraq in 2004 increased the visibility of PMCs to the world public. The mention of private soldiers in connection with the abuse of prisoners at the Iraqi Abu Ghraib prison in May 2004 has further exposed the presence of PMC employees in nearly every aspect of the efforts to bring peace to Iraq. These incidents will surely encourage the United States and other governments to further define the roles of PMCs and to develop controls and regulations for their actions.

appeal to the military audience. MPRI, ▱l, ITT, and many others post long lists of ▱the same manner as do publishing houses, ▱ufacturers, or other companies, large or ▱ Internet search yields more employment ▱or military contractor positions than an ap-▱d, much less prepare applications for.

▱with military training and experience con-▱he prime candidates for PMC employment, ▱cruiters actively advertise in unofficial mili-▱ations. The weekly editions of *Army Times,* ▱s, and *Air Force Times*—papers owned by the ▱es Publishing Company, a subsidiary of the ▱ompany, publisher of *USA Today*—carry one-▱d one-quarter-page ads under banners such as ▱ing the Free World" announcing positions for ▱tors for General Dynamics' Land Systems and ▱ promise to "Be Part of Something Bigger."

▱se weekly newspapers can be found at every check-▱unter at post and base exchanges around the world. ▱ also have a large subscription base of active and re-▱ military personnel and major civilian libraries.

▱he primary skills sought by the private military com-▱nies are those acquired by active duty soldiers, sailors, ▱rmen, and Marines. Veterans and retirees of the U.S. ▱pecial Operations Command and similar organizations ▱n other countries are the focus of many PMC recruitment efforts, but those proficient in the maintenance of military vehicles and aircraft are also important targets.

PMCs most actively recruit combat soldiers and maintenance technicians but there are ample opportunities for truck drivers, cooks, carpenters, and other skilled and semiskilled workers. These latter opportunities are numerous, but the competition is severe. On May 3, 2004, in the midst of news reports of dead and missing contractors in Iraq, Halliburton announced that it had one hundred

In addition to the philosophical concerns of the United Nations and individual countries about the actions of PMCs, there are practical aspects to the recruitment, activities, and efficiency of mercenaries. One of the greatest worries is about the effect contractors have on regular soldiers. While soldiers appreciate help from all sources on the battlefield, they are at the same time very much aware of the advantages in pay and benefits enjoyed by PMC employees over their own circumstances. Contractors commonly earn four to five times the wages of infantry privates or specialists. A contracted truck driver or mess cook with little education or experience receives higher wages than junior officers.

This disparity in pay is hard on morale and will surely lead to difficulties in discipline and retention. Senior enlisted members of the Special Forces, Delta Force, and SEALs earn about $50,000 per year and can retire with a pension in the range of $23,000 per year. For the same set of skills, PMCs offer six figure salaries.

The "bigger bucks" promised and delivered by the PMCs will continue to impact enlistment and reenlistment, but PMCs will certainly not destroy the regular military. Many, if not most, soldiers will turn down the increased pay for the security of remaining in uniform. The simple fact of serving one's country as a soldier rather than a contractor will also keep many in uniform.

Furthermore, cracks are beginning to show in the PMC model. Increased demand for all services has put the PMCs under pressure to deliver. In early 2004, complaints erupted that contractors in Iraq had difficulties delivering mail to the troops, one of the most important factors in soldiers' morale. In March of that year subcontractors of Halliburton revealed that they were not receiving timely payments and stated they might have to begin feeding soldiers sandwiches rather than hot meals. Contractors that fail to deliver the mail on time or interfere with the troops' chow may very well prove more disruptive to the future of PMCs than their direct actions on the battlefield.

Cost overruns and out-and-out gouging by contractors for fuel and other products in Iraq and Kuwait in 2004 have also brought additional attention on PMCs by the military, the government, and the American public. Just when and what actions will take place are still undetermined.

The conduct and performance of PMCs is an ongoing issue that will be highlighted, if not resolved, on the front pages of newspapers and on the airwaves of radio and television. There will be an increase in the awareness of PMCs and greater calls for legislation and regulation of their future activities.

Opport

Since the beginning of
there is no indication that
peoples, or religions are goin
long as there is war, there wi
there is always a need for hired
added numbers or their skills—or
someone else to fight in one's plac
fortune provide their services under
vate military companies, but these m
definitely the close kin of men who hav
naries through the ages. Employment
expanding, pay is great, and the future o
bright.

Private military companies, as separate cor
as subsidiaries of some of the largest busines
tions in the world, are the present and future for
cenary. The days of Hoare, Denard, and other indep
swashbucklers are past; suit-and-tie boardroom le
have replaced the camouflage and combat-boot merce
ies of old. Although a few "merc bars" still exist in se
eral South African cities, Los Angeles, Bangkok, and
few other places, soldiers for hire, and their opportunities,
are dwindling.

The out-of-the-way, mostly seedy establishments
where recruiting once took place have given way to employment announcements on the Internet and in major

publications that
DynCorp, Vinne
job vacancies in
automobile ma
small. A simpl
opportunities
plicant can re
Personnel
tinue to be
and their re
tary public
Navy Time
Army Ti
Gannet
eighth a
"Defen
contrac
KBR'
The
out c
The
tire

thousand applicants seeking employment with their organization. With pay opportunities of $75,000 for the minimally qualified and up to $200,000 for the technically proficient, the numbers of these job seekers is not likely to decrease, regardless of the hazards.

The major difference between the modern mercenaries and those of earlier times is that the modern version is gaining a respectability and acceptability previously unknown. For PMCs to continue to be accepted and to expand even more, they have only to do a few things. As with any business, they must be efficient and profitable to ensure that shareholders continue to receive dividends on their investments. They must avoid any hint of scandal that might draw comparisons to the mercenaries of the past. Last, and most important, they must meet the needs of their employers in successfully completing the requirements outlined in their contracts.

This is not the final word on the history of mercenaries and private military companies. Current activities are better found on the television news channels and on the front pages of world daily newspapers than in this or any other book. There is no ultimate answer, but excellent insight into the importance and future of PMCs were provided in interviews in the spring of 2004 with one of the profession's greatest innovators and practitioners.

Tim Spicer, the leader in establishing Sandline as the first major successful PMC, reflected on modern contractors, stating, "I believe there is a growing acceptance of the concept of the private sector operating in support of military forces. The best example of, and a catalyst for, this is Iraq. There are some 18,000 private military/security company personnel, armed and deployed in the country. They work for commercial clients and Government. They are generally very good at their jobs and have, in my view, proved the concept. They are involved in key point security, close protection, escort duties, and military training. They are in action every day, and frankly, the situation in Iraq would be untenable without their support. They allow the troops of the multinational divisions to get on with their primary role."

Spicer also discussed the future of PMCs. "There has been a lot of press comment about varying quality of the operators, their pay, etc., but this is inevitable. What I think Iraq will do is 'pave the way' for wider use of PMCs—possibly even by the UN. Use of 'contractors' has been long established in the U.S.—now other governments are beginning to see the value of the talent pool of former highly trained military and other government personnel. As long as they work for reputable, properly established companies in conjunction with government forces—the concept will continue to develop."

The need for soldiers of fortune has and will change little. Their organization into corporate-owned private military companies is a major evolution, but mercenaries will exist wherever warfare exists.

· APPENDIX A ·

Treaty between Great Britain and Hesse-Cassel (1776)

His Britannic Majesty, being desirous of employing in his service a body of 12,000 men, of the troops of his most serene highness the reigning landgrave of Hesse Cassel; and that prince, full of attachment for his Majesty, desiring nothing more than to give him proofs of it, his Majesty, in order to settle the objects relative to this alliance, has thought proper to send to Cassel the sieur William Faucitt, his minister plenipotentiary and colonel in his service, and his most serene highness has named, on his part, for the same purpose, the baron Martin Erneste de Schlieffen, his minister of state, lieutenant general and knight of his orders, who being furnished with requisite full powers, have agreed, that the Treaties formerly concluded between Great Britain and Hesse shall be made the basis of the present Treaty, and to adopt as much of them as shall be applicable to the present circumstances, or to determine by new articles such points as must be settled otherwise; every thing that shall not be differently regulated, shall be deemed to subsist in full force, as it shall appear to be declared in the abovementioned Treaties; and as it is not possible to specify each particular case, every thing that shall not be found regulated in a precise manner, neither in the present Treaty, nor in the former Treaties, ought to be settled with equity and good faith, conformably to the same principles which were agreed on each part to be pursued for regulating all such cases, whether during or after the last war.

I. There shall be therefore, by virtue of this Treaty, between his Majesty, the king of Great Britain and his most serene highness the landgrave of Hesse Cassel, their successors, and heirs, a strict friendship, and a sincere firm and constant union, insomuch that the one shall consider the interests of the other as his own, and shall apply himself with good faith to advance them to the utmost, and to prevent and avert mutually all trouble and loss.

II. To this end it is agreed, that all former Treaties, principally of guaranty, be deemed to be renewed and confirmed by their present Treaty, in all their points, articles and clauses, and shall be of the same force as if they were herein inserted word for word, so far as is not derogated from them by the present Treaty.

III. This body of 12,000 men of the troops of Hesse, which is to be employed in his Britannic Majesty's service, shall consist of four battalions of grenadiers, of four companies each, fifteen battalions of infantry, of five companies each, and two companies of chasseurs, the whole provided with general and other necessary officers. This corps shall be completely equipped and provided with tents and all accoutrements, of which it may stand in need; in a word, shall be put on the best footing possible, and none shall be admitted into it but men fit for service, and acknowledged for such by his Britannic Majesty's commissary. Formerly the signature of the Treaties has usually preceded, by some time, the requisition for the march of troops, but, as in the present circumstances, there is no time to be lost, the day of the signature of the present Treaty is deemed also to be the term of the requisition, and three battalions of grenadiers, six battalions of infantry, with one company of chasseurs, shall be in a condition to pass in review before his Britannic Majesty's commissary on the 14th of February, and shall begin to march on the day following, the 15th of February, for the place of embarkation. The rest shall be ready in four weeks after, if possible, and march in like manner. This body of troops shall not be separated, unless reasons of war require it, but shall remain under the orders of the general, to whom his most serene highness has entrusted the command; and the second division shall be conducted to the same places only, where the first shall actually be, if not contrary to the plan of operations.

IV. Each battalion of this body of troops shall be provided with two pieces of field artillery, with the officers, gunners, and other persons, and the train thereunto belonging, if his Majesty is desirous of it.

V. Towards defraying the expenses, in which the most serene landgrave shall be engaged, for the arming and putting in condition the said corps of 12,000 men, his Majesty, the king of Great Britain, promises to pay to his serene highness for each foot soldier 30 crowns Banco, levy money, as well for the infantry as for the chasseurs or artillery, if there should be any, the sum total of which shall be ascertained, according to the number of men composing this corps, and as they have been reckoned in former alliances. The sum of 180,000 crowns Banco, valued as in the following Article, shall be paid on account of this levy money, on the 10th of February, and the residue shall be paid when the second division of this corps shall begin their march.

VI. In all the former Treaties a certain number of years is stipulated for their duration; but, in the present, his Britannic Majesty, choosing rather not to engage himself for any longer time than he shall have occasion for these troops, consents, instead thereof, that the subsidy shall be double, from the day of the signature of the Treaty to its expiration; that is to say, that it shall amount for this body of 12,000 men to the sum of 450,000 crowns Banco per annum, the crown reckoned at 53 sols of Holland, or at 4s 93/4d. English money, and that the subsidy shall continue upon this foot during all the time that this body of troops shall remain in British pay. His Britannic Majesty engages also to give notice to the most serene landgrave of its determination, 12 months, or a whole year, before it shall take place, which notice shall not even be given before this body of troops is returned, and actually arrived in the dominions of the said prince, namely, in Hesse, properly so called: his Majesty shall continue equally to this corps the pay and other emoluments for the remainder of the month in which it shall repass the frontiers of Hesse, and his most serene highness reserves to himself, on his side, the liberty of recalling his troops at the end of four years, if they are not sent back before, or to agree with his Britannic Majesty at the end of that time for another term.

VII. With regard to the pay and treatment, as well ordinary as extraordinary, of the said troops, they shall be put on the same foot in all respects with the national British troops, and his Majesty's department of war shall deliver, without delay, to that of his most serene highness, an exact and faithful state of the pay and treatment enjoyed by those troops; which pay and treatment, in consideration that his most serene highness could not put this corps in a condition to march in so short a time, without extraordinary expenses, shall commence for the first division on the 1st day of February, and for the second seven days before it shall begin to march, and shall be paid into the military chest of Hesse, without any abatement or deduction, to be distributed according to the arrangements which shall be made for that purpose; and the sum of 20,000 sterling shall be advanced immediately on account of the said pay.

VIII. If it should happen, unfortunately, that any regiment or company of the said corps, should be ruined or destroyed, either by accidents on the sea, or otherwise, in the whole, or in part, or that the pieces of artillery, or other effects, with which they shall be provided, should be taken by the enemy, or lost on the sea, his Majesty, the king of Great Britain, shall cause to be paid the expenses of the necessary recruits, as well as the price of the said field pieces and effects, in order forthwith to reinstate the artillery, and the said regiment or companies; and the said recruits shall be settled likewise on the foot of those which were furnished to the Hessian officers, by the virtue of the Treaty of 1702, Article 5th, to the end that the corps may be always preserved and sent back in as good a state as it was delivered in. The recruits annually necessary shall be sent to the English commissary, disciplined and completely equipped, at the place of embarkation, at such time as this Britannic Majesty shall appoint.

IX. In Europe his Majesty shall make use of this body of troops by land, wherever he shall judge proper; but North America is the only country of the other parts of the globe where this body of troops shall be employed. They shall not serve on the sea; and they shall enjoy all the things, without any restriction whatsoever, the same pay and emoluments as are enjoyed by the English troops.

X. In case the most serene landgrave should be attacked or disturbed in the possession of his dominions, his Britannic Majesty promises and engages to give him all the succour that it shall be in his power to afford, which succour shall be continued to him until he shall have obtained an entire security and just indemnification: as the most serene landgrave promises likewise, on his part, that in the case his Majesty, the king of Great Britain, is attacked or disturbed in his kingdoms, dominions, lands, provinces, or towns, he will give him in like manner all the succour that it shall be in his power to afford, which succour shall likewise be continued to him until he shall have obtained a good and advantageous peace.

XI. In order to render this alliance and union the more perfect, and to leave no doubt with the parties about the certainty of the succour, which they have to expect by the virtue of this Treaty, it is expressly agreed, that to judge for the future whether the case of this alliance, and the stipulated succour, exists or not, it shall suffice that either of the parties is actually attacked by force of arms, without his having first used open force against him who attacks him.

XII. The sick of the Hessian corps shall remain under the care of their physicians, surgeons, and other persons, appointed for that purpose, under the orders of the general commanding the corps of that nation, and everything shall be allowed them that his Majesty allows to his own troops.

XIII. All the Hessian deserters shall be faithfully given up, wherever they shall be discovered, in the places dependent on his Britannic Majesty, and above all, as far as it is possible, no person whatever of that nation shall be permitted to establish himself in America without the consent of his sovereign.

XIV. All the transports for the troops, as well for the men as for the effects, shall be at the expense of his Britannic Majesty; and none belonging to the said corps shall pay any postage of letters in consideration of the distance of the places.

XV.   The Treaty shall be ratified by the high contracting parties, and the ratification thereof shall be exchanged as soon as possible.

In witness whereof, we, the undersigned, furnished with the full powers of his Majesty, the king of Great Britain on one part, and of his most serene highness the reigning landgrave of Hesse Cassel on the other part, have signed the present Treaty, and have caused the seals of our arms to be put thereon.

Done at Cassel, the 15th of January, in the year 1775.

   William Faucitt   M. de Schlieffen

French Foreign Legionnaire's Code of Honor

1. Legionnaire: You are a volunteer serving France faithfully and with honor.
2. Every Legionnaire is your brother-at-arms, irrespective of his nationality, race, or creed. You will demonstrate this by unwavering and straightforward solidarity which must always bind together members of the same family.
3. Respectful of the Legion's traditions, honoring your superiors, discipline, and comradeship are your strength, courage and loyalty your virtues.
4. Proud of your status as a Legionnaire, you will display the pride, by your turnout, always impeccable, your behavior ever worthy, though modest, your living quarters always tidy.
5. An elite soldier: You will train vigorously, you will maintain your weapon as if it were your most precious possession, you will keep your body in the peak of condition, always fit.
6. A mission once given to you becomes sacred to you. You will accomplish it to the end and at all costs.
7. In combat: You will act without relish of your tasks, or hatred; you will respect the vanquished enemy and will never abandon neither your wounded nor your dead, nor will you under circumstances surrender your arms.

Letter of Marque

To all who shall see these presents, greetings:

Be it known that in pursuance of an act of Congress passed on the fifth day of June one thousand eight hundred and twelve, I have commissioned, and by these presents do commission the private armed schooner named *Lucy* of the burden of twenty-five tons or thereabouts, owned by John Lawton in the city of Taunton state of Massachusetts mounting four carriage guns, and navigated by twenty-six men, hereby authorizing John Lawton Captain, and Perez Drinkwater Lieutenant of the said *Lucy* and the other officers and crew thereof to: Subdue, seize and take any armed or unarmed British vessel, public or private, which shall be found within the jurisdictional limits of the United States or elsewhere on the high seas, or within the waters of the British dominions.

And each captured vessel with her apparel, guns and appurtenances, and the goods or effects which shall be found on board the same, together with all the British persons and others who shall be found acting on board, within some port of the United States.

And also to retake any vessel, goods or effects of the people of the United States, which may have been captured by any British armed vessel, in order that proceedings may be had concerning each capture or recapture in due form of law, and as to right and justice shall appertain. The said John Lawton is further authorized to detain, seize, and take all vessels and effects, to whomsoever belonging, which shall be liable thereto according to the law of Nations and the rights of the United States as a power at war, and to bring the same within some port of the United States in order that due proceeding may be had thereon.

This commission to continue in force during the pleasure of the President of the United States for the time being.

Given under my hand and the seal of the United States of America at the city of Washington, the twenty second day of December in the year of our Lord, one thousand eight hundred and fourteen and the independence of the said states the thirty ninth.

By the President,   James Monroe,
James Madison   Secretary of State

Private Military Contract between Sandline International and Papua New Guinea (1997)

This Agreement is made this 31st day of January 1997 between the Independent State of Papua New Guinea (the State) of the one part and Sandline International (Sandline), whose UK representative office is 535 Kings Road, London SW10 OS2, of the other part.

WHEREAS

Sandline is a company specializing in rendering military and security services of an operational, training and support nature, particularly in situations of internal conflict, and only for and on the behalf of recognized Governments, in accord with international doctrines and in conformance with the Geneva Convention.

The State, engulfed in a state of conflict with the illegal and unrecognized Bougainville Revolutionary Army (BRA), requires such external military expertise to support its Armed Forces in the protection of its Sovereign territory and regain control over important national assets, specifically the Panguna mine. In particular, Sandline is contracted to provide personnel and related services and equipment to:

Train the State's Special Forces Unit (SFU) in tactical skills specific to the objective;

Gather intelligence to support effective deployment and operations;

Conduct offensive operations in Bougainville in conjunction with PNG defensive forces to render the BRA military ineffective and repossess the Panguna mine; and

Provide follow-up operational support, to be further specified and agreed between the parties and is subject to separate service provision levels and fee negotiations.

IT IS THEREFORE AGREED AS FOLLOWS:

The State hereby agrees to contract and utilize and employ the services of Sandline to provide all required and necessary services as are more particularly described hereafter.

Duration and Continuation

The duration of this contract shall be effective from the date of receipt of the initial payment, as defined in paragraph below, for a maximum initial period of three calendar months (the initial contract period) or achievement of the primary objective, being the rendering of the BRA militarily ineffective, whichever is the earlier. The State shall have the option of renewing this agreement either in part or in whole for further periods as may be required.

Notice of renewal, termination or proposed variation of this agreement is to be served on Sandline in writing by the State at least 45 days before the expiry of the current period. Non-communications by the State shall be regarded by Sandline as automatic renewal of the relevant parts of the agreement for a further three month period on the same terms and this precedent shall continue to apply thereafter.

Service Provision

Sandline shall provide the following manpower, equipment, and services:

(a) A 16 man Command, Admin and Training Team (CATT), to deploy in PNG and establish home bases at Jackson Airport and the Jungle Training Center at Wewac within one week of commencement of this agreement, which is deemed to be the date on which the initial payment relating thereto in accordance with paragraph below is deposited free and clear in Sandline's nominated bank account. The role of the CATT is to (i) establish links with PNG defense forces, (ii) develop the requisite logistics and communications infrastructure, (iii) secure and prepare facilities for the arrival of the contracted equipment, including air assets, (iv) initiate intelligence gathering operations, and (v) commence SFU training.

(b) Further Special Forces personnel which will deploy to PNG within 10 days of the arrival of the CATT, together with helicopter and fixed wing aircrew and engineers, intelligence and equipment operatives, mission operators, ground tech and medical support personnel. This force will absorb the CATT as part of its number, therefore bringing the total Strike Force head count to 70. This strike force shall be responsible for achieving the primary objective as specified in earlier paragraph of this agreement and the full complement will remain in country for the initial contract period as defined in the said paragraph.

Note: At no time will Sandline personnel cater the sovereign territory of another nation nor will they breach the laws and rules of engagement relating to armed conflict. Once the operation has been successfully concluded, Sandline personnel will be available to assist with the ongoing training, skills enhancement and equipping of the PNG defense forces.

(c) Weapons, ammunition and equipment, including helicopters and aircraft (serviceable for up to 50 hours flying time per machine per month), and electronic warfare equipment and communications systems, all as specified or equivalent to the items listed in Schedule.

    1. Upon termination of a contractual relationship between the States and Sandline and once all payments have been received and Sandline has withdrawn from theatre any remaining stock of equipment shall be handed over and become the property of the State. Selected Sandline personnel will remain in country to maintain and supplement such equipment subject to a separate agreement relating thereto.

    Note: Delivery into theatre of the contracted equipment shall be via air into Jackson Airport or such other facility as may be considered appropriate. The equipment will be delivered in full working order in accordance with manufacturers' specifications. After its delivery, any equipment lost, damaged or destroyed during Sandline's deployment shall be immediately replaced at the cost of the State.

(d) Personal kit, including U.S. pattern jungle fatigues, boots, and webbing, for Sandline personnel.

(e) All international transport arrangements for the shipment in/out of equipment and deployment in country of Sandline personnel but not for the movement of such equipment and personnel within the country if this needs to be achieved by way of commercial service providers.

(f) The provision of medical personnel to treat any Sandline casualties and their evacuation if necessary.

(g) A Project Coordinator who, together with the Strike Force Commander and his Senior Intelligence officer, shall maintain liaison with and provide strategic and operational briefings and advice to the Prime Minister, Defense Minister, NEC, NSC, the commander of the PNG defense forces and his delegated officers as may from time-to-time be required or requested.

Sandline shall ensure the enrollment of all personnel involved in this contract as Special Constables and that they carry appropriate ID cards in order to legally undertake their assigned roles.

Responsibilities of Sandline

Sandline will train SFU in tactical skills specific to the objective, such as live fire contact, ambush techniques and raiding drills, gather intelligence to support effective deployment and plan, direct, participate in and conduct such ground, air and sea operations which are required to achieve the primary objective.

Both parties hereto recognize and agree that the force capability to respond to all emergency and hostile situations will be constrained by the manpower and equipment level provided within the terms of this agreement. The achievement of the primary objective cannot be deemed to be a performance measure for the sake of this agreement if it can be demonstrated that for valid reasons it cannot be achieved within the given timescale and with the level of contracted resources provided.

Sandline shall supply all the personnel and maintain all services and equipment as specified in above paragraph to the approximate standards of proficiency and operational levels as is generally expected from a high caliber, professional armed force.

Sandline shall further provide a project coordinator to act as the liaison officer between the company's management and the nominated representatives of the State. This individual will convene and attend regular meetings at such venues as he may be so directed.

Sandline shall be responsible for any expense resulting from the loss or injury of any of its personnel for the duration of the agreement unless same is caused by the negligence of the State, its personnel or agents in which case all such costs will be fairly claimed against the State by Sandline and promptly paid for the benefit of the persons involved.

Sandline will ensure that the contents of this agreement shall remain strictly confidential and will not be disclosed to any third party. Sandline will not acknowledge the existence of this contract prior to the State issuing notifications in accordance with paragraph below and will not take credit for any successful action unless this is mutually agreed by the parties. Furthermore, Sandline and its personnel are well versed in the requirements to maintain absolute secrecy with regard to all aspects of its activities in order to guard against compromising operations and will apply the necessary safeguards.

Responsibilities of the State

Immediately on signing this agreement the State automatically grants to Sandline and its personnel all approvals, permissions, authorizations, licenses and permits to carry arms, conduct its operations and meet its contractual obligations without hindrance, including instructions to PNG defense force personnel to cooperate fully with Sandline commanders and their nominated representatives. All officers and personnel of Sandline assigned to this contract shall be enrolled as Special Constables, but hold military ranks commensurate with those they hold within the Sandline command structure and shall be entitled to give orders to junior ranks as may be necessary for the execution of their duties and responsibilities.

The State will ensure that full cooperation is provided from within its organization and that of the PNG defense forces. The commanders of the PNG defense forces and Sandline shall form a joint liaison and planning team for the duration of this agreement. The operational deployment of Sandline personnel and equipment is to be jointly determined by the commander, PNG defense forces and Sandline's commander, taking account of their assessment of the risk and value thereof.

The State recognizes that Sandline's commanders will have such powers as are required to efficiently and effectively undertake their given roles, including but not limited to the powers to engage and fight hostile forces, repel attacks therefrom, arrest any persons suspected of undertaking or conspiring to undertake a harmful act, secure Sovereign assets and territory, defend the general population from any threat, and proactively protect their own and State Forces from any form of aggression or threat. The State agrees to indemnify Sandline for the legitimate actions of the company's and its associates' personnel as specified herein and to assume any claims brought against the company arising out of this agreement.

The State shall pay or shall cause to be paid the fees and expenses relating to this agreement as set out in the following paragraph. Such fees and expenses to be paid as further specified without deduction of any taxes, charges or fees, and eligible to be freely exported from PNG. All payments to be made in U.S. dollars.

The State shall cause all importation of equipment and the provision of services to be free to Sandline (and any of its sister or associated companies as notified to the authorities) of any local, regional, or national taxes, withholding taxes, duties, fees, surcharges, storage charges and clearance expenses howsoever levied and shall allow such equipment to be processed through Customs without delay. Further, all Sandline personnel will be furnished with the necessary multiple entry visas without passport stamps and authorization to enter and leave the country free from hindrance at any time and shall be exempt from tax of any form on their remuneration from Sandline.

The State will promptly supply at no cost to Sandline and its sister and associated companies all End User Certificates and related documentation to facilitate the legitimate procurement and export of the specified equipment from countries of origin.

The State will provide suitable accommodation for all Sandline personnel together with all related amenities, support staff to undertake roles such as messengers and household duties, secure hangerage and storage facilities for equipment, qualified tradesmen and workmen to clear and prepare operation sites, all aviation and ground equipment fuel and lubricant needs, such vehicles and personnel carriers as reasonably specified for the field and staff use, foodstuffs and combat rations, fresh drinking water, and sanitary and other relevant services and ancillary equipment as Sandline may specify from time to time to undertake its activities without hindrance.

If any service, resource or equipment to be supplied by the State in accordance with this paragraph is not forthcoming then

Sandline will have the right to submit an additional invoice for the procurement and supply thereof and may curtail or reduce operations affected by its non-availability until payment has been made and the said equipment is in position.

The State agrees and undertakes that, during the period of this agreement and for a period of 12 months following the date of its expiration, it will not directly or indirectly offer employment to or employ any of the personnel provided hereunder or otherwise in the employment of Sandline and its associates. Any such employment will be construed as a continuation of the contract for the employees concerned and Sandline shall be entitled to be paid accordingly on a pro-rata basis.

The State and the PNG defense forces will ensure that information relating to planned operations, deployments and associated activities is restricted to only those personnel who have an essential need to be briefed in. Appropriate steps will be taken to prevent press reporting, both nationally and internationally, or any form of security breach or passage of information which may potentially threaten operational effectiveness and/or risk the lives of the persons involved. Sandline's commanders have the right to curtail any or all planned operations which they determine are compromised as a result of failure in security.

If deemed necessary due to external interest, the State shall be responsible for notifying and updating the International Community, including the United Nations and representatives of other Governments, at the appropriate time of the nature of this contract and the underlying intent to protect and keep safe from harm Papua New Guinea's sovereign territory, its population, mineral assets and investing community. The content and timing of all such formal communications will be discussed and agreed with Sandline before release.

Fees and Payments

Sandline's inclusive fee for the provision of the personnel and services in previous paragraphs and also in Schedule 1 (attached) for the initial contract period is $36 million (U.S. dollars).

Payment terms are as follows: All payments to be by way of cash funds, either in the form of electronic bank transfers or certified banker's checks.

On contract signing 50 percent of the overall fee, totaling

$18,000,000 (U.S. dollars) is immediately due and is deemed the "initial payment."

Within 30 days of deploying the CATT, the balance of $18,000,000 (U.S. dollars).

This contract is deemed to be enacted once the initial payment is received in full with value into such bank account as Sandline may nominate therefore. Payments are recognized as being received when they are credited as cleared funds in our account and payment receipt relies on this definition.

All fees for service rendered shall be paid in advance of the period to which they relate. Sandline reserves the right to withdraw from the theater in the event of nonpayment of fees for any renewal to the original contract period.

The financial impact of variations, additions or changes to the personnel provision and equipment supply specified herein will be agreed between the parties and any incremental payment will be made to Sandline before such change is deemed to take effect. There is no facility for rebate or refund in the event of a required reduction or early termination of service delivery within a given contract period.

Applicable Law

In the event of any dispute or difference arising out of or in relation to this agreement the parties shall in the first instance make an effort to resolve it amicably, taking account of the sensitive nature of this arrangement.

The aggrieved party shall notify the other by sending a notice of dispute in writing and, where amicable settlement is not possible within 30 days thereafter, refer the matter to arbitration in conformity with the UNCITRAL rules applying thereto.

This agreement shall be construed and governed in accordance with the Laws of England and the language of communication between the parties shall be English.

Agreements and Supplements

This agreement may only be altered, modified or amended by the parties hereto providing that such alteration, modification or amendment is in writing and signed by both parties.

Schedule 1 forms part of this agreement.

In witness thereof the parties hereto have set their hands on the day and year first written above.

For the Independent State of Papua New Guinea: Chris S. Haiveta and Vele Iamo

For Sandline International: Tim Spicer and J. N. Van Den Bergh

SCHEDULE 1
Sandline-PNG 1997 Contract

Item	Quantity	Cost (U.S. $)
Special Forces Team:		Subtotal $7,100,000
Manpower	40, plus 2 doctors	$4,500,000
Positioning		$100,000
Equipment:		$2,500,000
AK-47 Assault Rifle	100	
PKM Lt. Machine Gun	10	
RPG-7 Grenade Launcher	10	
60mm Mortar	10	
82mm Mortar	6	
AGS-17 30mm Automatic Grenade Launcher	4	
Makarov Pistol	20	
7.62×39 (for AK-47)	500,000	
AK-47 magazines	1,000	
7.62×54 (for PKM)	250,000	
12.7mm ball	100,000	
12.7mm tracer	25,000	
Ammo links	250,000	
PG-7 rocket grenades	1,000	

Item	Quantity	Cost (U.S. $)
30mm grenades (AGS-17)	2,000	
60mm HE mortar rounds	2,500	
82mm HE mortar rounds	2,500	
Illumination grenades	200	
Smoke/Frag grenades	800	
Personal kit and uniforms	100	
Mission Support:		Subtotal $29,170,000
Mi-24 Hind Attack Helicopter	2	$8,200,000
Ordnance:		$2,500,000
57mm rocket launcher pods	6	
57mm HE rocket	1,000	
23mm ball	20,000	
23mm tracer	5,000	
23mm links	125,000	
Mi-24 Aircrew	6	$680,000
Mi-17 Assault Helicopter	2	$3,000,000
Mi-17 Aircrew	6	$860,000
Spares— Helicopters		$1,500,000
Surveillance Platform— CASA-12	1	$2,400,000
"On Board Systems"	1	$4,850,000
SP Aircrew	4	$280,000
SP Trainers	included	$120,000

Item	Quantity	Cost (U.S. $)
SP Spares		$600,000
Ground System	1	$600,000
Mission Operators	5	$480,000
Ground Staff	5	$270,000
Electronic Warfare Trainers	included	$120,000
Project Coordinator	1	included
Personnel Equipment	30	$250,000
Personnel Movement		$250,000
Insurances		included
Logistics Support		Client Responsibility
Communications Equipment:		Subtotal $1,100,000
HF Radio System	1+15	$400,000
Hardened Tac Radio System	1+16	$500,000
Satellite Comms Units	15	$200,000
Contract Total		$37,370,000
Minus Package Price Reduction		−$1,370,000
FEE TO CLIENT		$36,000,000

Protocol Addition to the Geneva Convention of 12 August 1949 Relating to the Protection of Victims of International Armed Conflict Protocol I, 8 June 1977

Part III: Methods and Means of Warfare
Section II: Combat Prisoner of War Status
Article 47: Mercenaries

1. A mercenary shall not have the right to be a combatant or a prisoner of war.
2. A mercenary is any person who:
   (a) is specifically recruited locally or abroad in order to fight in an armed conflict;
   (b) does, in fact, take a direct part in the hostilities;
   (c) is motivated to take part in the hostilities essentially by the desire for private gain and, in fact, is promised, by or on behalf of a Party to the conflict, material compensation substantially in excess of that promised or paid to combatants of similar ranks and functions in the army forces of that Party;
   (d) is neither a national of the Party to the conflict nor a citizen of territory controlled by a Party to the conflict;
   (e) is not a member of the armed forces of a Party to the conflict; and
   (f) has not been sent by a State which is not a Party to the conflict on official duty as a member of its armed forces.

United Nations International Convention against Recruitment, Use, Financing, and Training of Mercenaries

THE STATES PARTIES TO THE PRESENT CONVENTION,

Reaffirming the purposes and principles enshrined in the Charter of the United Nations in the Declaration on the Principles of International Law concerning Friendly Relations and Cooperation among States with the Charter of the United Nations, *Being Aware* of the recruitment, use, financing and training of mercenaries for activities which violate principles of international law such as those of sovereign equality, political independence, territorial integrity of States and self-determination of peoples,

Affirming that the recruitment, use, financing and training of mercenaries should be considered as offenses of grave concern to all States and that any person committing any of these offenses should either be prosecuted or extradited,

Convinced of the necessity to develop and enhance international cooperation among States for the prevention, prosecution, and punishment of such offenses,

Expressing concern at new unlawful international activities linking drug traffickers and mercenaries in the perpetration of violent actions which undermine the constitutional order of States,

Also convinced that the adoption of a convention against the recruitment, use, financing and training of mercenaries would contribute to the eradication of these nefarious activities and thereby to the observance of the purposes and principles enshrined in the Charter of the United Nations,

Cognizant that matters not regulated by such a convention continue to be governed by the rules and principles of international law,

Have agreed as follows:

ARTICLE 1
For the purpose of the present convention,
1. A mercenary is any person who:
   a) Is specially recruited locally or abroad in order to fight in an armed conflict;
   b) Is motivated to take part in the hostilities essentially by the desire for private gain and, in fact, is promised, by or on behalf of a party to the conflict, material compensation substantially in excess of that promised or paid to combatants of similar rank and functions in the armed forces of that party;
   c) Is neither a national of a party to the conflict nor a resident of territory controlled by a party to the conflict;
   d) Is not a member of the armed forces of a party to the conflict; and
   e) Has not been sent by a State which is not a party to the conflict on official duty as a member of its armed force.
2. A mercenary is also any person who, in any other situation:
   a) Is specially recruited locally or abroad for the purpose of participating in a concerted act of violence aimed at:
      i) Overthrowing a Government or otherwise undermining the constitutional order of a State; or
      ii) Undermining the territorial integrity of a State;
   b) Is motivated to take part therein essentially by the desire for significant private gain and is prompted by the promise or payment of material compensation;
   c) Is neither a national nor a resident of the State against which such an action is directed;
   d) Has not been sent by a State on official duty; and
   e) Is not a member of the armed forces of the State on whose territory the act is undertaken.

ARTICLE 2
Any person who recruits, uses, finances or trains mercenaries, as defined in article 1 of the present Convention, commits an offense for the purposes of the Convention.

ARTICLE 3
1. A mercenary, as defined in article 1 of the present Conven-

tion, who participates directly in hostilities or in a concerted act of violence, as the case may be, commits an offense for the purposes of the Convention.

2. Nothing in this article limits the scope of application of article 4 of the present Convention.

ARTICLE 4

An offense is committed by any person who:

a) Attempts to commit one of the offenses set forth in the present Convention;

b) Is the accomplice of a person who commits or attempts to commit any of the offenses set forth in the present Convention.

ARTICLE 5

1. States Parties shall not recruit, use, finance or train mercenaries and shall prohibit such activities in accordance with the provisions of the present Convention.

2. States Parties shall not recruit, use, finance or train mercenaries for the purpose of opposing the legitimate exercise of the inalienable right of peoples to self-determination, as recognized by international law, and shall take, in conformity with international law, the appropriate measures to prevent the recruitment, use, financing or training of mercenaries for that purpose.

3. They shall make the offenses set forth in the present Convention punishable by appropriate penalties which take into account the grave nature of those offenses.

ARTICLE 6

State parties shall cooperate in the prevention of the offenses set forth in the present Convention, particularly by:

a) Taking all practical measures to prevent preparations in their respective territories for the commission of those offenses within or outside their territories, including the prohibition of illegal activities of persons, groups and organizations that encourage, instigate, organize or engage in the perpetration of such offenses.

b) Coordinating the tasking of administrative and other measures as appropriate to prevent the commission of those offenses.

ARTICLE 7

States Parties shall cooperate in taking the necessary measures for the implementation of the present Convention.

ARTICLE 8

Any State Party having reason to believe that one of the offenses set forth in the present Convention has been, is being or will be committed shall, in accordance with its national law, communicate the relevant information, as soon as it comes to its knowledge, directly or through the Secretary-General of the United Nations, to the States Parties affected.

ARTICLE 9

1. Each State Party shall take such measures as may be necessary to establish its jurisdiction over any of the offenses set forth in the present Convention which are committed:
   a) In its territory or on board a ship or aircraft registered in that state;
   b) By any of its nationals, or, if that State considers it appropriate, by those stateless persons who have their habitual residence in that territory.
2. Each State Party shall likewise take such measures as may be necessary to establish its jurisdiction over the offenses set forth in Articles 2, 3, and 4 of the present Convention in cases where the alleged offender is present in its territory and it does not extradite him to any of the States mentioned in paragraph 1 of this article.
3. The present Convention does not exclude any criminal jurisdiction exercised in accordance with national law.

ARTICLE 10

1. Upon being satisfied that the circumstances so warrant, any State Party in whose territory the alleged offender is present shall, in accordance with its laws, take him into custody or take such other measures to ensure his presence for such time as is necessary to enable any criminal or extradition proceedings to be instituted. The State Party shall immediately make a preliminary inquiry into the facts.
2. When a State Party, pursuant to this article, has taken a person into custody or has taken such other measures referred

to in paragraph 1 of this article, it shall notify without delay either directly or through the Secretary-General of the United Nations:

a) The State Party where the offense was committed;

b) The State Party against which the offense has been directed or attempted;

c) The State Party of which the natural or juridical person against whom the offense has been directed or attempted is a national;

d) The State Party of which the alleged offender is a national or, if he is a stateless person, in whose territory he has his habitual residence;

e) Any other interested State Party which it considers it appropriate to notify.

3. Any person regarding whom the measures referred to in paragraph 1 of this article are being taken shall be entitled:

a) To communicate without delay with the nearest appropriate representative of the State of which he is a national or which is otherwise entitled to protect his rights or, if he is a stateless person, the State in which territory he has his habitual residence.

b) To be visited by a representative of that State.

4. The provisions of paragraph 3 of this article shall be without prejudice to the right of any State Party having a claim to jurisdiction in accordance with Article 9, paragraph 1 (b), to invite the International Committee of the Red Cross to communicate with and visit the alleged offender.

5. The State which makes the preliminary inquiry contemplated in paragraph 1 of this article shall promptly report its findings to the States referred to in paragraph 2 of this article and indicate whether it intends to exercise jurisdiction.

ARTICLE 11

Any person regarding whom proceedings are being carried out in connection with any of the offenses set forth in the present Convention shall be guaranteed at all stages of the proceedings fair treatment and all the rights and guarantees provided for in the law of the State in question. Applicable norms of international law should be taken into account.

ARTICLE 12

The State Party in whose territory the alleged offender is found shall, if it does not extradite him, be obliged, without exception whatsoever and whether or not the offense was committed in its territory, to submit the case to its competent authorities for the purpose of prosecution, through proceedings in accordance with the laws of that State. Those authorities shall take their decision in the same matter as in the case of any other offense of a grave nature under the law of that State.

ARTICLE 13

1. State Parties shall afford one another the greatest measure of assistance in connection with criminal proceedings brought in respect of the offenses set forth in the present Convention, including the supply of all evidence at their disposal necessary for the proceedings. The law of the State whose assistance is requested shall apply in all cases.

2. The provisions of paragraph 1 of this article shall not affect obligations concerning mutual judicial assistance embodied in any other treaty.

ARTICLE 14

The State Party where the alleged offender is prosecuted shall in accordance with its laws communicate the final outcome of the proceedings to the Secretary-General of the United Nations, who shall transmit the information to the other States concerned.

ARTICLE 15

1. The offenses set forth in articles 2, 3, and 4 of the present Convention shall be deemed to be included as extraditable offenses in any extradition treaty existing between the State Parties. State Parties undertake to include such offenses as extraditable offenses in every extradition treaty to be concluded between them.

2. If a State Party which makes extradition conditional on the existence of a treaty receives a request for extradition from another State Party with which it has no extradition treaty, it may at its option consider the present Convention as the legal basis for extradition in respect of those offenses. Extra-

dition shall be subject to the other conditions provided by the law of the requested State.

3. State Parties which do not make extradition conditional on the existence of a treaty shall recognize those offenses as extraditable offenses between themselves, subject to the other conditions provided by the law of the requested State.

4. The offenses shall be treated, for the purpose of extradition between State Parties, as if they had been committed not only in the place in which they occurred but also in the territories of the States required to establish their jurisdiction in accordance with article 9 of the present Convention.

ARTICLE 16

The present Convention shall be applied without prejudice to:

a) The rules relating to the international responsibility of States;

b) The law of armed conflict and international humanitarian law, including the provisions relating to the status of combatants or of prisoners of war.

ARTICLE 17

1. Any dispute between two or more State Parties concerning the interpretation or application of the present Convention which is not settled by negotiation shall, at the request of one of them, be submitted to arbitration. If, within six months from the date of request for arbitration, the parties are unable to agree on the organization of the arbitration, any one of those parties may refer the dispute to the International Court of Justice by a request in conformity with the Statute of the Court.

2. Each State may, at the time of the signature or ratification of the present Convention or accession thereto, declare that it does not consider itself bound by paragraph 1 of the article. The other State Parties shall not be bound by paragraph 1 of this article with respect to any State Party which has made such a reservation.

3. Any State Party which has made a reservation in accordance with paragraph 2 of this article may at any time withdraw that reservation by notification to the Secretary-General of the United Nations.

ARTICLE 18

1. The present Convention shall be open for signature of all States until 31 December 1990 at United Nations Headquarters in New York.
2. The present Convention shall be subject to ratification. The instruments of ratification shall be deposited with the Secretary-General of the United Nations.
3. The present Convention shall remain open for accession by any State. The instruments of accession shall be deposited with the Secretary-General of the United Nations.

ARTICLE 19

1. The present Convention shall enter into force on the thirtieth day following the date of deposit of the twenty-second instrument or ratification or accession with the Secretary-General of the United Nations.
2. For each State ratifying or acceding to the Convention after the deposit of the twenty-second instrument of ratification or accession, the Convention shall enter into force on the thirtieth day after the deposit by such State of its instrument of ratification or accession.

ARTICLE 20

1. Any State Party may denounce the present Convention by written notification to the Secretary-General of the United Nations.
2. Denunciation shall take effect one year after the date on which the notification is received by the Secretary-General of the United Nations.

ARTICLE 21

The original of the present Convention, of which the Arabic, Chinese, English, French, Russian and Spanish texts are equally authentic, shall be deposited with the Secretary-General of the United Nations, who shall send certified copies thereof to all States.

IN WITNESS WHEREOF the undersigned, being duly authorized thereto by their respective governments, have signed the present treaty.

BIBLIOGRAPHY

Andrews, Kenneth R. *Elizabethan Privateering: English Privateering during the Spanish War, 1585–1603.* New York: Cambridge University Press, 1964.

Arnold, Guy. *Mercenaries: The Scourge of the Third World.* New York: St. Martin's, 1999.

Banks, John. *The Wages of War: The Life of a Modern Mercenary.* London: Cooper, 1978.

Bayley, C. C. *Mercenaries for the Crimea: The German, Swiss, and Italian Legions in British Service.* Montreal: McGill-Queens University, 1977.

Baylor, Paul. *Manual of the Mercenary Soldier.* New York: Dell, 1988.

Bergner, David. *In the Land of Magic Soldiers: A Story of White and Black in West Africa.* New York: Farrar, Straus & Giroux, 2003.

Bidwell, Shelford. *Swords for Hire: European Mercenaries in Eighteenth Century India.* London: Murray, 1971.

Blackburn, Robert M. *Mercenaries and Lyndon Johnson's "More Flags": The Hiring of Korean, Filipino, and Thai Soldiers in the Vietnam War.* Jefferson, NC: McFarland and Company, 1994.

Bocca, Geoffrey. *La Legion! The French Foreign Legion and the Men Who Made It Glorious.* New York: Thomas Y. Crowell, 1964.

Briody, Dan. *The Halliburton Agenda: The Politics of Oil and Money.* Hoboken, NJ: John Wiley and Sons, 2004.

Chennault, Chaire L. *Way of a Fighter.* New York: G. P. Putnam's Sons, 1949.

Cocks, Chris. *Fireforce: One Man's War in the Rhodesian Light Infantry.* Pretoria, South Africa: Covos Day, 2001.

Coggeshall, George. *The History of the American Privateers and Letters of Marque During Our War with England in the Years 1812, '13 and '14*. New York: George Coggeshall, 1856.

Cole, Barbara. *The Elite: The Story of the Rhodesian Special Air Service*. Traskei, South Africa: Three Knights, 1988.

Contamine, Phillipe. *War in the Middle Ages*. New York: Basil Blackwell, 1984.

Cook, Fred J. *The Privateers of Seventy-six*. Indianapolis: Bobbs-Merrill, 1976.

Cottrell, Leonard. *Hannibal: Enemy of Rome*. New York: Da Capo Press, 1992.

Crabites, Pierre. *Americans in the Egyptian Army*. London: Routledge, 1938.

Davis, James R. *Fortune's Warriors: Private Armies and the New World Order*. Vancouver, BC: Douglas & McIntyre, 2002.

Davis, Richard H. *Real Soldiers of Fortune*. New York: Scribner's, 1912.

Dorney, Sean. *The Sandline Affair: Politics and Mercenaries in the Bougainville Crisis*. Sydney: ABC Books, 1998.

Eggenberger, David. *An Encyclopedia of Battles: Accounts of Over 1,560 Battles from 1479 B.C. to the Present*. New York: Dover Publications, 1985.

Farwell, Byron. *The Gurkhas*. New York: W. W. Norton, 1984.

Fawcett, Bill, ed. *Mercs: True Stories of Mercenaries in Action*. New York: Avon Books, 1999.

Fowler, Kenneth A. *Medieval Mercenaries: The Great Companies*. Oxford: Backwell, 2001.

Glubb, John. *Soldiers of Fortune: The Story of the Mamlukes*. New York: Stein & Day, 1973.

Griffith, G. T. *The Mercenaries of the Hellenistic World*. London: Cambridge University, 1935.

Hasbrouck, Alfred. *Foreign Legionaries in the Liberation of Spanish South America*. New York: Columbia, 1928.

Hempstone, Frederick A. *Mercenaries and Dividends: The Katanga Story*. New York: Praeger, 1972.

Hennessy, Maurice. *The Wild Geese: The Irish Soldier in Exile*. Old Greenwich, CT: Devin-Adair, 1973.

Hoare, Mike. *Congo Mercenary*. New York: Robert Hale, 1967.

———. *Mercenary*. London: Corgi Books, 1968.

———. *The Seychelles Affair*. New York: Bantam, 1986.

Hooper, Jim. *Bloodsong: First-Hand Accounts of a Modern Private Army in Action*. London: Harper-Collins, 2002.

Ingaro, Charles W. *The Hessian Mercenary State: Ideas, Institutions, and Reform under Frederick II, 1760–1785*. New York: Cambridge University Press, 1987.

James, Harold D. *The Gurkhas*. Harrisburg, PA: Stackpole, 1966.

Kagay, Donald J., and L. J. Andrew Villalon, eds. *The Circle of War in the Middle Ages: Essays on Medieval Military and Naval History*. Rochester, NY: Boydell Press, 2000.

Langley, Lester D., and Thomas Schoonover. *The Banana Men: American Mercenaries and Entrepreneurs in Central America, 1880–1930*. Lexington, KY: University Press of Kentucky, 1995.

Larsen, Stanley Robert, and James Lawton Collins. *Allied Participation in Vietnam*. Washington DC: Department of the Army, 1975.

Lonn, Ella. *Foreigners in the Confederacy*. Chapel Hill, NC: University of North Carolina Press, 1940.

———. *Foreigners in the Union Army and Navy*. Baton Rouge, LA: Louisiana State University Press, 1951.

Lydon, James G. *Pirates, Privateers, and Profits*. Upper Saddle River, NJ: Gregg, 1970.

Machiavelli, Niccolo. *The Prince*. Translated by Hill Thompson. New York: Heritage Press, 1954.

Maclay, Edgar Stanton. *A History of American Privateers*. New York: Appleton, 1899.

Mallet, Michael E. *Mercenaries and Their Masters: Warfare in Renaissance Italy*. Totowa, NJ: Rowman and Littlefield, 1974.

Mallin, Jay, and Robert K. Brown. *Merc: American Soldiers of Fortune*. New York: Macmillan, 1979.

McCormick, John. *One Million Mercenaries: Swiss Soldiers in the Armies of the World*. London: Leo Cooper, 1993.

Mockler, Anthony. *The Mercenaries: The Men Who Fight for Profit—from the Free Companies of Feudal France to the White Adventurers in the Congo*. New York: Macmillan, 1970.

———. *The New Mercenaries: The History of the Mercenary from the Congo to the Seychelles*. London: Sidgwick & Jackson, 1985.

Moscati, Sabatino, coordinator. *The Celts*. New York: Rizzoli International, 1999.

Murray, Simon. *Legionnaire*. New York: Times Books, 1978.

Nicholson, J. B. *The Gurkhas Rifles*. New York: Hippocrene, 1974.

O'Brien, Conor Cruise. *To Katanga and Back*. New York: Simon & Schuster, 1962.

Park, H. W. *Greek Mercenary Soldiers: From the Earliest Times to the Battle of Ipus*. Oxford: Oxford University Press, 1933.

Pelton, Robert Young. *The Hunter, The Hammer, and Heaven*. Guilford, CT: Lyons Press, 2002.

Pettengill, Ray Waldron. *Letters from America, 1776–1779: Being Letters of Brunswick, Hessian, and Waldeck*

Officers with the British Armies during the Revolution. Boston: Houghton Mifflin, 1924.

Porch, Douglas. *The French Foreign Legion: A Complete History of the Legendary Fighting Force*. New York: HarperCollins, 1991.

Prevas, John. *Xenophon's March into the Lair of the Persian Lion*. Cambridge, MA: Da Capo Press, 2002.

Ripley, Tim. *Mercenaries: Soldiers of Fortune*. Bristol, GB: Parragon, 1997.

Roebuck, Derek, and Wilfred Burchett. *Whores of War: Mercenaries Today*. New York: Viking Penguin, 1977.

Rogers, Anthony. *Someone Else's War: Mercenaries from 1960 to the Present*. London: HarperCollins, 1998.

Ryan, James W. *The French Foreign Legion's Greatest Battle: Camerone*. Westport, CT: Greenwood, 1996.

Scott, Peter. *The Lost Crusade: America's Secret Cambodia Mercenaries*. Annapolis, MD: Naval Institute Press, 1998.

Seagrave, Sterling. *Soldiers of Fortune*. Alexandria, VA: Time-Life Books, 1981.

Shand, Alexander. *Soldiers of Fortune in Camp and Court*. New York: Dutton, 1907.

Shearer, David. *Private Armies and Military Intervention*. New York: Oxford University Press, 1998.

Silverstein, Ken. *Private Warriors*. New York: Verso, 2000.

Simpson, Howard R. *The Paratroopers of the French Foreign Legion*. Washington, DC: Brassey's, 1997.

Singer, P. W. *Corporate Warriors: The Rise of the Privatized Military Industry*. Ithaca, NY: Cornell University Press, 2003.

Spicer, Tim. *An Unorthodox Soldier: Peace and War and the Sandline Affair*. Edinburgh: Mainstream, 1999.

Stradling, R. A. *The Spanish Monarchy and Irish Mercenaries: The Wild Geese in Spain, 1618–1668*. Dublin: Irish Academic Press, 1994.

Szuscikiewicz, Paul. *Flying Tigers*. New York: Gallery Books, 1990.

Thomas, Gerry S. *Mercenary Troops in Modern Africa*. Boulder, CO: Westview, 1984.

Thomas, Hugh. *The Spanish Civil War*. New York: Harper & Row, 1977.

Thompson, Leroy. *Uniforms of the Soldiers of Fortune*. New York: Blandford Press, 1985.

Thomson, Janice E. *Mercenaries, Pirates, and Sovereigns: State-Building and Extraterritorial Violence in Early Modern Europe*. Princeton, NJ: Princeton University Press, 1994.

Tickler, Peter. *The Modern Mercenary: Dog of War or Soldier of Honour?* Wellingborough, UK: Stephens, 1987.

Toland, John. *The Flying Tigers*. New York: Dell, 1963.

Trease, Geoffrey. *The Condottieri: Soldiers of Fortune*. New York: Holt, Rinehart & Winston, 1971.

Weinberg, Samantha. *Last of the Pirates: The Search for Bob Denard*. New York: Random House, 1995.

Xenophon. *Anabasis*. Translated by Carleton L. Brownson. Cambridge, MA: Harvard University Press, 1922.

Yalichev, Serge. *Mercenaries of the Ancient World*. London: Constable, 1997.

Young, John Robert. *The French Foreign Legion: The Inside Story of the World-Famous Fighting Force*. London: Thames & Hudson, 1984.